Other Books and Series by Jeff Bowen

Applications for Enrollment of Chickasaw Newborn Act of 1905
Volumes I thru VII

Cherokee Intermarried White 1906 Volume I thru X

Applications for Enrollment of Creek Newborn Act of 1905
Volumes I, II, III, IV, V, VI, VII, VIII, IX & X

Visit our website at **www.nativestudy.com** to learn more about these and other books and series by Jeff Bowen

APPLICATIONS FOR ENROLLMENT OF CREEK NEWBORN ACT OF 1905 VOLUME XI

TRANSCRIBED BY
JEFF BOWEN
NATIVE STUDY
Gallipolis, Ohio
USA

Other Books and Series by Jeff Bowen

1901-1907 Native American Census Seneca, Eastern Shawnee, Miami, Modoc, Ottawa, Peoria, Quapaw, and Wyandotte Indians (Under Seneca School, Indian Territory)

1932 Census of The Standing Rock Sioux Reservation with Births And Deaths 1924-1932

Census of The Blackfeet, Montana, 1897- 1901 Expanded Edition

Eastern Cherokee by Blood, 1906-1910, Volumes I thru XIII

Choctaw of Mississippi Indian Census 1929-1932 with Births and Deaths 1924-1931 Volume I
Choctaw of Mississippi Indian Census 1933, 1934 & 1937, Supplemental Rolls to 1934 & 1935 with Births and Deaths 1932-1938, and Marriages 1936-1938 Volume II

Eastern Cherokee Census Cherokee, North Carolina 1930-1939 Census 1930-1931 with Births And Deaths 1924-1931 Taken By Agent L. W. Page Volume I
Eastern Cherokee Census Cherokee, North Carolina 1930-1939 Census 1932-1933 with Births And Deaths 1930-1932 Taken By Agent R. L. Spalsbury Volume II
Eastern Cherokee Census Cherokee, North Carolina 1930-1939 Census 1934-1937 with Births and Deaths 1925-1938 and Marriages 1936 & 1938 Taken by Agents R. L. Spalsbury And Harold W. Foght Volume III

Seminole of Florida Indian Census, 1930-1940 with Birth and Death Records, 1930-1938

Texas Cherokees 1820-1839 A Document For Litigation 1921

Choctaw By Blood Enrollment Cards 1898-1914 Volumes I thru XVII

Starr Roll 1894 (Cherokee Payment Rolls) Districts: Canadian, Cooweescoowee, and Delaware Volume One
Starr Roll 1894 (Cherokee Payment Rolls) Districts: Flint, Going Snake, and Illinois Volume Two
Starr Roll 1894 (Cherokee Payment Rolls) Districts: Saline, Sequoyah, and Tahlequah; Including Orphan Roll Volume Three

Cherokee Intruder Cases Dockets of Hearings 1901-1909 Volumes I & II

Indian Wills, 1911-1921 Records of the Bureau of Indian Affairs Books One thru Seven;
Native American Wills & Probate Records 1911-1921

Other Books and Series by Jeff Bowen

Turtle Mountain Reservation Chippewa Indians 1932 Census with Births & Deaths, 1924-1932

Chickasaw By Blood Enrollment Cards 1898-1914 Volume I thru V

Cherokee Descendants East An Index to the Guion Miller Applications Volume I
Cherokee Descendants West An Index to the Guion Miller Applications Volume II (A-M)
Cherokee Descendants West An Index to the Guion Miller Applications Volume III (N-Z)

Applications for Enrollment of Seminole Newborn Freedmen, Act of 1905

Eastern Cherokee Census, Cherokee, North Carolina, 1915-1922, Taken by Agent James E. Henderson   Volume I (1915-1916)
Volume II (1917-1918)
Volume III (1919-1920)
Volume IV (1921-1922)

Complete Delaware Roll of 1898

Eastern Cherokee Census, Cherokee, North Carolina, 1923-1929, Taken by Agent James E. Henderson   Volume I (1923-1924)
Volume II (1925-1926)
Volume III (1927-1929)

Applications for Enrollment of Seminole Newborn Act of 1905 Volumes I & II

North Carolina Eastern Cherokee Indian Census 1898-1899, 1904, 1906, 1909-1912, 1914 Revised and Expanded Edition

1932 Hopi and Navajo Native American Census with Birth & Death Rolls (1925-1931) Volume 1 - Hopi
1932 Hopi and Navajo Native American Census with Birth & Death Rolls (1930-1932) Volume 2 - Navajo

Western Navajo Reservation Navajo, Hopi and Paiute 1933 Census with Birth & Death Rolls 1925-1933

Cherokee Citizenship Commission Dockets 1880-1884 and 1887-1889 Volumes I thru V

Copyright © 2012
by Jeff Bowen

ALL RIGHTS RESERVED
No part of this publication may be reproduced
or used in any form or manner whatsoever
without previous written permission from the
copyright holder or publisher.

Originally published:
Baltimore, Maryland
2012

Reprinted by:

Native Study LLC
Gallipolis, OH
www.nativestudy.com
2020

Library of Congress Control Number: 2020917992

ISBN: 978-1-64968-090-7

Made in the United States of America.

This series is dedicated to the descendants of the Creek newborn listed in these applications.

DEPARTMENT OF THE INTERIOR.

Commissioner to the Five Civilized Tribes.

NOTICE.

Opening of Land Office at Wewoka,
IN THE SEMINOLE NATION, INDIAN TERRITORY.

Notice is hereby given that on Monday, September 4, 1905, the Commissioner to the Five Civilized Tribes will establish a land office at Wewoka, in the Seminole Nation, Indian Territory, for the purpose of allowing citizens and freedmen of the Seminole Nation to select allotments of land for their minor children enrolled under the Act of Congress approved March 3, 1905 (33 Stat. L 1060), and for the further purpose of allowing citizens and freedmen of the Seminole Nation, whose allotments are incomplete, to select additional land in order to bring the value of their allotments up to the standard of $309.09, as nearly as may be practicable.

Each child whose enrollment in accordance with the Act of March 3, 1905, has been duly approved by the Secretary of the Interior, is entitled to receive an alllotment of forty acres without regard to the character or value of the land selected.

Selection of allotments for minor children must be made by their citizen or freedmen parents or by a duly appointed guardian, or curator, or by a duly appointed administrator.

TAMS BIXBY,
Commissioner.

Muskogee, Indian Territory,
July 29, 1905.

This particular notice makes mention of the Act of 1905. The Creek and Seminole were closely related tribes. Both tribes' notices were similar in nature.

DEPARTMENT OF THE INTERIOR,

Commission to the Five Civilized Tribes.

Closing of Citizenship Rolls

OF THE MUSKOGEE OR CREEK NATION.

WHEREAS, on June 13, 1904, the Secretary of the Interior, under the authority in him vested by the provisions of the act of Congress approved March 3, 1901, (31 Stat., 1058) ordered that September 1, 1904, be and the same is hereby fixed as the time when the rolls of the Muskogee or Creek Nation shall be closed:

Notice is hereby given that the Commission to the Five Civilized Tribes will, at its office in Muskogee, Indian Territory, up to and inclusive of September 1, 1904, receive applications for the enrollment of citizens and freedmen of the Muskogee or Creek Nation, and that after that date the application of no person whomsoever for enrollment as a citizen or freedman of said nation will be received by the Commission.

Commission to the Five Civilized Tribes,
TAMS BIXBY, Chairman,
T. B. NEEDLES,
C. R. BRECKINRIDGE,
Commissioners.

Muskogee, Indian Territory,
June 25, 1904.

A notice like this was printed in newspapers and posted throughout Indian Territory.

INTRODUCTION

This series concerns Applications for Enrollment of Creek Newborn, National Archive film M-1301 (Act of 1905), as described in the National Archives publication *American Indians*. It falls under the heading Applications for Enrollment of the Commission to the Five Civilized Tribes, 1898-1914, M-1301 and is transcribed from microfilm rolls 414-419. This shows the application forms filled out by individuals applying for enrollment in the Five Civilized Tribes under the Dawes Commission. These applications contain additional information that wasn't abstracted to the census cards that you find in series M-1186. This particular roll (Creek by Birth) contains its own series of numbers separate from M-1186. To find each party's roll number you would have to reference M-1186. On July 25, 1898, there was an Indian Territory Division created in the Office of the Department of Interior. This division was created because of the increased work caused by what was called the Curtis Act, named after Senator Charles Curtis. Basically, this law stated that the tribal rolls needed to be descriptive and pointed out that each tribal roll was without description and had to be redone. At this point there was such a struggle among the Creeks to accept that the Government was going to change their way of life, again, that their leaders were refusing to cooperate in handing over their census information. The Commission had found that enrolling the Creeks was a difficult task not only because the Creek feared what was coming but also because their tribal structure was consistent with being a confederacy with forty-four different bands whose tribesmen lived in different towns of which each had a king that was supposed to keep track of their citizenry. The Commission reported that there was very little evidence of any census that existed and what there was had been kept carelessly. There were attempts and tribal conflicts along the way, but the Curtis Act would make it so they had to do it again no matter what effort from the past. In 1899, Agent Wesley Smith educated Washington to the fact that it was difficult to verify Creek eligibility. The acts passed by the Creeks themselves concerning enrollment since 1893 had been strewn amongst the archives of the Creek Council in Muskogee, I.T., and there was no provision ever approved for the printing of the those enrollments. There was confusion and difficulty let alone the fact that surnames were practically unknown among the Creek. But there was no confusion on March 9, 1905, when the Commission stated they would come to seven towns in the Creek Nation and accept applications that had to be made on a standardized blank form and contain a notarized affidavit from the mother and the attending doctor or midwife. A few by mail, but most of them were offered to a field party led by Commissioner Needles. The Commission took in applications for 2,410 children by the deadline of midnight, May 2, 1905.

This series contains applications and correspondence from 1,171 of those claimants. Realizing there were over 2,400 applicants originally, it is understood that not all were accepted. Also included are names of doctors, lawyers, mid-wives, and others who attended to the Creek Nation before and during this time in history.

Jeff Bowen
Gallipolis, Ohio
NativeStudy.com

Applications for Enrollment of Creek Newborn
Act of 1905   Volume XI

Sapulpa, I. T.
April 29 1905

Commission to Five Tribes
Muskogee, I. T.

Gentlemen:

On April 24, 1905, there was forwarded the application for enrollment of Sam Ispokogee, Creek Infant, father Belcher Ispokogee, mother Jennie Ispokogee.

You are advised that the correct surname of the family is "Ispokogee" this part was ascertained today upon the reappearance of the mother and father to complete application for another child not Ispokogee.

Respfy.
David Shelby.

Muskogee, Indian Territory, October 21, 1905.

Jennie Ispokogee,
 Care Belcher Ispokogee,
  Sapulpa, Indian Territory.

Dear Madam:

In the matter of the application for the enrollment of Sam Ispokogee, born July 2, 1904, as a citizen by blood of the Creek Nation, you sign your name to an affidavit executed April 24, 1905, relative to the birth of said child, Jennie Spokogee, you give the name of the child as Sam Spokogee and the name of the father of said child as Belcher Spokogee.

Your name appears on the final roll of citizens by blood of the Creek Nation as Jennie Ispokogee and the name of the father Belcher Ispokogee appears on said roll. It, therefore, necessarily follows that the name of said child is San Ispokogee.

There is herewith enclosed form of birth affidavit properly filled out and you are requested to have same executed before a notary public, care being taken that he affix his name and notarial seal, and return to this office in the enclosed envelope.

Respectfully,
AG-844-Env.   Commissioner.

Applications for Enrollment of Creek Newborn
Act of 1905 Volume XI

BIRTH AFFIDAVIT.
DEPARTMENT OF THE INTERIOR.
COMMISSION TO THE FIVE CIVILIZED TRIBES.

IN RE APPLICATION FOR ENROLLMENT, as a citizen of the Creek Nation, of Sam Spokogee, born on the 2 day of July, 1904

Name of Father: Belcher Spokogee   a citizen of the Creek Nation.
Name of Mother: Jennie Spokogee   a citizen of the Creek Nation.

Postoffice   Sapulpa I.Ty.

AFFIDAVIT OF MOTHER.   Child present

UNITED STATES OF AMERICA, Indian Territory,
Western   DISTRICT.

I, Jennie Spokogee, on oath state that I am 23 years of age and a citizen by blood, of the Creek Nation; that I am the lawful wife of Belcher Spokogee, who is a citizen, by blood of the Creek Nation; that a male child was born to me on 2 day of July, 1904, that said child has been named Sam Spokogee, and was living March 4, 1905.

                                             Jennie Spokogee
Witnesses To Mark:
{

Subscribed and sworn to before me this 24" day of April, 1905.

(Seal)   J McDermott
                                     Notary Public.

AFFIDAVIT OF ATTENDING PHYSICIAN OR MID-WIFE.

UNITED STATES OF AMERICA, Indian Territory,
Western   DISTRICT.

I, Lucinda Bruner, a midwife, on oath state that I attended on Mrs. Jennie Spokogee, wife of Belcher Spokogee on the 2 day of July, 1904; that there was born to her on said date a *(blank)* child; that said child was living March 4, 1905, and is said to have been named Sam Spokogee

                                             Lucinda Bruner
Witnesses To Mark:
{

Applications for Enrollment of Creek Newborn
Act of 1905 Volume XI

Subscribed and sworn to before me this 24" day of April, 1905.

(Seal)   J McDermott
   Notary Public.

BIRTH AFFIDAVIT.
DEPARTMENT OF THE INTERIOR.
COMMISSION TO THE FIVE CIVILIZED TRIBES.

IN RE APPLICATION FOR ENROLLMENT, as a citizen of the Creek Nation, of Sam Ispokogee, born on the 2 day of July, 1904

Name of Father: Belcher Ispokogee   a citizen of the Creek Nation.
Name of Mother: Jennie Ispokogee   a citizen of the Creek Nation.

Postoffice   Sapulpa

AFFIDAVIT OF MOTHER.   Child present

UNITED STATES OF AMERICA, Indian Territory,
   Western   DISTRICT.

I, Jennie Ispokogee, on oath state that I am 23 years of age and a citizen by blood, of the Creek Nation; that I am the lawful wife of Belcher Ispokogee, who is a citizen, by blood of the Creek Nation; that a male child was born to me on 2 day of July, 1904, that said child has been named Sam Ispokogee, and was living March 4, 1905.

   Jennie Ispokogee
Witnesses To Mark:
{ James J Mars
{ Lucinda Bruner

Subscribed and sworn to before me this 31st day of October, 1905.

My commission expires May 7, 1907.   James J Mars
   Notary Public.

AFFIDAVIT OF ATTENDING PHYSICIAN OR MID-WIFE.

UNITED STATES OF AMERICA, Indian Territory,
   Western   DISTRICT.

I, Lucinda Bruner, a midwife, on oath state that I attended on Mrs. Jennie Ispokogee, wife of Belcher Ispokogee on the 2 day of July, 1904; that there was

Applications for Enrollment of Creek Newborn
Act of 1905   Volume XI

born to her on said date a   male   child; that said child was living March 4, 1905, and is said to have been named Sam Ispokogee

Lucinda Bruner

Witnesses To Mark:

{

Subscribed and sworn to before me this 31st day of October, 1905.

My commission expires May 7, 1907.   James J Mars
Notary Public.

BIRTH AFFIDAVIT.
DEPARTMENT OF THE INTERIOR.
COMMISSION TO THE FIVE CIVILIZED TRIBES.

IN RE APPLICATION FOR ENROLLMENT, as a citizen of the Creek. - - - - - - - - - - - Nation, of Elma Glenn, - - - - - - - - - - -------- - , born on the 19th, day of June, - - - , 1904
non

Name of Father: R.J. Glenn, - - - - - - - - - - - - -   a citizen of the C R E E K,- -Nation.
Name of Mother: Ida Estella, Glenn, - - - - - - -   a citizen of the C R E E K,- - Nation.
(Broken Arrow)
Postoffice   Praper, I.T.

AFFIDAVIT OF MOTHER.

Child Brought in 5/24/05

UNITED STATES OF AMERICA, Indian Territory, }   Gr.
Western - - - - - - - - - DISTRICT.

I, Ida Estella Glenn, - - - - - - - - - - - - - - - , on oath state that I am Twenty four years of age and a citizen by Blood - - - - - - , of the Creek - - - - - - - - - - - - Nation; that I am the lawful wife of R.J. Glenn - , who is not citizen, by - - - - - - - - - of the Creek - - - - - - - - - - Nation; that a female   child was born to me on 19th - - - - day of June - - - - - - - - - - - - - - , 1904, that said child has been named Elma Glenn - - - - - - - - , and was living March 4, 1905.

Ida Estella Glenn

Witnesses To Mark:

{

4

Applications for Enrollment of Creek Newborn
Act of 1905   Volume XI

Subscribed and sworn to before me this 22nd day of April - - - - - - - - , 1905.

My Commission expires Feb. 21, 1907.

B Barton
Notary Public.

AFFIDAVIT OF ATTENDING PHYSICIAN OR MID-WIFE.

UNITED STATES OF AMERICA, Indian Territory,
Western - - - - - - - DISTRICT.

I, M.D. Taylor - - - - - - - - - - - - - , a Physician, - - - , on oath state that I attended on Mrs. Ida Estella Glenn - - - - - , wife of R.J. Glenn - - - - - - on the 19th day of June - - - - - , 1904 ; that there was born to her on said date a female child; that said child was living March 4, 1905, and is said to have been named Elma Glenn - - - - -

M. D. Taylor, M.D.
Witnesses To Mark:

Subscribed and sworn to before me this 22nd day of April - - - - - - - - , 1905.

My Commission expires Feb. 21, 1907.

B Barton
Notary Public.

BIRTH AFFIDAVIT.

DEPARTMENT OF THE INTERIOR.
COMMISSION TO THE FIVE CIVILIZED TRIBES.

IN RE APPLICATION FOR ENROLLMENT, as a citizen of the Muskogee Nation, of L. Beatrice Bruner, born on the 1st day of February , 1902

Name of Father: Richard Bruner   a citizen of the Muskogee   Nation.
Name of Mother: Sarah Bruner   a citizen of the Muskogee   Nation.

Postoffice   Coweta, Ind. Terry

Applications for Enrollment of Creek Newborn
Act of 1905 Volume XI

AFFIDAVIT OF MOTHER.

UNITED STATES OF AMERICA, Indian Territory, ⎫
    Western   DISTRICT.   ⎬

I, Sarah Bruner , on oath state that I am 25 years of age and a citizen by blood , of the Muskogee Nation; that I am the lawful wife of Richard Bruner , who is a citizen, by blood of the Muskogee Nation; that a girl child was born to me on 1st day of February , 1902 , that said child has been named Lady Beatrice Bruner , and is now living.

Sarah Bruner

Witnesses To Mark:
{

Subscribed and sworn to before me this 10th day of April , 1905.

Bert J Beavers
Notary Public.

My commission expires Dec 19- 1908

AFFIDAVIT OF ATTENDING PHYSICIAN OR MID-WIFE.

UNITED STATES OF AMERICA, Indian Territory, ⎫
    Western   DISTRICT.   ⎬

I, Susan Sarty , a Midwife , on oath state that I attended on Mrs. Sarah Bruner , wife of Richard Bruner on the 1st day of February , 1902 ; that there was born to her on said date a girl child; that said child is now living and is said to have been named Lady Beatrice Bruner

her
Susan x Sarty
mark

Witnesses To Mark:
{ Sadie Chissoe
  (Name Illegible)

Subscribed and sworn to before me this 10th day of April , 1905.

Bert J Beavers
Notary Public.

My commission expires Dec 19- 1908

Applications for Enrollment of Creek Newborn
Act of 1905   Volume XI

BIRTH AFFIDAVIT.
DEPARTMENT OF THE INTERIOR.
COMMISSION TO THE FIVE CIVILIZED TRIBES.

IN RE APPLICATION FOR ENROLLMENT, as a citizen of the Creek Nation, of Nina E. Posey, born on the 12th day of May, 1904

Name of Father: Albert W. Posey a citizen of the Creek Nation.
Name of Mother: Mary A. Posey a citizen of the United States Nation.

Postoffice Basin Idaho at present time

AFFIDAVIT OF MOTHER.

UNITED STATES OF AMERICA, Indian Territory,
State of Idaho   DISTRICT.
County of Cassia

I, Mary A Posey , on oath state that I am 29 years of age and a citizen ~~by~~ of the United , ~~of the~~ States ~~Nation~~; that I am the lawful wife of Albert W Posey , who is a citizen, by birth of the Creek Nation; that a Female child was born to me on 12th day of May , 1904 , that said child has been named Nina E Posey , and was living March 4, 1905.

                                                Mary A Posey
Witnesses To Mark:
 { W.A. Martindale
   J.A. Martindale

Subscribed and sworn to before me this 24th day of April , 1905.

                                                B.P. Howells
                                                Notary Public.

AFFIDAVIT OF ATTENDING PHYSICIAN OR MID-WIFE.

UNITED STATES OF AMERICA, Indian Territory,
State of Idaho   DISTRICT.
County of Cassia

I, Dr. J J Hannberg , a Physician , on oath state that I attended on Mrs. Mary A Posey , wife of Albert W Posey on the 12th day of May , 1904 ; that there was born to her on said date a Female child; that said child was living March 4, 1905, and is said to have been named Nina E Posey

                                                J J Hannberg
Witnesses To Mark:
 { Mamie Hannberg
   E.B. Dayley

Applications for Enrollment of Creek Newborn
Act of 1905 Volume XI

Subscribed and sworn to before me 24th day of April, 1905.

B.P. Howells
Notary Public.

CERTIFICATE OF MARRIAGE:

STATE OF IDAHO)
COUNTY OF CASSIA) SS

I, B. P. Howells, a Justice of the Peace in and for the County of Cassia, State of Idaho, do hereby certify that on the eighth day of December, 1893.
Mr. Albert W. Posey of Basin, Idaho.

and
Miss Mary A Dayley, of Basin, Idaho,
were by me joined together IN THE BONDS OF MATRIMONY at James Dayley in said Cassia County, State of Idaho, in accordance with the laws of the United States and of said State of Idaho, and that I, as such officiating Justice, satisfied my self that neither of the parties to such marriage had living, at the date thereof, any legal husband or wife, and that no other impediment existed to hinder the said marriage.

B.P. Howells,
John H. Rothery   Justice of the Peace.
J.N. Dayley.

We, the parties in the foregoing certified named as having contracted marriage at the time and place therein mentioned, do hereby certify and declare that all of the facts in said certificate set forth are true and correct.

Albert W. Posey,
Witnesses: John H. Rothery   Mary A. Dayley.
J.N. Dayley
Dated Dec. 8th, 1893.

CERTIFICATE OF MARRIAGE.

Mr. Albert W. Posey of Basin, Idaho, and Miss Mary M[sic]. Dayley, of Basin Idaho, B.P. Howells, Officiating. Filed _____189____

_____Probate Judge.

Lona Merrick, being duly sworn, states that she copied the above and foregoing and that the same is a true and correct copy of the original.

Lona Merrick

Applications for Enrollment of Creek Newborn
Act of 1905 Volume XI

Subscribed and sworn to before me this 2nd day of August, 1906.

HG Hains
Notary Public.

J.D.

Muskogee, Indian Territory, April 27, 1905.

Albert W. Posey,
　　Basin,
　　　　Cassia County, Idaho.

Dear Sir:

　　The Commission acknowledges receipt of your letter of April 19, 1905, in which you request blank form of birth affidavit for your twelve months old child, Ninna[sic] Posey. You also state that you are the father of a child who died November, 1898, and you ask if said deceased child is entitled to enrollment as a citizen of the Creek Nation.

　　In accordance with your request there is herewith enclosed one blank of the description desired.

　　In having these applications executed care should be exercised to see that all blanks are properly filled, all names written in full and in the event that either of the persons signing the affidavit is unable to write, signatures by mark must be attested by two witnesses. Each affidavit must be executed before a Notary Public and the notarial seal and signature of the officer must be attached to each separate affidavit.

　　You are further advised that persons who died before April 1, 1899, are not entitled to enrollment as citizens of the Creek Nation.

　　　　　　　　　　　　　　Respectfully,
1 B A　　　　　　　　　　　　　　　　　　　Chairman.

NC-847.

Muskogee, Indian Territory, October 19, 1905.

Mary A. Posey,
　　Basin, Idaho.

Dear Madam:

　　In the matter of the application for the enrollment of your minor child, Nina E. Posey, born May 12, 1904, as a citizen by blood of the Creek Nation, You are advised

Applications for Enrollment of Creek Newborn
Act of 1905   Volume XI

that it will be necessary for you to furnish this office with evidence of your marriage to Albert W. Posey, the father of said child.

Such evidence may consist of either the original or a certified copy of your marriage license and certificate.

Respectfully,

Commissioner.

J.D.

Muskogee, Indian Territory, April 20, 1905.

Peter Boon,
    Beggs, Indian Territory.

Dear Sir:

The Commission is in receipt of your letter, dated April 19, 1905, in which you ask if affidavits relating to the birth of your twin children, Ikey and Isaac Boon, have been received by the Commission.

In reply you are advised said affidavits have been filed with the Commission and are considered as an application for the enrollment of said Ikey and Isaac Boon as citizens of the Creek Nation. It is stated in said affidavits that the parents of Ikey and Isaac Boon are Peter and Martha Boon, who, it is claimed, are citizens of the Creek Nation.

You are further advised that the records of the Commission have been examined and the names of Peter and Martha Boon, or either of them, do not appear on the approved roll of citizens by blood of the Creek Nation.

You are requested to advise the Commission as to the names and roll numbers appearing on the deeds or allotment certificates of yourself and your wife, Martha Boon, in case deeds or allotment certificates have been issued.

Respectfully,

Chairman.

Applications for Enrollment of Creek Newborn
Act of 1905   Volume XI

(The letter below copied as given.)

Beggs I.T.
April 26 <u>05</u>

Com. To the five Civilize Tribe
Muskogee, I.T.

Sir inclose you will find number of Deeds of which you requsted of me My Town is *(Illegible)* Town My Deed show this Roll nomber 4848   You will my name Peter Boon

Before my wife was married she went by the name of Martha Adams and her Land was allotted to he[sic] in that name so her Roll Nomber on her deed is 2147

She is the mother of Wm Washington Decese. Allso she are the mother of Isaac Boon and Ikey Boon The little Twin boys

I am yours
Truly Peter Boon
Beggs I. T.

BIRTH AFFIDAVIT.

DEPARTMENT OF THE INTERIOR.
COMMISSION TO THE FIVE CIVILIZED TRIBES.

IN RE APPLICATION FOR ENROLLMENT, as a citizen of the Creek Nation, of Isaac Boon , born on the 16th day of March , 1903

Name of Father: Peter Boon	a citizen of the	Creek	Nation.
Name of Mother: Martha Boon	a citizen of the	Creek	Nation.

Postoffice   Beggs, I.T.

AFFIDAVIT OF MOTHER.

UNITED STATES OF AMERICA, Indian Territory, ⎫
    Western   DISTRICT.   ⎭

I, Martha Boon , on oath state that I am 20 years of age and a citizen by blood , of the Creek Nation; that I am the lawful wife of Peter Boon , who is a citizen, by blood of the Creek Nation; that a male child was born to me on Sixteenth day of March , 1903 , that said child has been named Isaac Boon , and was living March 4, 1905.

Martha Boon

Applications for Enrollment of Creek Newborn
Act of 1905   Volume XI

Witnesses To Mark:
{ Wm F A Gierkes
{ Lewis Adams

Subscribed and sworn to before me this 8<u>th</u> day of April, 1905.

W^mFA Gierkes
Notary Public.
My Commission Expires June 29, 1908

AFFIDAVIT OF ATTENDING PHYSICIAN OR MID-WIFE.

UNITED STATES OF AMERICA, Indian Territory, }
 Western   DISTRICT.

I, Annie Adams, a midwife, on oath state that I attended on Mrs. Martha Boon, wife of Peter Boon on the Sixteenth day of March, 1903 ; that there was born to her on said date a male child; that said child was living March 4, 1905, and is said to have been named Isaac Boon

Annie Adams

Witnesses To Mark:
{ Wm F A Gierkes
{ Lewis Adams

Subscribed and sworn to before me this 8<u>th</u> day of April, 1905.

W^mFA Gierkes
Notary Public.
My Commission Expires June 29, 1908

BIRTH AFFIDAVIT.

DEPARTMENT OF THE INTERIOR.
COMMISSION TO THE FIVE CIVILIZED TRIBES.

IN RE APPLICATION FOR ENROLLMENT, as a citizen of the Creek Nation, of Ikey Boon, born on the 16th day of March, 1903

Name of Father: Peter Boon   a citizen of the   Creek   Nation.
Name of Mother: Martha Boon   a citizen of the   Creek   Nation.

Postoffice   Beggs, I.T.

Applications for Enrollment of Creek Newborn
Act of 1905 Volume XI

AFFIDAVIT OF MOTHER.

UNITED STATES OF AMERICA, Indian Territory, ⎫
    Western   DISTRICT.   ⎬

    I, Martha Boon, on oath state that I am 20 years of age and a citizen by blood, of the Creek Nation; that I am the lawful wife of Peter Boon, who is a citizen, by blood of the Creek Nation; that a male child was born to me on Sixteenth day of March, 1903, that said child has been named Ikey Boon, and was living March 4, 1905.

                             Martha Boon

Witnesses To Mark:
⎰ Wm F A Gierkes
⎱ Lewis Adams

    Subscribed and sworn to before me this 8$^{\underline{th}}$ day of April, 1905.

                             W^{m}FA Gierkes
                             Notary Public.
               My Commission Expires June 29, 1908

AFFIDAVIT OF ATTENDING PHYSICIAN OR MID-WIFE.

UNITED STATES OF AMERICA, Indian Territory, ⎫
    Western   DISTRICT.   ⎬

    I, Annie Adams, a midwife, on oath state that I attended on Mrs. Martha Boon, wife of Peter Boon on the Sixteenth day of March, 1903; that there was born to her on said date a male child; that said child was living March 4, 1905, and is said to have been named Ikey Boon

                             Annie Adams

Witnesses To Mark:
⎰ Wm F A Gierkes
⎱ Lewis Adams

    Subscribed and sworn to before me this 8$^{\underline{th}}$ day of April, 1905.

                             W^{m}FA Gierkes
                             Notary Public.
               My Commission Expires June 29, 1908

Applications for Enrollment of Creek Newborn
Act of 1905 Volume XI

Cr BA-2250 1/2-B

Muskogee, Indian Territory, May 5, 1905.

Vicy Dansby,
    Care of Walter Dansby,
        Braggs, Indian Territory.

Dear Madam:

    The Commission is in receipt of an affidavit executed by you relative to the birth of your minor child, Lucinda Dansby; it is stated in said affidavit that you are a citizen by adoption of the Creek Nation.

    Without further information, the Commission is unable to identify you on the approved roll of Creek Freedmen. You are therefore requested to inform the Commission as to your roll number as the same appears on your deeds or allotment certificate.

        Respectfully,

                Chairman.

NC. 849.

Muskogee, Indian Territory, July 15, 1905.

Chief Clerk,
    Cherokee Enrollment Division,
        Muskogee, Indian Territory.

Dear Sir:

    April 28, 1905, application was made to the Commission to the Five Civilized Tribes for the enrollment of Lucinda Dansby, born June 2, 1901, as a citizen by blood of the Creek Nation. It is stated in said application that the father of said child is Walter Dansby, a citizen of the Cherokee Nation, and that the mother is Vicey Dansby, a citizen of the Creek Nation.

    You are requested to inform the Creek Enrollment Division as to whether application has been made for the enrollment of said Lucinda Dansby, as a citizen of the Cherokee Nation, and if so, what disposition has been made of the same.

        Respectfully,

                Commissioner.

Applications for Enrollment of Creek Newborn
Act of 1905 Volume XI

REFER IN REPLY TO THE FOLLOWING:

DEPARTMENT OF THE INTERIOR,
COMMISSIONER TO THE FIVE CIVILIZED TRIBES.

Muskogee, Indian Territory, July 18, 1905.

Chief Clerk,
   Creek Enrollment Division,
      Muskogee, Indian Territory.

Dear Sir:

    Replying to your letter of July 18, 1905, (NC. 849) asking to be advised whether or not any application has ever been made for the enrollment, as a citizen of the Cherokee Nation, of Lucinda Dansby, a child of Walter Dansby, a citizen of the Cherokee Nation, and Vicey Dansby, a citizen of the Creek Nation, you are advised that from an examination of the records of the Cherokee Enrollment Division it does not appear that any application has ever been made for the enrollment of said child as a citizen of that nation.

                          Respectfully,
                          Tams Bixby   Commissioner.

GHL

NC 849

Muskogee, Indian Territory, November 18, 1906.

Chief Clerk,
   Cherokee Enrollment Division,
      General Office.

Dear Sir:

    You are hereby advised that the name of Lucinda Dausby[sic] born June 2, 1901 to Walter Dausby (or Dansby) an alleged citizen of the Cherokee Nation and Vicy[sic] Dansby, a citizen by blood of the Creek Nation, is contained in schedule or minor citizens by blood of the Creek Nation, approved by the Secretary of the Interior, November 27, 1905, opposite Roll Number 813.

                          Respectfully,
                                    Commissioner.

Applications for Enrollment of Creek Newborn
Act of 1905   Volume XI

BIRTH AFFIDAVIT.
DEPARTMENT OF THE INTERIOR.
COMMISSION TO THE FIVE CIVILIZED TRIBES.

IN RE APPLICATION FOR ENROLLMENT, as a citizen of the Creek Nation, of Lucinda Dansby, born on the 2nd day of June, 1901

Name of Father: Walter Dansby   a citizen of the   Cherokee   Nation.
Name of Mother: Vicy Dansby   a citizen of the   Creek   Nation.

Postoffice   Braggs Ind. Ter.

AFFIDAVIT OF MOTHER.

UNITED STATES OF AMERICA, Indian Territory,
Western   DISTRICT.

about
I, Vicy Dansby, on oath state that I am 33 years of age and a citizen by adoption, of the Creek Nation; that I am the lawful wife of Walter Dansby, who is a citizen, by adoption of the Cherokee Nation; that a Female child was born to me on 2nd day of June, 1901, that said child has been named Lucinda Dansby, and was living March 4, 1905.

                                   her
                              Vicy x Dansby
Witnesses To Mark: mark
   { Elmer Coon
   { Walter Smith

Subscribed and sworn to before me this 29 day of April, 1905.

                              Edward McLain
                              Notary Public.

AFFIDAVIT OF ATTENDING PHYSICIAN OR MID-WIFE.

UNITED STATES OF AMERICA, Indian Territory,
Western   DISTRICT.

I, Gracie Crossland, a midwife, on oath state that I attended on Mrs. Vicy Dansby, wife of Walter Dansby on the 2 day of June, 1901; that there was born to her on said date a Female child; that said child was living March 4, 1905, and is said to have been named Lucinda Dansby

                               her
                          Gracie x Crossland
Witnesses To Mark: mark
   { Elmer Coon
   { Walter Smith

Applications for Enrollment of Creek Newborn
Act of 1905 Volume XI

Subscribed and sworn to before me 29 day of April, 1905.

                                Edward McLain
                                Notary Public.

BIRTH AFFIDAVIT.
DEPARTMENT OF THE INTERIOR.
COMMISSION TO THE FIVE CIVILIZED TRIBES.

IN RE APPLICATION FOR ENROLLMENT, as a citizen of the Creek Nation, of Lucinda Dausby, born on the 2 day of June, 1901

Name of Father: Walter Dausby	a citizen of the Cherokee Nation.
Name of Mother: Vicey Dausby	a citizen of the Creek Nation.

                        Postoffice   Braggs

AFFIDAVIT OF MOTHER.

UNITED STATES OF AMERICA, Indian Territory,
    Western   **DISTRICT.**

    I, Vicey Dausby , on oath state that I am 32 years of age and a citizen by blood, of the Creek Nation; that I am the lawful wife of Walter Dausby , who is a citizen, by adoption of the Cherokee Nation; that a female child was born to me on 2 day of June , 1901 , that said child has been named Lucinda Dausby , and was living March 4, 1905.   My

                                        Vicey x Dausby
Witnesses To Mark: Mark
   { Zera E Parrish
     JY Miller

    Subscribed and sworn to before me this 28$^{\underline{th}}$ day of April , 1905.

                                  Zera E Parrish
                                  Notary Public.

Applications for Enrollment of Creek Newborn
Act of 1905   Volume XI

BIRTH AFFIDAVIT.

DEPARTMENT OF THE INTERIOR.
COMMISSION TO THE FIVE CIVILIZED TRIBES.

    IN RE APPLICATION FOR ENROLLMENT, as a citizen of the Creek Nation, of Leola May Berryhill, born on the 24 day of May, 1904

Name of Father: Pleasant Berryhill   a citizen of the   Creek   Nation.
Broken Arrow Town
Name of Mother: Jeanetta Berryhill   a citizen of the   Creek   Nation.
Osoche Town
                          Postoffice   Okmulgee, Ind. Ter.

AFFIDAVIT OF MOTHER.

UNITED STATES OF AMERICA, Indian Territory, }   Child is present
     Western   DISTRICT.

    I, Jeanetta Berryhill, on oath state that I am 24 years of age and a citizen by blood, of the Creek Nation; that I am the lawful wife of Pleasant Berryhill, who is a citizen, by blood of the Creek Nation; that a female child was born to me on 24 day of November, 1904, that said child has been named Leola May Berryhill, and was living March 4, 1905.

                                         Jeanetta Berryhill
Witnesses To Mark:
{

     Subscribed and sworn to before me this 10 day of April, 1905.

                                         Drennan C Skaggs
                                             Notary Public.

AFFIDAVIT OF ATTENDING PHYSICIAN OR MID-WIFE.

UNITED STATES OF AMERICA, Indian Territory, }
     Western   DISTRICT.

    I, F. M. Logan, a physician, on oath state that I attended on Mrs. Jeanetta Berryhill, wife of Pleasant Berryhill on the 24 day of May, 1901; that there was born to her on said date a female child; that said child was living March 4, 1905, and is said to have been named Leola May Berryhill
                                         F M Logan
Witnesses To Mark:
{

Applications for Enrollment of Creek Newborn
Act of 1905 Volume XI

Subscribed and sworn to before me this 10 day of April, 1905.

                                Drennan C Skaggs
                                Notary Public.

BIRTH AFFIDAVIT.

                Mother Creek Roll N° 7301
                Father Creek Roll N° 7145

DEPARTMENT OF THE INTERIOR.
COMMISSION TO THE FIVE CIVILIZED TRIBES.

IN RE APPLICATION FOR ENROLLMENT, as a citizen of the Creek Nation, of Ollie Grayson, born on the 14 day of June, 1902

Name of Father: Buck Grayson   a citizen of the Creek Nation.
(Lochopaka)
Name of Mother: Menene Grayson   a citizen of the Creek Nation.
(Hitchite)
                        Postoffice   Fry

AFFIDAVIT OF MOTHER.

                                          Child Present

UNITED STATES OF AMERICA, Indian Territory,
    Western   DISTRICT.

    I, Menene Grayson, on oath state that I am about 30 years of age and a citizen by blood, of the Creek Nation; that I am the lawful wife of Buck Grayson, who is a citizen, by blood of the Creek Nation; that a female child was born to me on 14 day of June, 1902, that said child has been named Ollie Grayson, and was living March 4, 1905.   Her

                                   Menene x Grayson
Witnesses To Mark: mark
    David Shelby
    EC Griesel

Subscribed and sworn to before me this 24 day of April, 1905.

(Seal)   Edw C Griesel
                                              Notary Public.

Applications for Enrollment of Creek Newborn
Act of 1905   Volume XI

AFFIDAVIT OF ATTENDING ~~PHYSICIAN OR MID-WIFE~~.
Father

UNITED STATES OF AMERICA, Indian Territory,
   Western   DISTRICT.

I, Buck Grayson , ~~a~~ *(blank)* , on oath state that I attended on Mrs. Menaney Grayson , my wife ~~of~~ *(blank)* on the 14 day of June , 1902 ; that there was born to her on said date a female child; that said child was living March 4, 1905, and is said to have been named Ollie Grayson

Buck Grayson

Witnesses To Mark:

Subscribed and sworn to before me this 24 day of April , 1905.

(Seal)   Edw C Griesel
                                       Notary Public.

Mother Cr Roll No 7301
Father Cr   "   " 7145

BIRTH AFFIDAVIT.

DEPARTMENT OF THE INTERIOR.
COMMISSION TO THE FIVE CIVILIZED TRIBES.

IN RE APPLICATION FOR ENROLLMENT, as a citizen of the Creek Nation, of Lillie Grayson, born on the 8 day of Feb, 1904

Name of Father: Buck Grayson   a citizen of the   Creek   Nation.
(Lochopocha)
Name of Mother: ~~Menaney~~ Grayson   a citizen of the   Creek   Nation.
(Hitchite)   Menene
                              Postoffice   Fry, I. T.

AFFIDAVIT OF MOTHER.
Child Present

UNITED STATES OF AMERICA, Indian Territory,
   Western   DISTRICT.

            enene
I, ~~Menaney~~ Grayson , on oath state that I am about 30 years of age and a citizen by blood , of the Creek Nation; that I am the lawful wife of Buck Grayson , who is a citizen, by blood of the Creek Nation; that a female child was born to me on 8 day of Feb , 1904 , that said child has been named Lillie Grayson , and was living March 4, 1905.

Applications for Enrollment of Creek Newborn
Act of 1905   Volume XI

                                                          enene   Her

                                            M~~enaney~~ x Grayson

Witnesses To Mark: mark
{ David Shelby
  Jesse McDermott

Subscribed and sworn to before me this 24 day of April , 1905.

(Seal)   Edw C Griesel
                                                      Notary Public.

AFFIDAVIT OF ATTENDING ~~PHYSICIAN OR MID-WIFE~~.
                                         Father

UNITED STATES OF AMERICA, Indian Territory,
     Western   **DISTRICT.**

     I, Buck Grayson , ~~a~~ *(blank)* , on oath state that I attended on Mrs. Menaney Grayson , my wife ~~of~~ *(blank)* on the 8 day of Feb , 1904 ; that there was born to her on said date a female child; that said child was living March 4, 1905, and is said to have been named Lillie Grayson

                                               Buck Grayson
Witnesses To Mark:

{

Subscribed and sworn to before me this 24 day of April , 1905.

(Seal)   Edw C Griesel
                                                      Notary Public.

Applications for Enrollment of Creek Newborn
Act of 1905 Volume XI

NC-852.

Muskogee, Indian Territory, October 19, 1905.

Jennie Cosar,
    Sapulpa, Indian Territory.

Dear Madam:

    In the matter of the application for the enrollment of your minor child, Galvos Cosar, born November 4, 1902, as a citizen by blood of the Creek Nation, this office requires the affidavit of the physician or midwife who attended at the birth of said Galvos Cosar and a blank for that purpose is inclosed herewith.

    If there was no physician or midwife in attendance when said child was born it will be necessary for you to furnish this office with the affidavits of two disinterested persons relative to the birth of said child. Said affidavits to set forth said child's name, the date of his birth, the names of his parents and whether or not he was living on March 4, 1905.

    This matter should receive your immediate attention.

                        Respectfully,

                                         Commissioner.

B C
Env.

AFFIDAVIT OF ATTENDING PHYSICIAN OR MID-WIFE.

UNITED STATES OF AMERICA, Indian Territory,
    Western   DISTRICT.

    I, Toochee Standwaitie, a *(blank)*, on oath state that I attended on Mrs. Jennie Cosar, wife of Tom Cosar on the 4th day of Nov, 1902; that there was born to her on said date a male child; that said child is now living and is said to have been named Galvos Cosar

                                                her
                                  Toochee x Standwaitie
Witnesses To Mark: mark
  (Name Illegible)
  W A Sapulpa

    Subscribed and sworn to before me this 7 day of Nov, 1906.

My Commission expires 10/20-1906   Joseph Bruner
                                                     Notary Public.

Applications for Enrollment of Creek Newborn
Act of 1905 Volume XI

BIRTH AFFIDAVIT.
DEPARTMENT OF THE INTERIOR.
COMMISSION TO THE FIVE CIVILIZED TRIBES.

IN RE APPLICATION FOR ENROLLMENT, as a citizen of the Creek Nation, of Galvos Cosar, born on the 4th day of November, 1902

Name of Father: Tom Cosar   a citizen of the   Creek   Nation.
Name of Mother: Jennie Cosar   a citizen of the   Creek   Nation.

                       Postoffice   Sapulpa I.T.

AFFIDAVIT OF MOTHER.
                                      Child present
UNITED STATES OF AMERICA, Indian Territory, ⎫
     Western   DISTRICT. ⎭

      I, Jennie Cosar, on oath state that I am about 33 years of age and a citizen by blood, of the Creek Nation; that I am the lawful wife of Tom Cosar, who is a citizen, by blood of the Creek Nation; that a male child was born to me on 4th day of November, 1902, that said child has been named Galvos Cosar, and was living March 4, 1905.
                                                  her
                                           Jennie x Cosar
Witnesses To Mark: mark
    ⎰ David Shelby
    ⎱ Jesse McDermott

      Subscribed and sworn to before me this 24 day of April, 1905.

(Seal)   Edw C Griesel
                                             Notary Public.

AFFIDAVIT OF ~~ATTENDING PHYSICIAN OR MID-WIFE~~. father

UNITED STATES OF AMERICA, Indian Territory, ⎫   Child present
     Western   DISTRICT. ⎭

      I, Tom Cosar, ~~a (blank)~~, on oath state that I attended on Mrs. Jennie Cosar my, wife of ~~(blank)~~ on the 4th day of November, 1902; that there was born to her on said date a male child; that said child was living March 4, 1905, and is said to have been named Galvos Cosar
                                       Tom Cosar
Witnesses To Mark:
    ⎰
    ⎱

Applications for Enrollment of Creek Newborn
Act of 1905 Volume XI

Subscribed and sworn to before me this 24 day of April, 1905.

(Seal)   Edw C Griesel
                                             Notary Public.

BIRTH AFFIDAVIT.

DEPARTMENT OF THE INTERIOR.
COMMISSION TO THE FIVE CIVILIZED TRIBES.

IN RE APPLICATION FOR ENROLLMENT, as a citizen of the Creek Nation, of Hattie Crabtree, born on the 17 day of June, 1902

Name of Father: George Crabtree   a citizen of the Creek Nation.
Name of Mother: Tooka Hutton   a citizen of the Creek Nation.

                             Postoffice   Huttonville I.T.

AFFIDAVIT OF MOTHER.

UNITED STATES OF AMERICA, Indian Territory,
     Western   DISTRICT.

     I, Tooka Hutton, on oath state that I am 28 years of age and a citizen by Blood, of the Creek Nation; that I am not ~~the lawful~~ wife of George Crabtree, who is a citizen, by blood of the Creek Nation; that a Female child was born to me on 17 day of June, 1902, that said child has been named Hattie Crabtree, and was living March 4, 1905.

                                      Tooka Hutton
Witnesses To Mark:

{

     Subscribed and sworn to before me this 20 day of Apr, 1905.

                                     L.G. McIntosh
                                       Notary Public.

Applications for Enrollment of Creek Newborn
Act of 1905 Volume XI

AFFIDAVIT OF ATTENDING PHYSICIAN OR MID-WIFE.

UNITED STATES OF AMERICA, Indian Territory,
Western DISTRICT.

I, Judie Grayson , a midwife , on oath state that I attended on Mrs. Tooka Hutton , ~~wife of~~ she has no Husband on the 17 day of June , 1902 ; that there was born to her on said date a Female child; that said child was living March 4, 1905, and is said to have been named Hattie Crabtree

Judie Grayson her x mark

Witnesses To Mark:
- Sam Haynes
- Adline Stidham

Subscribed and sworn to before me 20 day of April, 1905.

L.G. McIntosh
Notary Public.

(Illegible) Town Rolle[sic]

BIRTH AFFIDAVIT.

DEPARTMENT OF THE INTERIOR.
COMMISSION TO THE FIVE CIVILIZED TRIBES.

IN RE APPLICATION FOR ENROLLMENT, as a citizen of the Creek Nation, of Rebecca Crabtree , born on the 24 day of Dec , 1904

Name of Father: George Crabtree   a citizen of the Creek Nation.
Name of Mother: Tooka Hutton   a citizen of the Creek Nation.

Postoffice   Hutton Ville I.T.

AFFIDAVIT OF MOTHER.

UNITED STATES OF AMERICA, Indian Territory,
Western DISTRICT.

I, Tooka Hutton , on oath state that I am 28 years of age and a citizen by blood, of the Creek Nation; that I am not a ~~the lawful~~ wife of George Crabtree , who is a citizen, by blood of the Creek Nation; that a Female child was born to me on 24 day of December , 1904 , that said child has been named Rebecca Crabtree , and was living March 4, 1905.

Tooka Hutton

Witnesses To Mark:

Applications for Enrollment of Creek Newborn
Act of 1905   Volume XI

Subscribed and sworn to before me this 20 day of Apr , 1905.

                                    L.G. McIntosh
                                    Notary Public.

AFFIDAVIT OF ATTENDING PHYSICIAN OR MID-WIFE.

UNITED STATES OF AMERICA, Indian Territory, }
    Western   DISTRICT.

                                                                          iss

I, Harriet Kizzee , a midwife , on oath state that I attended on M~~rs~~. Tooka Hutton , ~~wife of~~ she has no Husband on the 24 day of December , 1904 ; that there was born to her on said date a Female child; that said child was living March 4, 1905, and is said to have been named Rebecca Crabtree

                                  Harriet Kizzee   her x mark

Witnesses To Mark:
  { Sam Haynes
    Adline Stidham

Subscribed and sworn to before me 20 day of April, 1905.

                                  L.G. McIntosh
                                  Notary Public.

(Illegible) Town Rolle[sic]

BIRTH AFFIDAVIT.

DEPARTMENT OF THE INTERIOR.
COMMISSION TO THE FIVE CIVILIZED TRIBES.

IN RE APPLICATION FOR ENROLLMENT, as a citizen of the Creek Nation, of Katie Berryhill , born on the 5 day of March , 1903

Name of Father: Aleck Berryhill   a citizen of the Creek Nation.
Concharte Town
Name of Mother: Annie Berryhill   a citizen of the Creek Nation.
Cussehta Town

                          Postoffice   Okmulgee, Ind. Ter.

Applications for Enrollment of Creek Newborn
Act of 1905 Volume XI

AFFIDAVIT OF MOTHER.

UNITED STATES OF AMERICA, Indian Territory, } Child is present
Western DISTRICT.

I, Annie Berryhill , on oath state that I am about 28 years of age and a citizen by blood , of the Creek Nation; that I am the lawful wife of Aleck Berryhill , who is a citizen, by blood of the Creek Nation; that a female child was born to me on 5 day of March , 1903 , that said child has been named Katie Berryhill , and was living March 4, 1905.

                                                   her
                                      Annie x Berryhill
Witnesses To Mark: mark
{ Alex Posey
{ DC Skaggs

Subscribed and sworn to before me this 10 day of April , 1905.

                                      Drennan C Skaggs
                                      Notary Public.

AFFIDAVIT OF ATTENDING PHYSICIAN OR MID-WIFE.

UNITED STATES OF AMERICA, Indian Territory, }
Western DISTRICT.

I, Effie Miller , a——, on oath state that I attended on Mrs. Annie Berryhill , wife of Aleck Berryhill on the 5 day of March , 1903 ; that there was born to her on said date a female child; that said child was living March 4, 1905, and is said to have been named Katie Berryhill
                                       her
                                      Effie x Miller
Witnesses To Mark: mark
{ Alex Posey
{ DC Skaggs

Subscribed and sworn to before me 10 day of April, 1905.

                                      Drennan C Skaggs
                                      Notary Public.

Applications for Enrollment of Creek Newborn
Act of 1905 Volume XI

N.C. 855

DEPARTMENT OF THE INTERIOR,
COMMISSIONER TO THE FIVE CIVILIZED TRIBES.

Muskogee, Indian Territory, October 18, 1905.

In the matter of the application for the enrollment of Elsie West as a citizen by blood of the Creek Nation.

Robert West, being duly sworn, testified as follows (through Jesse McDermott, Official Interpreter):

EXAMINATION BY THE COMMISSIONER:
Q What is your name? A Robert West.
Q How old are you? A I am about 35.
Q What is your postoffice? A Okfuske.
Q Have you a child for whom you made application this year? A No, I did not make application myself.
Q What is the name of the child that you were applying for? A The mother of the child made application and named it Elsie.
Q Is Elsie living? A Yes sir.
Q When was Elsie born? A I wasn't living with her at the time the child was born, and I don't know.
Q Havn't[sic] you any idea at all when this child was born? A No sir, I didn't hear of the birth of the child until sometime after it was born.
Q How old is that child now? A Nearly two years old.
Q Who is the mother of that child? A Parsinda West.
Q Is she a citizen of the Creek Nation? A Yes sir.
Q You are a citizen of the Creek Nation, are you not? A Yes sir.
Q Were you lawfully married to Parsinda? A We were not married according to United States laws--according to the Indian custom.
Q But you were married according to the Indian custom? A Yes sir.
Q Has she possession of the child now? A Yes sir
Q Is her postoffice address Okfuske? A Morse.
Q Then you cannot swear now whether that child was born March or April, 1904, can you? A No sir.
Q Do you know whether or not any one attended her at the birth of the child? A There is a physician at Morse who attended her at the birth of the child, and I understand that he made affidavit about the birth.
Q What is that physician's name? A I don't know his name.

INDIAN TERRITORY, Western District.

I, J. Y. Miller, a stenographer to the Commissioner to the Five Civilized Tribes, do hereby certify that the above and foregoing is a true and complete translation of my notes as same appear in my stenographic report of this case.

JY Miller

Applications for Enrollment of Creek Newborn
Act of 1905   Volume XI

Sworn to and subscribed before me
this the 18th day of October,
1905.   Edw C Griesel
                                        Notary Public.

N.C. 855.
N.B.A. 2654.

DEPARTMENT OF THE INTERIOR,
COMMISSIONER TO THE FIVE CIVILIZED TRIBES.
Muskogee, I. T., February 8, 1906.

In the matter of the application for the enrollment of Elsie West as a citizen by blood of the Creek Nation.

CHOFOLUP HARJO, being duly sworn, testified as follows:

Through Alex Posey Official Interpreter:

BY THE COMMISSIONER:
Q What is your name? A Chofolup Harjo.
Q What is your post office address? A Morse.
Q Do you remember when the Field Party was out in your neighborhood and you stated that Fuscinda[sic], of Nuyaka Town, had a child about a year old? A Yes, sir. At that time I thought the parents were "Snakes" and I gave in the name for that reason, by since that time I have found that the mother made an application for it and that her application is in here.
Q What is the name of that woman who made the application? A Parsinder[sic]. I did know her sir-name but have forgot it.
Q Do you know the name of Parsinder's father? A Locher Fixico.

Said party s identified as Parcinder West opposite Creek Indian Roll No. 4589.

Q What is the name of Parcinder's mother? A Chinah.
Q Was she ever called Nosey? A Chenah is the only name by which I knew her.
Q Has Parcinder any other children? A She has two others.
Q Name then? A The oldest is Malissa and the next is Lonie.
Q Did you know a child of hers by the name of Feney West? A Yes, sir, that child is now dead.
Q What was the name of the father of Feney? A It was generally reported that Robert West was the father of the child but I don't know of my own knowledge that that is a fact.
Q Do you know whether Parcinder was ever married to Robert West? A They lived together. I don't think that he was ever formally married to her.
Q Is this child of Parcinder's living? A Yes, sir.

---oooOOOooo---

Applications for Enrollment of Creek Newborn
Act of 1905 Volume XI

I, D. C. Skaggs, on oath state that the above and foregoing is a full and true transcript of my stenographic notes as taken in said cause on said date.

D. C. Skaggs

Subscribed and sworn to before me this 8" day of Feb. 1906.

J. McDermott
Notary Public.

BIRTH AFFIDAVIT.

DEPARTMENT OF THE INTERIOR.
COMMISSION TO THE FIVE CIVILIZED TRIBES.

IN RE APPLICATION FOR ENROLLMENT, as a citizen of the Creek Nation, of Elsie West, born on the 25 day of March, 1904

Name of Father: Robert West	a citizen of the Creek	Nation.
Name of Mother: Parsinder West	a citizen of the Creek	Nation.

Postoffice Morse, IT

AFFIDAVIT OF MOTHER.

UNITED STATES OF AMERICA, Indian Territory,
Western DISTRICT.

I, Parsinder West, on oath state that I am about 38 years of age and a citizen by blood, of the Creek Nation; that I am not the lawful wife of Robert West, who is a citizen, by blood of the Creek Nation; that a female child was born to me on 25" day of March, 1904, that said child has been named Elsie West, and was living March 4, 1905.

her
Parsinder West x
mark

Witnesses To Mark:
 { John H. Phillips
 { M.L. Chenault

Subscribed and sworn to before me this 26 day of Feb., 1906.

John H. Phillips
Notary Public.

My Commission Expires Sept. 6th 1906

Applications for Enrollment of Creek Newborn
Act of 1905 Volume XI

AFFIDAVIT OF ATTENDING PHYSICIAN OR MID-WIFE.

UNITED STATES OF AMERICA, Indian Territory, }
Western DISTRICT.

I, JA. Kennedy , a Physician , on oath state that I attended on Mrs. Parsindie West , wife of   X   on the 25th day of March , 1904 ; that there was born to her on said date a Female child; that said child was living March 4, 1905, and is said to have been named Elsie West

                 J.A. Kennedy M.D.
Witnesses To Mark:
{

  Subscribed and sworn to before me 2 day of March, 1906.

                C.C. Eskridge
My Commission Expires March 5th 1908.   Notary Public.

BIRTH AFFIDAVIT.
DEPARTMENT OF THE INTERIOR.
COMMISSION TO THE FIVE CIVILIZED TRIBES.

  IN RE APPLICATION FOR ENROLLMENT, as a citizen of the CREEK Nation, of Elsie West , born on the *(blank)* day of April , 1904

Name of Father: Robert West   a citizen of the   Creek   Nation.
Name of Mother: Parsinder West   a citizen of the   Creek   Nation.

         Postoffice   Morse I.T.

AFFIDAVIT OF MOTHER.

UNITED STATES OF AMERICA, Indian Territory, }
  WESTERN   DISTRICT.

  I, Parsinder West , on oath state that I am 35   years of age and a citizen by Blood , of the Creek Nation; ~~that I am the lawful wife of~~ Robert West , who is a citizen, by Blood of the Creek Nation; that a Female   child was born to me on *(blank)* day of April , 1904 , that said child has been named Elsie West , and is now living.   her
                Parsinder x West
Witnesses To Mark: mark
{ F W *(Illegible)*
 C. C. Eskridge

Applications for Enrollment of Creek Newborn
Act of 1905 Volume XI

Subscribed and sworn to before me this 12 day of April, 1905.

My Commission Expires Sept. 6th 1906

John H. Phillips
Notary Public.

BIRTH AFFIDAVIT.

DEPARTMENT OF THE INTERIOR.
COMMISSION TO THE FIVE CIVILIZED TRIBES.

IN RE APPLICATION FOR ENROLLMENT, as a citizen of the Creek Nation, of Elsie West, born on the 25 day of March, 1904

Name of Father: Robert West   a citizen of the   Creek   Nation.
Name of Mother: Parsinder West   a citizen of the   Creek   Nation.

Postoffice   Morse, IT

AFFIDAVIT OF MOTHER.

UNITED STATES OF AMERICA, Indian Territory,
Western   DISTRICT.

I, Parsinder West, on oath state that I am *(blank)* years of age and a citizen by Blood, of the Creek Nation; that I am the lawful wife of *(blank)*, who is a citizen, by *(blank)* of the *(blank)* Nation; that a Female child was born to me on 25 day of March, 1904, that said child has been named Elsie West, and was living March 4, 1905.

                                her
                        Parsinder x West
Witnesses To Mark: mark
  Edward Foster
  William Benson

Subscribed and sworn to before me this 26 day of Apr., 1905.

                        C.C. Eskridge
My Commission Expires March 5th, 1908.   Notary Public.

Applications for Enrollment of Creek Newborn
Act of 1905   Volume XI

AFFIDAVIT OF ATTENDING PHYSICIAN OR MID-WIFE.

UNITED STATES OF AMERICA, Indian Territory,
Western   DISTRICT.

I, JA. Kennedy , a Physician , on oath state that I attended on Mrs. Parsinder West , wife of *(blank)* on the 25 day of March , 1904 ; that there was born to her on said date a Female child; that said child was living March 4, 1905, and is said to have been named Elsie West

J.A. Kennedy M.D.

Witnesses To Mark:

{

Subscribed and sworn to before me this 26 day of Apr. , 1905.

C.C. Eskridge

My Commission Expires March 5th, 1908.   Notary Public.

NC-855.

Muskogee, Indian Territory, October 19, 1905.

Parsender West,
        Morse, Indian Territory.

Dear Madam:

In the matter of the application for the enrollment of your minor child, Elsie West, born March 25, 1904, as a citizen by blood of the Creek Nation, you do not state in your affidavits, relative to the birth of said child, whether or not you are the lawful wife of Robert West who, it is stated in the captions of said affidavits, is the father of said Elsie West. Your name is signed to the affidavits in said case Parsinder West and you are identified upon the final roll of citizens by blood of the Creek Nation as Parsender West. You state in your affidavit, executed April 12, 1905, that said Elsie West was born on the blank day of April 1904, and you and the physician, who attended at the birth of said child, state in your affidavits, executed April 26, 1905, that said Elsie West was born March 25, 1904.

There is inclosed herewith blank form of birth affidavit which you are requested to execute and return to this office in the inclosed envelope. If March 25, 1904 is the correct date of the birth of said child it will not be necessary for you to again secure the affidavit of the physician, who attended at the birth of said child, but if some other date is given you should have the blank for the attending physician or midwife properly filled out and executed before a notary public giving the correct date of the birth of said child.

Applications for Enrollment of Creek Newborn
Act of 1905   Volume XI

Respectfully,
Tams Bixby
Commissioner.

B C
Env.

NC-855

Muskogee, Indian Territory, December 15, 1905.

Parsender West,
   Care of Robert West,
      Okfuskee, Indian Territory.

Dear Madam:

In the matter of the application for the enrollment of your minor child, Elsie West, born March 25, 1904, as a citizen by blood of the Creek Nation, you do not state in your affidavit relative to the birth of said child whether or not you are the lawful wife of Robert West, who, it is states in the caption of said affidavit, is the father of said Elsie West. Your name is signed in said affidavit "Parsinder" West, and you are identified on the final rolls of citizens of the Creek Nation as "Parsender." You state in your affidavit executed April 12, 1905, that said Elsie West was born on the ____ day of April, 1904; and you and the physician who attended at the birth of said Elsie West, state in your affidavit executed April 26, 1905, that said child was born March 25, 1904. Robert West, the father of said child, in his testimony of October 18, 1905, states that said child was born in 1904, but that he does not know whether it was in March or April of that year.

There is herewith enclosed blank form of birth affidavit which you are requested to execute and return to this Office in the enclosed envelope. If March 25, 1904, is the correct date of the birth of said child, it will not be necessary for you to again secure the affidavit of the physician or midwife who attended at the birth of said child; but if some other date is given, you will have the blank for the attending physician or midwife properly filled out and executed before a notary public, giving the correct date of said child's birth, returning affidavit to this Office.

This matter should receive your immediate attention.

Respectfully,
Tams Bixby
Commissioner.

1 B A

Applications for Enrollment of Creek Newborn
Act of 1905   Volume XI

C 856

DEPARTMENT OF THE INTERIOR,
COMMISSION TO THE FIVE CIVILIZED TRIBES.

Okmulgee, I. T., April 10, 1905.

In the matter of the application for the enrollment of Pearlie Bosen as a citizen by blood of the Creek Nation.

JOSIE ASBURY, being duly sworn, testified as follows:

BY COMMISSION:
Q What is your name? A Josie Asbury.
Q How old are you? A Twenty-two.
Q What is your post office address? A Okmulgee.
Q Are you a citizen of the Creek Nation? A Yes, sir.
Q To what town do you belong? A Cheyarha.
Q Do you make application for the enrollment of your minor child, Pearlie Bosen, as a citizen of the Creek Nation? A Yes, sir.
Q What is the name of the father of this child? A George Bosen.
Q Is he living? A Yes, sir.
Q Is he your lawful husband? A No, sir.
Q Were you ever married to him? A No, sir.
Q To what town in the Creek Nation does he belong? A Tulsa Canadian
Q Did you ever live together as man and wife? A Yes, sir.
Q How long did you live together as man and wife? A About a year.
Q Was[sic] you married to him according to Indian Custom? A Yes, sir.
Q Does he acknowledge the child as his own? A Yes, sir.
Q Did you live together before the child was born? A Yes, sir.
Q Does he support the child? A He did but he got married and quit.

---oooOOOooo---

I, D. C. Skaggs, on oath state that the above and foregoing is a full and true transcript of my stenographic notes as taken in said cause on said date.

D. C. Skaggs

Subscribed and sworn to before me this 24 day of July, 1905.

J McDermott
Notary Public.

Applications for Enrollment of Creek Newborn
Act of 1905   Volume XI

JJB

Muskogee, Indian Territory, October 4, 1904.

Barclay Morgan,
    Henryetta, Indian Territory.

Dear Sir:

    Your letter dated September 1, 1904, inclosing an affidavit relative to the birth of Pearlie Bosen, was received by the Commission September 2, 1904. It appears from the affidavit that said Pearlie Bosen is the child of Josephine Asbury, a citizen of the Creek Nation.

    In support of the application the Commission desires the affidavit of one, and if possible, two persons, showing when this application was deposited in the United States Mail for transmission to the Commission.

        Respectfully,

                          Chairman.

J.J.B

BA. 283.

Muskogee, Indian Territory, December 28, 1904.

Josephine Asbury,
    Okmulgee, Indian Territory.

Dear Madam:

    There is on file with the Commission an affidavit relative to the birth of your child, Pearlie Bozen[sic], who it is claimed is entitled to enrollment as a citizen of the Creek Nation.

    You are advised that it will be necessary for you to appear before the Commission at its office in Muskogee, Indian Territory, with two witnesses who know the date of birth of said child, for the purpose of being examined under oath.

        Respectfully,

                          Chairman.

Applications for Enrollment of Creek Newborn
Act of 1905 Volume XI

NC-856.

Muskogee, Indian Territory, October 21, 1905.

Josephine Asbury,
 Okmulbee[sic], Indian Territory.

Dear Madam:

In the matter of the application for the enrollment of your minor child, Pearlie Bosen, as a citizen by blood of the Creek Nation, it appears from your affidavit and the affidavit of the midwife, executed September 1, 1904, that said Pearlie Bosen was born December 26, 1900, and it appears from the affidavits of the same persons, executed April 11, 1905, that said Pearlie Bosen was born December 26, 1901.

In order that this discrepancy may be explained you are notified to appear at the office of the Commissioner to the Five Civilized [sic] at Muskogee, Indian Territory, within fifteen days from date with the midwife in attendance at the birth of said Pearlie Bosen and at least one other witness who knows the exact date of the birth of said child.

Respectfully,

Commissioner.

NC-856

DEPARTMENT OF THE INTERIOR,
COMMISSIONER TO THE FIVE CIVILIZED TRIBES.

Muskogee, Indian Territory, November 4, 1905.

In the matter of the application for the enrollment of Pearlie Bosen as a citizen by blood of the Creek Nation.

Josephine Asbury, being duly sworn, testified as follows:

EXAMINATION BY THE COMMISSIONER:
Q What is your name? A Josephine Asbury.
Q Sometimes called Josie, are you? A Yes sir.
Q But your correct name if Josephine? A Yes sir.
Q What is the name of your father? A Jesse Asbury.
Q What is the name of your mother? A Mary Asbury, now Grayson.

The witness is identified as Josephine Asbury, on Creek Indian card, field No. 1401, opposite Roll No. 4446.

Q How old are you? A I am 22.
Q What is your postoffice address? A Okmulgee.

Applications for Enrollment of Creek Newborn
Act of 1905   Volume XI

Q What is the name of this child you have here? A Pearlie Bosen.
Q What is the name of the father of this child? A George Bosen.

George Bosen is identified on Creek Indian care, field No. 1950, opposite Roll No. 6100.

Q When was this child here born? A 1901, December 26.
Q You have made two affidavits; in one of them you give this date, but in the second one you and the midwife give the year 1900; is that a mistake? A Yes sir.
Q The correct date is 1901? A Yes sir.
Q December 26, next Christmas, 1905, how old will it be? A She will be four years old the coming December 26.
Q You are sure of that? A Yes sir.

Josephine Thompson, being duly sworn, testified as follows:

EXAMINATION BY THE COMMISSIONER:
Q What is your name? A Josephine Thompson.
Q How old are you? A About 67.
Q What is your postoffice? A Okmulgee.
Q Are you a citizen of the Creek Nation? A Yes sir.
Q Are you the grandmother of Josephine Asbury? A Yes sir.
Q She was not married to George Bosen, was she? A No sir.
Q You know that child, Pearlie? A Yes sir.
Q Is that it? A Yes sir.
Q You made out two affidavits; in one of them you gave December 26, 1900, as the date of the birth of this child; was that a mistake? A Yes sir. I don't know about 19's and 18's.
Q How old will it be--? A Four years old this December 26.
Q You are sure of that? A Yes sir.
Q And that is the child there? A Yes sir.

Josephine Asbury, recalled.

Q You are not married? A No sir.
Q Never was married, were you? A No sir.
Q Illegitimate child. But it is your child? A Yes sir.

INDIAN TERRITORY, Western District.
    I, J. Y. Miller, a stenographer to the Commissioner to the Five Civilized Tribes, do hereby certify that the above and foregoing is a true and complete translation of my notes as same appear in my stenographic report of this case.

JY Miller

Applications for Enrollment of Creek Newborn
Act of 1905 Volume XI

Sworn to and subscribed before me
this the 14th day of November,
1905.

                                          J McDermott
                                          Notary Public.

DEPARTMENT OF THE INTERIOR,
COMMISSION TO THE FIVE CIVILIZED TRIBES.
----o----

In the Matter of the Birth)	
Affidavit of Pearlie Bozen[sic],)	
a citizen of the Creek Nation,)	-AFFIDAVIT-
	---o---
making applicayion[sic] for enrollment.)	

United States of America)
Western District   )SS:-
Indian Territory.   )

    I, Mark L. Bozarth, being first duly sworn upon my oath, depose and say, ~~that~~, that the affidavit in relation to the birth of Pearlie Bozen was prepared by me in the office of Phillips and Bozarth at Okmulgee, Indian Territory, on the 1st, day of September, 1904; that I addressed an envelope containing said affidavit to the Commission to the Five Civilized Tribes on said date, and handed the same to Mr W.B. Morgan, to be mailed the evening of September 1st, 1904.

                                            Mark L. Bozarth

Subscribed and sworn to before me this 26th day of October, 1904.

                                            Fred H. Smith
                                            Notary Public.

My Commission Expires Mch 12" 1907

Applications for Enrollment of Creek Newborn
Act of 1905   Volume XI

DEPARTMENT OF THE INTERIOR,
COMMISSION TO THE FIVE CIVILIZED TRIBES.
------o-------

In the matter of the birth)
affidavit of Pearlie Bozen[sic], a) AFFIDAVIT
Citizen of the Creek Nation,) ---o---
making application for enrollment.)

United States of America)

Western District) SS:-

Indian Territory)

     I, Charles L. Phillips, being first duly sworn, upon my oath, depose and say, that I was present at the time the affidavit relating to the birth of Pearlie Bozen was prepared by Mark L. Bozarth; that said affidavit was prepared in the office of Phillips and Bozarth at Okmulgee, Indian Territory, September 1st, 1904, and I saw Mark L. Bozarth address an envelope containing said affidavit to the Commission to the Five Civilized tribes[sic] at Muskogee, Indian Territory, and handed the same to W.B. Morgan to be mailed in the evening of the day above mentioned.

                                               Chas. L. Phillips

Subscribed and sworn to before me this 26 day of October, 1904.

                                               Fred H. Smith
My Commission Ex. Mch 12" 1907   Notary Public.

W.B. Morgan on oath says that he mailed the affidavit relating to the birth of Pearlie Bozen above mentioned between the hours two and four o'clock, September 1st, 1904, P.M. at the Post Officer at Okmulgee, Indian Territory; and that same was properly addressed to the Commission to the Five Civilized Tribes at Muskogee, Indian Territory, and that no one else was present when said affidavit was mailed.

                                               W.B. Morgan

Subscribed and sworn to before me this 26th, day of October, 1904.

                                               Fred H. Smith
My Commission Ex. Mch 12" 1907   Notary Public.

Applications for Enrollment of Creek Newborn
Act of 1905   Volume XI

-DEPARTMENT-OF-THE-INTERIOR-
-COMMISSION-TO-THE-FIVE-CIVILIZED-TRIBES-

In Re Application for Enrollment, as a citizen of the Creek Nation, of Pearlie Bozen   born on   26th day of   December 1900   Name of father   George Bozen   citizen of the   Creek   Nation, name of mother Josephine Asbury   a citizen of the Creek Nation.

PostOffice   Okmulgee, Indian Territory.

-AFFIDAVIT-OF-MOTHER-

United States of America   )
Indian Territory   )
Western Judicial District   )

I,   Josephine Asbury   , on oath state that I am   24   years of age and a citizen, by blood   , of the   Creek   Nation; that I am the lawful wife of ----------------   , who is a citizen, by ---------   , of the   -----------   Nation; that a   female   child was born to me on   26th day of   December 1900   ; that said child has been named   Pearlie Bozen   and is now living.

                                         her
Witness to Mark   Josephine x Asbury
T.W. Morton   mark
Chas. L. Phillips   Subscribed and sworn to before me this
                              the   1st day of   September   1904.

                                William B. Morgan
          My Com Ex April 22, 1908.   Notary Public.

Affidavit of Attending Physician or Mid-Wife.

United States of America, Indian Territory   )
Western Judicial District   )

I,   Josephine Thompson, a   Mid-wife   , on oath state that I attended on Miss Josephine Asbury   , wife of -------------   on the 26th day of   December , 1900 ; that there was born to her on said date a   female   child; that said child is now living and is said to have been named   Pearlie Bozen
                                         her
                                Josephine x Thompson
                                       mark
Witnesses to Mark.
T.W. Morton
Chas. L. Phillips

Applications for Enrollment of Creek Newborn
Act of 1905   Volume XI

Subscribed and sworn to before me this 1ˢᵗ day of September 1904.

My Commission Ex 22 April 1908.   William B. Morgan
                                          Notary Public.

BIRTH AFFIDAVIT.

DEPARTMENT OF THE INTERIOR.
COMMISSION TO THE FIVE CIVILIZED TRIBES.

  IN RE APPLICATION FOR ENROLLMENT, as a citizen of the Creek Nation, of Pearlie Bosen, born on the 26 day of December , 1901

Name of Father: George Bosen   a citizen of the   Creek   Nation.
Tulsa Canadian Town
Name of Mother: Josie Asbery   a citizen of the   Creek   Nation.
Cheyatha Town
         Postoffice   Okmulgee, I. T.

AFFIDAVIT OF MOTHER.
               Child present.

UNITED STATES OF AMERICA, Indian Territory,
   Western   **DISTRICT.**

  I, Josie Asbery , on oath state that I am 22 years of age and a citizen by blood , of the Creek   Nation; that I am not the lawful wife of George Bosen , who is a citizen, by blood of the Creek   Nation; that a female   child was born to me on 26 day of December , 1901 , that said child has been named Pearlie Bosen , and was living March 4, 1905.

               Josie Asbury

Witnesses To Mark:
{

  Subscribed and sworn to before me this 10 day of April , 1905.

              Drennan C Skaggs
              Notary Public.

AFFIDAVIT OF ATTENDING PHYSICIAN OR MID-WIFE.

UNITED STATES OF AMERICA, Indian Territory,
   Western   **DISTRICT.**

  I, Josephine Thompson , a mid-wife , on oath state that I attended on ~~Mrs.~~Miss Josie Asbery , ~~wife of~~ ———on the 26 day of December , 1901 ; that there was born

Applications for Enrollment of Creek Newborn
Act of 1905   Volume XI

to her on said date a female child; that said child was living March 4, 1905, and is said to have been named Pearlie Bosen

Witnesses To Mark:
{ DC Skaggs
  Alex Posey

Josephine x Thompson
mark

Subscribed and sworn to before me 10 day of April, 1905.

Drennan C Skaggs
Notary Public.

BIRTH AFFIDAVIT.

DEPARTMENT OF THE INTERIOR,
COMMISSION TO THE FIVE CIVILIZED TRIBES.

IN RE APPLICATION FOR ENROLLMENT, as a citizen of the Creek Nation, of Pearlie Bosen , born on the 26 day of December, 1901

Name of Father: George Bosen   a citizen of the   Creek   Nation.
Name of Mother: Josephine Asbury   a citizen of the   Creek   Nation.

Post-Office : Okmulgee I.T.

AFFIDAVIT OF MOTHER.

UNITED STATES OF AMERICA,
INDIAN TERRITORY,
Western   District.

I, Josephine Asbury , on oath state that I am 22   years of age and a citizen by blood , of the Creek   Nation; that I am not the lawful wife of George Bosen , who is a citizen, by blood of the Creek   Nation; that a female   child was born to me on the 26" day of December , 1901 , that said child has been named Pearlie Bosen , and is now living.

Josephine Asbury

WITNESSES TO MARK:
{

Subscribed and sworn to before me this 4" day of   November , 1905.

Henry G. Hains
NOTARY PUBLIC.

Applications for Enrollment of Creek Newborn
Act of 1905   Volume XI

AFFIDAVIT OF ATTENDING PHYSICIAN OR MID-WIFE.

UNITED STATES OF AMERICA,
   INDIAN TERRITORY,
   Western   District.

   I, Josephine Thompson , a midwife , on oath state that I attended on ~~Mrs~~. Josephine Asbury , ~~wife of~~ on the 26" day of December , 1901; that there was born to her on said date a female child; that said child is now living and is said to have been named Pearlie Bosen

                                              her
                               Josephine x Thompson

WITNESSES TO MARK: mark
   { H.G. Hains
   { EC Griesel

   Subscribed and sworn to before me this 4" day of November , 1905.

                                   Henry G. Hains
                                      NOTARY PUBLIC.

BIRTH AFFIDAVIT.

DEPARTMENT OF THE INTERIOR.
COMMISSION TO THE FIVE CIVILIZED TRIBES.

   IN RE APPLICATION FOR ENROLLMENT, as a citizen of the Creek Nation[sic] Nation, of William Thomas Carter , born on the 5th day of Feby , 1903

Name of Father: Joe Carter   a citizen of the *(blank)*   Nation.
Name of Mother: Anna Carter   a citizen of the Creek   Nation.

                    Postoffice   Okmulgee I.T.

AFFIDAVIT OF MOTHER.

UNITED STATES OF AMERICA, Indian Territory,
   Western   DISTRICT.

   I, Anna Carter , on oath state that I am 22 years of age and a citizen by Birth , of the Creek Nation[sic] Nation; that I am the lawful wife of Joe Carter , who is not a citizen, by Birth of the Creek Nation; that a male child was born to me on 5th day

Applications for Enrollment of Creek Newborn
Act of 1905   Volume XI

of Feby , 1903 , that said child has been named William Thomas Carter , and was living March 4, 1905.

Witnesses To Mark:
{ Wilford E. Wood
{ Fred. E. Barnhill

her
Anna x Carter
mark

Subscribed and sworn to before me this 24 day of April , 1905.

My Commission Expires July 29, 1907.   WM Jackson
                                              Notary Public.

AFFIDAVIT OF ATTENDING PHYSICIAN OR MID-WIFE.

UNITED STATES OF AMERICA, Indian Territory, }
   Western   DISTRICT.   }

Anna Carter
I, E. T. Hensley , a Physician , on oath state that I attended on Mrs. ~~Joe Carter~~ , wife of   Joe Carter on the 5th day of February , 1903 ; that there was born to her on said date a male child; that said child was living March 4, 1905, and is said to have been named William Thomas Carter

E. T. Hensley

Witnesses To Mark:
{ Wilford E. Wood
{ Fred. E. Barnhill

Subscribed and sworn to before me this 24 day of April , 1905.

My Commission Expires July 29, 1907.   WM Jackson
                                              Notary Public.

Applications for Enrollment of Creek Newborn
Act of 1905   Volume XI

N.C. 858

DEPARTMENT OF THE INTERIOR,
COMMISSIONER TO THE FIVE CIVILIZED TRIBES.
Muskogee, Indian Territory, March 10, 1906.

In the matter of the application for the enrollment of Roman Burgess as a citizen by blood of the Creek Nation.

William Burgess, being duly sworn, testified as follows through Jesse McDermott, official interpreter.

Q What is your name? A William Burgess.
Q What is your age? A I don't know; I have no record of it. (witness appears to be about twenty three).
Q What is your post office address? A Schulter.
Q How long have you lived there? A Since the 24th of last January.
Q Was Senora your post office before that? A Yes, sir.
Q Is your wife Fannie there with you now? A Yes, sir.
Q Is your child Roman Burgess with you? A Yes
Q Are you the father of Roman? A Yes
Q You are a Seminole are you? A Yes.
Q If it should be found that this child Roman has rights in either the Creek or Seminole Nations, in which nation do you elect for him to be enrolled and receive his allotment of land? A Creek.

Witness is again advised as he and his wife have been by letter heretofore that this office requires the affidavit of two disinterested witnesses in lieu of the affidavit of the midwife.

Q What was the name of your wife's former husband? [sic] Wash Kanard.
Q And after Wash died you married her? A Yes
Q What was her maiden name? A Watson.

Fannie, the mother of said child, is identified as Fannie Kanard opposite Creek roll No. 6526

I, Anna Garrigues, on oath state that the above and foregoing is a true and correct transcript of my stenographic notes as taken in said cause on said date.

Anna Garrigues

Subscribed and sworn to before me this 13 day of March 1906.

J McDermott
Notary Public.

Applications for Enrollment of Creek Newborn
Act of 1905 Volume XI

Indian Territory   )
)
Western District   ) SS

We, the undersigned, on oath state that we are personally acquainted with Fannie Burgess wife of William Burgess and that on or about the 19 day of May , 1904, a male child was born to them and has been named Roman Burgess , and that said child was living March 4, 1905.

We further state that we have no interest in the above case.

her
Elie Randall x
mark
Jim Burgess

Witnesses to mark:
M.F. Graham
DM Smith

_____

Subscribed and sworn to before me this 12th day of Mch 1906.

My Com Ex Oct 9th 1907

M.F. Graham
Notary Public.

BIRTH AFFIDAVIT.

DEPARTMENT OF THE INTERIOR.
COMMISSION TO THE FIVE CIVILIZED TRIBES.

IN RE APPLICATION FOR ENROLLMENT, as a citizen of the Creek Nation, of Roman Burgess, born on the 19th day of May , 1904

Name of Father: William Burgess   a citizen of the   Seminole   Nation.
Name of Mother: Fannie Burgess   a citizen of the   Creek   Nation.

Postoffice   Senora Ind Ter.

AFFIDAVIT OF MOTHER.

UNITED STATES OF AMERICA, Indian Territory, ⎫
     Western   DISTRICT.   ⎭

I, Fannie Burgess , on oath state that I am 27 years of age and a citizen by Blood , of the Creek Nation; that I am the lawful wife of William Burgess , who is a

Applications for Enrollment of Creek Newborn
Act of 1905 Volume XI

citizen, by Blood of the Seminole Nation; that a Male child was born to me on 19th day of May , 1904 , that said child has been named Roman Burgess , and was living March 4, 1905.

Fannie Burgess

Witnesses To Mark:
{

Subscribed and sworn to before me this 17th day of August , 1905.

My Commission Expires July 13th, 1908   J. W. Fowler
Notary Public.

AFFIDAVIT OF ATTENDING PHYSICIAN OR MID-WIFE.

UNITED STATES OF AMERICA, Indian Territory,
Western   DISTRICT.

I, William Burgess Acting Commissioner as a , a Mid wife , on oath state that I attended on Mrs. Fannie Burgess , wife of William Burgess on the 19th day of May , 1904 ; that there was born to her on said date a Male child; that said child was living March 4, 1905, and is said to have been named Roman Burgess

William Burgess

Witnesses To Mark:
{

Subscribed and sworn to before me this 17th day of August , 1905.

My Commission Expires July 13th, 1908   J. W. Fowler
Notary Public.

BIRTH AFFIDAVIT.

DEPARTMENT OF THE INTERIOR.
COMMISSION TO THE FIVE CIVILIZED TRIBES.

IN RE APPLICATION FOR ENROLLMENT, as a citizen of the Creek Nation, of Roman Burgess, born on the 19 day of May , 1904

Name of Father: William Burgess   a citizen of the   Seminole   Nation.
Name of Mother: Fanny Burgess (nee Watson) a citizen of the   Creek   Nation.
Eufaula Deep Fork Town
Postoffice   Senora, Ind Ter.

Applications for Enrollment of Creek Newborn
Act of 1905   Volume XI

AFFIDAVIT OF MOTHER.

UNITED STATES OF AMERICA, Indian Territory, }   Child is present
Western   DISTRICT.

I, Fanny Burgess , on oath state that I am 27 years of age and a citizen by blood , of the Creek Nation; that I am the lawful wife of William Burgess , who is a citizen, by blood of the Seminole Nation; that a male child was born to me on 19 day of May , 1904 , that said child has been named Roman Burgess , and was living March 4, 1905.

                                       Fannie Burgess

Witnesses To Mark:
{

Subscribed and sworn to before me this 10 day of April , 1905.

                                       Drennan C Skaggs
                                       Notary Public.

AFFIDAVIT OF ATTENDING PHYSICIAN OR MID-WIFE.

UNITED STATES OF AMERICA, Indian Territory, }
Western   DISTRICT.

                                       my wife
I, William Burgess , a~~ (blank)~~ , on oath state that I attended on ^ Mrs. Fanny Burgess , wife of William Burgess on the 19 day of May , 1904 ; that there was born to her on said date a male child; that said child was living March 4, 1905, and is said to have been named Roman Burgess

                                       William Burgess

Witnesses To Mark:
{

Subscribed and sworn to before me this 10 day of April , 1905.

                                       Drennan C Skaggs
                                       Notary Public.

Applications for Enrollment of Creek Newborn
Act of 1905 Volume XI

NC. 858.

Muskogee, Indian Territory, July 15, 1905.

Chief Clerk,
    Seminole Enrollment Division,
        Muskogee, Indian Territory.

Dear Sir:

    April 12, 1905, application was made to the Commission to the Five Civilized Tribes for the enrollment of Roman Burgess, born May 19, 1904, as a citizen by blood of the Creek Nation. It is stated in said application that the father of said child is William Burgess, a citizen of the Seminole Nation, and that the mother is Fanny Burgess, a citizen of the Creek Nation.

    You are requested to inform the Creek Enrollment Division as to whether application has been made for the enrollment of said Roman Burgess as a citizen of the Seminole Nation, and if so, what disposition has been made of the same.

                Respectfully,
                              Commissioner.

                            858
                      NC. ~~832~~.

Muskogee, Indian Territory, July 17, 1905.

Fannie Burgess,
    Senora, Indian Territory.

Dear Madam:

    In the matter of the application for the enrollment of your minor child, Roman Burgess, as a citizen of the Creek Nation, you are advised that without further information it is impossible for this office to identify you on its rolls of citizens of said Nation.

    You are requested to state your maiden name, the names of your parents, the Creek Indian Town to which you belong, and, if possible the roll numbers which appear on your deeds to land in the Creek Nation, and any other information that will help to identify you as a citizen of the Creek Nation.

    You are further advised that this office requires the affidavits of two disinterested witnesses as to the birth of said child. It is states that William Burgess, the father of said child, is a citizen of the Seminole Nation.

Applications for Enrollment of Creek Newborn
Act of 1905 Volume XI

You will be allowed fifteen days from date hereof which to appear before this office to elect whether you desire said child to be enrolled in the Creek or Seminole Nation.

Respectfully,

Commissioner.

W.F.

DEPARTMENT OF THE INTERIOR.
COMMISSION TO THE FIVE CIVILIZED TRIBES.

Muskogee, Indian Territory, July 19, 1905.

Chief Clerk,
    Creek Enrollment Division.

Dear Sir:

Receipt is acknowledged of your letter of July 15, 1905. (NC-858) stating that application was made to the Commission to the Five Civilized Tribes for the enrollment of Roman Burgess, born May 19, 1904, child of William Burgess, a citizen of the Seminole Nation, and Fanny Burgess, a citizen of the Creek Nation, as a citizen by blood of the Creek Nation and requesting to be informed as to whether application has been made for the enrollment of said child as a citizen of the Seminole Nation.

In reply to your letter you are advised that it does not appear from an examination of the records of this office that any application was made for the enrollment of said Roman Burgess as a citizen of the Seminole Nation.

Respectfully,
Tams Bixby
Commissioner.

NC-858.

Muskogee, Indian Territory, October 21, 1905.

Fanny Burgess,
    c/o William Burgess,
        Senora, Indian Territory.

Dear Madam:

In the matter of the application for the enrollment of your minor child, Roman Burgess, born May 19, 1904, as a citizen by blood of the Creek Nation, this office requires the affidavits of two disinterested witnesses relative to the birth of said child. Said affidavits to set forth said child's name, the date of his birth, the names of his parents and whether or not he was living on March 4, 1905.

Applications for Enrollment of Creek Newborn
Act of 1905   Volume XI

You are further advised that this office requires the joint affidavit of your self and your husband, William Burgess, who is a citizen of the Seminole Nation, electing whether you will have said Roman Burgess enrolled as a citizen of the Creek or Seminole Nation.

Respectfully,

Commissioner.

REFER IN REPLY TO THE FOLLOWING:

DEPARTMENT OF THE INTERIOR,
COMMISSIONER TO THE FIVE CIVILIZED TRIBES.

Muskogee, Indian Territory, August 21, 1906.

Chief Clerk,
    Creek Enrollment Division,
        Muskogee, Indian Territory.

Dear Sir:

Receipt is hereby acknowledged of your letter of August 21, 1906, asking if application has been made for enrollment as a citizen of the Seminole Nation of Roman Burgess, child of William Burgess, a citizen of the Seminole nation, and Fanny Burgess, a citizen of the Creek Nation.

In reply you are advised that it does not appear from the records of this office that application has been made on behalf of Roman Burgess for enrollment as a new born citizen of the Seminole Nation under the Act of Congress approved March 3, 1905.

Respectfully,

W^m. O. Beall
Acting Commissioner.

NC 858/[sic]

Muskogee, Indian Territory, October 31, 1906.

Chief Clerk,
    Seminole Enrollment Division,
        Muskogee, Indian Territory.

Dear Sir:

There is on file in this office an application for the enrollment of Roman Burgess, born May 19, 1904, to William Burgess, a citizen of the Seminole Nation, and Fannie Burgess, who is identified on the rolls of citizens by blood of the Creek Nation as Fannie Kanard, opposite Creek Indian Roll No. 6526.

Applications for Enrollment of Creek Newborn
Act of 1905 Volume XI

You are advised that the name of said child is contained in a partial list of new born citizens by blood of the Creek Nation, approved by the Secretary of the Interior October 15, 1906, opposite roll number 1075.

Respectfully,

Commissioner.

BIRTH AFFIDAVIT.

DEPARTMENT OF THE INTERIOR.
COMMISSION TO THE FIVE CIVILIZED TRIBES.

IN RE APPLICATION FOR ENROLLMENT, as a citizen of the Creek Nation, of Eli Postoak, born on the 7 day of September, 1903

Name of Father: Lincoln Postoak   a citizen of the   Creek   Nation.
Name of Mother: Patty Bridges   a citizen of the   Creek   Nation.

Postoffice   Sapulpa, I.T.

AFFIDAVIT OF MOTHER.

UNITED STATES OF AMERICA, Indian Territory, }
       Western   DISTRICT.

I, Patty Bridges, on oath state that I am 18 years of age and a citizen by blood, of the Creek Nation; that I am not the lawful wife of Lincoln Postoak, who is a citizen, by blood of the Creek Nation; that a male child was born to me on 7th day of September, 1903, that said child has been named Eli Postoak, and was living March 4, 1905.

Patty Bridges

Witnesses To Mark:

Subscribed and sworn to before me this 30th day of October A.D., 1905. My commission expires on the 11th day of July A.D. 1906

P. L. Mars
Notary Public.

Applications for Enrollment of Creek Newborn
Act of 1905   Volume XI

(The Birth Affidavit below typed as given.)

BIRTH AFFIDAVIT.
DEPARTMENT OF THE INTERIOR.
COMMISSION TO THE FIVE CIVILIZED TRIBES.

IN RE APPLICATION FOR ENROLLMENT, as a citizen of the Creek Nation, of Eli Postoak, born on the 7th day of September, 1903

Name of Father: Lincoln Postoak   a citizen of the   Creek   Nation.
                  Bridges
Name of Mother: Bettie ~~Burgess~~   a citizen of the   Creek   Nation.

               Postoffice   Sapulpa, Ind. Ter.

AFFIDAVIT OF MOTHER.

UNITED STATES OF AMERICA, Indian Territory,
    Western   DISTRICT.
               Bridges
    I, Bettie ~~Burgess~~, on oath state that I am 18 years of age and a citizen by blood, of the Creek Nation; that I am the lawful wife of Wade ~~Burgess~~ Bridges, who is a citizen, by birth of the U. S. Nation; that a male child was born to me on 7th day of September, 1903, that said child has been named Eli Postoak, and was living March 4, 1905.

                               Bettie Bridges
Witnesses To Mark:

    Subscribed and sworn to before me this 18th day of April, 1905.

                               Allen Henry
                               Notary Public.
My Commission expires Oct. 19, 1907.

AFFIDAVIT OF ATTENDING PHYSICIAN OR MID-WIFE.

UNITED STATES OF AMERICA, Indian Territory,
    Western   DISTRICT.

    I, Maria Postoak, a mid-wife, on oath state that I attended on Mrs. Bettie Bridges, wife of Wade Bridges on the 7th day of September, 1903; that there was born to her on said date a male child; that said child was living March 4, 1905, and is said to have been named Eli Postoak

Applications for Enrollment of Creek Newborn
Act of 1905   Volume XI

Witnesses To Mark:
{ W E Bridges
{ T.A. Henry

her
Maria x Postoak
mark

Subscribed and sworn to before me this 24th day of April, 1905.

Allen Henry
Notary Public.

My Commission expires Oct. 19, 1907.

NC-859.

Muskogee, Indian Territory, October 21, 1905.

Bettie Bridges,
   Sapulpa, Indian Territory.

Dear Madam:

In the matter of the application for the enrollment of your minor child, Eli Postoak, born September 7, 1903, as a citizen by blood of the Creek Nation, it is stated in the caption of said affidavit that the father of said child is Lincoln Postoak. In the affidavits themselves you and the midwife, who attended at the birth of said Eli Postoak, state that you are the wife of Wade Bridges, a citizen of the United States. You do not state whether you were ever the wife of Lincoln Postoak or whether said Eli Postoak is an illegitimate child.

There is herewith inclosed form of birth affidavit which has been partial filled out. If you are the widow or divorced wife of Lincoln Postoak you will insert that statement where the form reads "I am the lawful wife of". If said Eli Postoak is an illegitimate child you will insert the word "not" between the words "m" and "the" on said Form. In the latter case it will be necessary for you to furnish this office with the affidavit of Lincoln Postoak, the alleged father of said child, setting forth said child's name, the date of his birth, whether or not he was living March 4, 1905 and acknowledging that he, Lincoln Postoak, is the father of your said child.

This office had been unable to identify you upon the final roll of citizens by blood of the Creek Nation. In order that you may be so identified you are requested to state the name under which you were finally enrolled, the names of your parents and other members of your family, the Creek Indian town to which you belong and your final roll number as the same appears upon your allotment certificate and deeds.

Respectfully,

CTD-12.
Env.

Commissioner.

Applications for Enrollment of Creek Newborn
Act of 1905   Volume XI

(The letter below typed as given.)

Sapulpa, I.T. October, 28th. 1905.

Hon. Tams Bixby,
    Muskogee, I.T.

Dear Sir:

    Answering your communication of October, 21st. stating that you was unable to identify me upon the final roll as a citizen by blood of the Creek Nation, will say that my brothers are Arlinger Bruner and Magully Bruner, and Lincoln Postoak is my uncle. My allottment deeds are now at Muskogee in the hands of the Commission on file with an application to remove restrictions, and I can not give you my roll number, but my allotment is the Southeast Quarter of section six (6) Township 18, Range 11, and I was finally enrolled under the name of Patty Bruner.

                          Patty Bruner Bridges

Subscribed and sworn to before me this the 30 day of October, 1905.

                          P. L. Mars
                          Notary Public Western District
                          of Indian Territory.

My commission expires 11$\underline{th}$ day of July A.D. 1906.

NC 859

                          Muskogee, Indian Territory, August 4, 1906.

Patty Bruner Bridges,
    Sapulpa, Indian Territory.

Dear Madam:

    Replying to your letter of August 1, 1906, you are advised that the name of your minor child, Eli Postoak is contained in a partial list of creek[sic] citizens approved by the Secretary of the Interior, January 4, 1906, opposite new born creek[sic] Indian Roll No. 979, and that a selection of land in the Creek nation[sic] may now be made for said child at the Creek Land Office in Muskogee, Indian Territory.

                        Respectfully,
                                Commissioner.

Applications for Enrollment of Creek Newborn
Act of 1905 Volume XI

N.C. 860.

DEPARTMENT OF THE INTERIOR,
COMMISSIONER TO THE FIVE CIVILIZED TRIBES.
Muskogee, I. T., January 29, 1906

In the matter of the application for the enrollment of Martin Johnson as a citizen by blood of the Creek Nation.

SANDY JOHNSON, being duly sworn, testified as follows:

BY THE COMMISSIONER:
Q What is your name? A Sandy Johnson.
Q How old are you? A About thirty-five or thirty-six.
Q What is your post office address? A Sapulpa.
Q Are you a citizen by blood of the Creek Nation? A Yes, sir.
Q What is the name of your wife? A Jennie Johnson.
Q Is she a citizen by blood of the Creek Nation? A Yes, sir.
Q Is she living? A Yes, sir

On November 7, 1905, there was filed with this office an affidavit in the matter of the birth of Martin Johnson, it being stated in said affidavit that said child was born on the 4th day of January, 1905. Said affidavit further stated "that said child has been named Martin Johnson and is now living."

Q When was Martin Johnson born? A The 4th day of January.
Q Is Martin Johnson living at the present time? A He was pretty sick when I fixed the paper and when he died the lawyers told me to take the papers on down there and they would fix it up.
Q Is Martin living now? A No, sir.
Q When did he die? A On the 24th day of October, 1905.
Q This affidavit seems to have been signed by Jennie Johnson, the mother, on March 1, 1905, and attested by P. L. Mars, notary public. The affidavit also bears the signature of Salina Land as mid-wife, subscribed before John M. Weeks, notary public, on October 28, 1905. These affidavits were signed by your wife and Salina Land on different dates, were they? A Yes, sir. We couldn't find the mid-wife until several days later. She was out in the country.
Q t was seven months later, wasn't it, before Salina Land signed this affidavit? A No, sir, I don't think so.
Q Just a few days? A I think so.
Q Then do you think the date as given in the affidavit signed by Salina Land, October 28, 1905, is a mistake? A Mr. Weeks made a mistake in the date and in the name?
Q Was this child living on October 28, 1905? A No, sir, he died on the 24th.
Q Then this affidavit, signed by Salina Land, before John M. Weeks, notary public, is not correct in stating that this child was living on October 28, 1905? A They fixed the paper out. He was dead but they fixed the paper out and they told me to come before the Commissioner here and you would fix this up.

Applications for Enrollment of Creek Newborn
Act of 1905   Volume XI

I, D. C. Skaggs, on oath state that the above and foregoing is a full and true transcript of my stenographic notes as taken in said cause on said date.

D. C. Skaggs

Subscribed and sworn to before me this 29 day of January, 1906.

J McDermott
Notary Public.

(A note on a small piece of torn paper)

This is certainly meant for Emma: the mother's name being erroneously inserted for that of the child. See N.C. 860.

BIRTH AFFIDAVIT.

DEPARTMENT OF THE INTERIOR,
COMMISSION TO THE FIVE CIVILIZED TRIBES.

IN RE Application for Enrollment, as a citizen of the Creek Nation, of Emma Johnson, born on the 29 day of Dec , 1901

Name of Father: Sandy Johnson	a citizen of the Creek	Nation.
Name of Mother: Jennie Johnson	a citizen of the Creek	Nation.

Post-office: Tulsa I.T.

AFFIDAVIT OF MOTHER.

UNITED STATES OF AMERICA, ⎤
    INDIAN TERRITORY.   ⎬
    Western   District. ⎦

I, Jennie Johnson , on oath state that I am 18 years of age and a citizen by Birth, of the Creek Nation; that I am the lawful wife of Sandy Johnson , who is a citizen, by Birth of the Creek Nation; that a Female child was born to me on 29 day of Dec , 1901 , that said child has been named Jennie Johnson , and is now living.

her
Jennie x Johnson
mark

WITNESSES TO MARK:
{ George W Henry
{ L.L. Lewis

Applications for Enrollment of Creek Newborn
Act of 1905 Volume XI

Subscribed and sworn to before me this 30 *day of* Sept , *1902.*

Com Ex 7/3/1906　　　　　　　　　Robert E. Lynch
　　　　　　　　　　　　　　　　　　　NOTARY PUBLIC.

AFFIDAVIT OF ATTENDING PHYSICIAN OR MID-WIFE.

UNITED STATES OF AMERICA,
　INDIAN TERRITORY.
　　Western　　　District.

　　I, Elizabeth Clements , a Midwife , on oath state that I attended on Mrs. Jennie Johnson , wife of Sandy Johnson on the 29 day of December , 1901 ; that there was born to her on said date a Female child; that said child is now living and is said to have been named Jennie Johnson　　　　　　　　　　　her
　　　　　　　　　　　　　　　　　　　Elizabeth x Clements
WITNESSES TO MARK:　　　　　　　　　　　mark
　{ George W Henry
　　L.L. Lewis

Subscribed and sworn to before me this 30 *day of* Sept , *1902.*

Com Ex 7/3/1906　　　　　　　　　Robert E. Lynch
　　　　　　　　　　　　　　　　　　　NOTARY PUBLIC.

BIRTH AFFIDAVIT.
　　　　　　　　　　DEPARTMENT OF THE INTERIOR.
　　　　　　　COMMISSION TO THE FIVE CIVILIZED TRIBES.

　　IN RE APPLICATION FOR ENROLLMENT, as a citizen of the Creek Nation, of Martin Johnson , born on the 4th day of Jany , 1905

Name of Father: Sandy Johnson　　　　a citizen of the　Creek　　Nation.
　　　　　　　　　　　Thewarle
Name of Mother: Jennie Johnson　　　　a citizen of the　Creek　　Nation.
　　　　　　　　　　　Lochapok
　　　　　　　　　　　　　Postoffice　　Sapulpa I.T.

Applications for Enrollment of Creek Newborn
Act of 1905   Volume XI

AFFIDAVIT OF MOTHER.

Child present

UNITED STATES OF AMERICA, Indian Territory, ⎱
   Western   **DISTRICT.** ⎰

   I, Jennie Johnson , on oath state that I am 28 years of age and a citizen by blood , of the Creek   Nation; that I am the lawful wife of Sandy Johnson , who is a citizen, by blood of the Creek   Nation; that a male   child was born to me on 4th day of January , 1905 , that said child has been named   Martin Johnson , and was living March 4, 1905.

                                                   her
                                         Jennie x Johnson

Witnesses To Mark: mark
⎰ David Shelby
⎱ Jesse McDermott

   Subscribed and sworn to before me this 24th day of April , 1905.

(Seal)   Edw C Griesel
                                                 Notary Public.

AFFIDAVIT OF ~~ATTENDING PHYSICIAN OR MID-WIFE~~.
                                husband

UNITED STATES OF AMERICA, Indian Territory, ⎱   Child present
   Western   **DISTRICT.** ⎰

   I, Sandy Johnson , ~~a (blank)~~ , on oath state that I attended on Mrs. Jennie Johnson my, wife of   ~~(blank)~~   on the   4th day of   Jany , 1905 ; that there was born to her on said date a   male   child; that said child was living March 4, 1905, and is said to have been named Martin Johnson

                                             Sandy Johnson

Witnesses To Mark:
⎰
⎱

   Subscribed and sworn to before me this 24th day of April , 1905.

(Seal)   Edw C Griesel
                                                 Notary Public.

Applications for Enrollment of Creek Newborn
Act of 1905   Volume XI

BIRTH AFFIDAVIT.

DEPARTMENT OF THE INTERIOR.
COMMISSION TO THE FIVE CIVILIZED TRIBES.

                                                    Creek

IN RE APPLICATION FOR ENROLLMENT, as a citizen of the ~~Martin Johnson~~ Nation, of Martin Johnson, born on the 4th day of January, 1905

Name of Father: Sandy Johnson	a citizen of the	Creek	Nation.
Name of Mother: Jennie Johnson	a citizen of the	Creek	Nation.

                    Postoffice   Sapulpa I.T.

AFFIDAVIT OF MOTHER.

UNITED STATES OF AMERICA, Indian Territory, }
    Western   DISTRICT.

    I, Jennie Johnson, on oath state that I am 26 years of age and a citizen by blood, of the Creek Nation; that I am the lawful wife of Sandy Johnson, who is a citizen, by blood of the Creek Nation; that a male child was born to me on 4th day of January A.D., 1905, that said child has been named Martin Johnson, and was living March 4, 1905.

                                                  Her
                                        Jennie x Johnson
Witnesses To Mark: mark
  { John *(Illegible)*
    F.L. Mars

    Subscribed and sworn to before me this 11th day of March, A.D., 1905.

My Commission expires July 11, 1908.   F.L. Mars
                                                  Notary Public.

AFFIDAVIT OF ATTENDING PHYSICIAN OR MID-WIFE.

UNITED STATES OF AMERICA, Indian Territory, }
    Western   DISTRICT.

    I, Salina Land, a Midwife, on oath state that I attended on Mrs. Jennie Johnson my, wife of Sandy Johnson on the 4th day of January, A.D., 1905; that there was born to her on said date a male child; that said child was living March 4, 1905, and is said to have been named Martin Johnson

                                                    her
                    have party sign here - Salina x Land
                                                  mark

Applications for Enrollment of Creek Newborn
Act of 1905   Volume XI

Witnesses To Mark:
    { Belchee *(Illegible)*   must two witnesses witness
      George Bosen   the mark

(Seal) Subscribed and sworn to before me this 28 day of October A.D., 1905.

My Commission Expires July 8th. 1906.   John M. Weeks
My commission expires on   Notary Public.
the …….. day of ……., A.D. 190…

DEPARTMENT OF THE INTERIOR.
COMMISSION TO THE FIVE CIVILIZED TRIBES.

In the matter of the death of Martin Johnson a citizen of the Creek Nation, who formerly resided at or near Sapulpa , Ind. Ter., and died on the 24 day of October , 1905

AFFIDAVIT OF RELATIVE.

UNITED STATES OF AMERICA, Indian Territory,
     Western   DISTRICT.

I, Sandy Johnson , on oath state that I am 35 years of age and a citizen by blood , of the Creek Nation; that my postoffice address is Sapulpa , Ind. Ter.; that I am father of Martin Johnson who was a citizen, by blood , of the Creek Nation and that said Martin Johnson died on the 24 day of October , 1905

                         Sandy Johnson

Witnesses To Mark:
     {

Subscribed and sworn to before me this 16" day of January, 1906.

                         Henry G. Hains
                         Notary Public.

Applications for Enrollment of Creek Newborn
Act of 1905 Volume XI

BIRTH AFFIDAVIT.

DEPARTMENT OF THE INTERIOR.
COMMISSION TO THE FIVE CIVILIZED TRIBES.

IN RE APPLICATION FOR ENROLLMENT, as a citizen of the Creek Nation, of Emma Johnson, born on the 29th day of January, 1902

Name of Father: Sandy Johnson   a citizen of the   Creek   Nation.
Name of Mother: Jennie Johnson   a citizen of the   Creek   Nation.

Postoffice   Sapulpa, Ind. Ter.

AFFIDAVIT OF MOTHER.

UNITED STATES OF AMERICA, Indian Territory,
    Western   DISTRICT.

I, Jennie Johnson, on oath state that I am 26 years of age and a citizen by blood, of the Creek Nation; that I am the lawful wife of Sandy Johnson, who is a citizen, by blood of the Creek Nation; that a Female child was born to me on 29th day of January A.D., 1902, that said child has been named Emma Johnson, and is now living.

                                       Her
                            Jennie x Johnson
Witnesses To Mark: mark
    { John *(Illegible)*
       F.L. Mars

Subscribed and sworn to before me this 11th day of March, A.D., 1905.

My Commission expires July 11, 1908.   F.L. Mars
                                            Notary Public.

AFFIDAVIT OF ATTENDING PHYSICIAN OR MID-WIFE.

UNITED STATES OF AMERICA, Indian Territory,
    Western   DISTRICT.

I, *(blank)*, a notary public, on oath state that I attended on Mrs. Jennie Johnson, wife of Sandy Johnson on the 29th day of January A.D., 1902; that there was born to her on said date a female child; that said child is now living and is said to have been named Emma Johnson

                         sign here   Bettie Clement

Applications for Enrollment of Creek Newborn
Act of 1905 Volume XI

Witnesses To Mark:
    her
{ Lizzie x *(Illegible)*   two witnesses to her mark
  mark
?. C. Clement

Subscribed and sworn to before me this *(blank)* day of April A.D. , 1905.

My commission expires on   *(No Signature Given)*
the ….. day of ….. A.D. 190….   Notary Public.

BIRTH AFFIDAVIT.

See former application

DEPARTMENT OF THE INTERIOR.
COMMISSION TO THE FIVE CIVILIZED TRIBES.

IN RE APPLICATION FOR ENROLLMENT, as a citizen of the Creek Nation, of Emma Johnson , born on the 29th day of Jany , 1902

Name of Father: Sandy Johnson   a citizen of the   Creek   Nation.
                      Thewarle
Name of Mother: Jennie Johnson   a citizen of the   Creek   Nation.
                      Lochapoka
                             Postoffice   Sapulpa I.T.

AFFIDAVIT OF MOTHER.

UNITED STATES OF AMERICA, Indian Territory, }
     Western   **DISTRICT.**

    I, Sandy Johnson , on oath state that I am 35 years of age and a citizen by blood , of the Creek Nation; that I am the lawful ~~wife~~ husband of Jennie Johnson, who is a citizen, by blood of the Creek Nation; that a female child was born to ~~me~~ her on 29th day of January , 1902 , that said child has been named Emma Johnson , and was living March 4, 1905.

                                      Sandy Johnson
Witnesses To Mark:
{

Subscribed and sworn to before me this 24th day of April, 1905.

    (Seal)   Edw C Griesel
                                        Notary Public.

Applications for Enrollment of Creek Newborn
Act of 1905   Volume XI

BIRTH AFFIDAVIT.

DEPARTMENT OF THE INTERIOR.
COMMISSION TO THE FIVE CIVILIZED TRIBES.

IN RE APPLICATION FOR ENROLLMENT, as a citizen of the Creek Nation, of Emma Johnson , born on the 29th day of January, 1902

Name of Father: Sandy Johnson	a citizen of the Creek	Nation.
Name of Mother: Jennie Johnson	a citizen of the Creek	Nation.

Postoffice   Sapulpa, Ind. Ter.

AFFIDAVIT OF MOTHER.

UNITED STATES OF AMERICA, Indian Territory,
   Western   DISTRICT.

I, Jennie Johnson , on oath state that I am 26   years of age and a citizen by blood, of the Creek   Nation; that I am the lawful wife of   Sandy Johnson , who is a citizen, by blood of the Creek   Nation; that a Female   child was born to me on 29th day of January A.D. , 1902 , that said child has been named   Emma Johnson , and was living March 4, 1905.

                                            her
                                   Jennie x Johnson
Witnesses To Mark: mark
  { Henry Campbell
    C.A. Vaughn

Subscribed and sworn to before me this 28 day of October A.D. , 1905.

My Commission Expires July 8th. 1906.   John M. Weeks

AFFIDAVIT OF ATTENDING PHYSICIAN OR MID-WIFE.

UNITED STATES OF AMERICA, Indian Territory,
   Western   DISTRICT.

I, Bettie Clement   , a midwife , on oath state that I attended on Mrs. Jennie Johnson , wife of Sandy Johnson on the 29 day of January , 1902 ; that there was born to her on said date a female child; that said child was living March 4, 1905, and is said to have been named Emma Johnson

                                     Bettie Clement
Witnesses To Mark:
  { Geo W Allen
    N.D. Christian

Applications for Enrollment of Creek Newborn
Act of 1905   Volume XI

Subscribed and sworn to before me this 31" day of October , 1905.

My Com Ex 7/3/1906

Robert E. Lynch
Notary Public.

(The above Birth Affidavit given again.)

NC-860.

Muskogee, Indian Territory, October 21. 1905.

Jennie Johnson,
    c/o Sandy Johnson,
        Sapulpa, Indian Territory.

Dear Madam:

    In the matter of the application for the enrollment of your minor child, Martin Johnson, born June 4, 1905, as a citizen by blood of the Creek Nation this office desires the affidavit of the midwife who attended at the birth of said child, and a blank for that purpose is inclosed herewith.

    If there was no physician or midwife in attendance when said Martin Johnson was born it will be necessary for you to furnish this office with the affidavits of two disinterested witnesses relative to the birth of said child. Said affidavits to set forth said child's name, the date of his birth, the names of his parents and whether or not he was living March 4, 1905.

    In the matter of the application for the enrollment of your minor child, Emma Johnson, born January 29, 1902, the affidavit of the midwife is defective in that Bettie Clement, by whom it is signed, describes herself as a notary public, and also because same is not sworn to.

    There is herewith inclosed form of birth affidavit which has been partially filled out. If the same correctly states the facts you are requested to have it executed and when so executed return it to this office in the inclosed envelope. Be careful to see that the notary public before whom the affidavits are sworn to attaches his name and seal to each affidavit. In case any signature is by mark the same must be attested by two disinterested witnesses.

                      Respectfully,
                                        Commissioner.

CTD-12.
Env.

Applications for Enrollment of Creek Newborn
Act of 1905 Volume XI

NC 860
~~BANE 186~~

Muskogee, Indian Territory, January 23, 1906.

Jinnie[sic] Johnson,
    Care Sandy Johnson,
        Sapulpa, Indian Territory.

Dear Madam:

    There is on file in this office your affidavit executed September 30, 1902 relative to your child born December 29, 1901; it is presumed that the name Jennie was inserted in the affidavit as the name of the child when as a matter of fact the correct name of said child is Emma.

    You are requested to write this office at an early date stating whether you have a child named Jennie Johnson, born on the date given, also as to whether the child born December 29, 1901 is not identical with Emma Johnson, born January 29, 1902 and for whom lands in the Creek Nation have been recently allotted.

                       Respectfully,

                                            Commissioner.

Mars and Mars
    Lawyers
F.L. Mars   J.J. Mars   Sapulpa, Ind. Ter. January 25th, 1906.

Hon. Tams Bixby,
    Muskogee, Ind. Ty.

Dear Sir:

    Replying to your favor of the 23rd inst relative to the affidavit executed September 30th 1902, in which you state said affidavit shows the child to have been born December 29th, 1901, and name Jennie, inserted, to which I desire to reply that the child was born January 29th, 1902 and the correct name of said child is Emma Johnson and Jinnie is the mother of said child.

    I have no child that was born on the 92th[sic] of December, 1901 and have no child named Jennie, and the name of the child is Emma Johnson who was born on the 29th day of January 1902.

    I presume if an affidavit of this kind was filed in your department the name of Jennie Johnson as referred to is the mother of Emma Johnson.

    I trust this will be satisfactory to your department.

Applications for Enrollment of Creek Newborn
Act of 1905 Volume XI

I hold a correct copy of the affidavit made of the birth and application of enrollment of this child, with Sandy Johnson as father and Jennie Johnson, mother, executed before F.L. Mars, Notary Public, September 30th, 1902.

                        Yours respectfully,
                                Sandy Johnson

BIRTH AFFIDAVIT.

DEPARTMENT OF THE INTERIOR.
COMMISSION TO THE FIVE CIVILIZED TRIBES.

IN RE APPLICATION FOR ENROLLMENT, as a citizen of the Creek Nation, of Ruby Chamblen, born on the 10th day of Dec, 1904

                                                                     Delaware
Name of Father: John C. Chamblen   a citizen of the Cherokee   Nation.
Name of Mother: Susie Chamblen   a citizen of the   Creek   Nation.

                        Postoffice   Broken Arrow, I.T.

AFFIDAVIT OF MOTHER.

UNITED STATES OF AMERICA, Indian Territory, }
    Western   DISTRICT. }

I, Susie Chamblen, on oath state that I am 29 years of age and a citizen by Blood, of the Creek Nation; that I am the lawful wife of John C. Chamblen, who is a citizen, by Blood of the Cherokee Delaware Nation; that a female child was born to me on 10th day of Dec, 1904, that said child has been named Ruby Chamblen, and was living March 4, 1905.
                                     Her
                              Susie x Chamblen
Witnesses To Mark: mark
  { John N Day
  { Chas Haley

    Subscribed and sworn to before me this 8th day of April, 1905.

       Com Ex 7/3/1906   Robert E Lynch
                                                   Notary Public.

Applications for Enrollment of Creek Newborn
Act of 1905   Volume XI

AFFIDAVIT OF ATTENDING PHYSICIAN OR MID-WIFE.

UNITED STATES OF AMERICA, Indian Territory,
Western DISTRICT.

I, Sarah Chamblen , a Midwife , on oath state that I attended on Mrs. Susie Chamblen , wife of Jno C. Chamblen on the 10th day of Dec , 1904; that there was born to her on said date a female child; that said child was living March 4, 1905, and is said to have been named Ruby Chamblen

Sarah Chamblen

Witnesses To Mark:
{

Subscribed and sworn to before me 18th day of March, 1905.

N.N. Barker
Notary Public.

My Com. Ex. 7/14-1906.

BIRTH AFFIDAVIT.

DEPARTMENT OF THE INTERIOR.
COMMISSION TO THE FIVE CIVILIZED TRIBES.

IN RE APPLICATION FOR ENROLLMENT, as a citizen of the Creek Nation, of Dewey Chamblen , born on the 30th day of September , 1902

Cherokee
Name of Father: John C. Chamblen   a citizen of the Deleware[sic]Nation.
Name of Mother: Susie Chamblen   a citizen of the   Creek   Nation.

Postoffice   Broken Arrow, I.T.

AFFIDAVIT OF MOTHER.

UNITED STATES OF AMERICA, Indian Territory,
Western DISTRICT.

I, Susie Chamblen , on oath state that I am 29 years of age and a citizen by Blood , of the Creek Nation; that I am the lawful wife of John C. Chamblen , who is a citizen, by Blood of the Cherokee Delaware Nation; that a Male child was born to me on 30" day of September, 1902 , that said child has been named Dewey Chamblen, and was living March 4, 1905.
Her
Susie x Chamblen
mark

Witnesses To Mark:
{ John N Day
  Chas Haley

Applications for Enrollment of Creek Newborn
Act of 1905   Volume XI

Subscribed and sworn to before me this 8th day of April, 1905.

Com Ex 7/3/1906   Robert E Lynch
                                   Notary Public.

AFFIDAVIT OF ATTENDING PHYSICIAN OR MID-WIFE.

UNITED STATES OF AMERICA, Indian Territory, ⎫
   Western   DISTRICT.   ⎭

I, Lizzie Gillis, a Cherokee, on oath state that I attended on Mrs. Susie Chamblen, wife of Jno C. Chamblen on the 30th day of September, 1902; that there was born to her on said date a male child; that said child was living March 4, 1905, and is said to have been named Dewey Chamblen   her
                                                               Lizzie x Gillis
Witnesses To Mark: mark
 ⎰ J ? Kirkpatrick
 ⎱ Benjamin F. Rice Jr.

Subscribed and sworn to before me 15th day of March, 1905.

                                   Benjamin F. Rice Jr.
                                   Notary Public.
My Com. Ex. 9/19/08

NC. 861.

Muskogee, Indian Territory, July 15, 1905.

Chief Clerk,
   Cherokee Enrollment Division,
      Muskogee, Indian Territory.

Dear Sir:

April 12, 1905, application was made to the Commission to the Five Civilized Tribes for the enrollment of Dewey Chamblen, born September 30, 1902, and Ruby Chamblen, born December 10, 1904, as citizens by blood of the Creek Nation. It is stated in said application that the father of said children is John C. Chamblen, a citizen of the Cherokee Nation, and that the mother is Susie Chamblen, identified as Susie Chamberlain, a citizen of the Creek Nation.

You are requested to inform the Creek Enrollment Division as to whether application has been made for the enrollment of said children as citizens of the Cherokee Nation, and if so, what disposition has been made of the same.

Applications for Enrollment of Creek Newborn
Act of 1905   Volume XI

Respectfully,

Commissioner.

REFER IN REPLY TO THE FOLLOWING:

**DEPARTMENT OF THE INTERIOR,
COMMISSIONER TO THE FIVE CIVILIZED TRIBES.**

Muskogee, Indian Territory, July 18, 1905.

Chief Clerk,
    Creek Enrollment Division,
        Muskogee, Indian Territory.

Dear Sir:

    Replying to your letter of July 15, 1905, (NC. 861) asking to be advised whether or not any application has ever been made for the enrollment, as citizens of the Cherokee Nation, of Dewey Chamblen and Ruby Chamblen, children of John C. Chamblen, a citizen of the Cherokee Nation, and Susie Chamblen, a citizen of the Creek Nation, you are advised that from an examination of the records of the Cherokee Enrollment Division it does not appear that any application has ever been made for the enrollment of said children as citizens of that nation.

Respectfully,

GHL

Tams Bixby   Commissioner.

N.C. 861

Muskogee, Indian Territory, October 19, 1905.

Chief Clerk,
    Cherokee Enrollment Division.

Dear Sir:

    April 12, 1905 application was made to the Commission to the Five Civilized Tribes for the enrollment of Dewey Chamblen, born September 30, 1902, and Ruby Chamblen, born December 10, 1904, as citizens by blood of the Creek Nation.

    It is stated in said application that the father of said child is John Chamblen, a Cherokee Delaware, and that the mother is Susie, identified as Susie Chamberlain, a citizen of the Creek Nation.

Applications for Enrollment of Creek Newborn
Act of 1905   Volume XI

You are requested to inform the Creek Enrollment Division whether application has been made for the enrollment of said children as Cherokee Delawares and if so what disposition has been made of the same.

Respectfully,

Commissioner.

REFER IN REPLY TO THE FOLLOWING:

DEPARTMENT OF THE INTERIOR,
COMMISSIONER TO THE FIVE CIVILIZED TRIBES.

Muskogee, Indian Territory, October 23, 1905.

Chief Clerk,
    Creek Enrollment Division.

Dear Sir:

    In reply to your letter of October 19, (N.C. 861), asking to be advised if any application has been made for the enrollment, as citizens of the Cherokee Nation, of Dewey Chamblen, born September 30, 1902, and Rubey[sic] Chamblen, born December 10, 1904, children of John Chamblen, an alleged Delaware-Cherokee, and Susie Chamberlain, a citizen of the Creek Nation, you are advised that it does not appear from an examination of the records of the Cherokee Enrollment Division that any application has ever been made for the enrollment of said child as a citizen of the Cherokee Nation. the records of this office that any application has ever been made for the enrollment, as citizens of the Cherokee Nation, of said children; neither can their father be identified as an applicant for enrollment as a citizen of that Nation.

Respectfully,
Tams Bixby   Commissioner.

LS

NC 861

Muskogee, Indian Territory, November 13, 1906.

Chief Clerk,
    Cherokee Enrollment Division,
        General Office.

Dear Sir:

    You are hereby advised that the names of Dewey and Ruby Chamberlain, children of John C. Chamberlain, an alleged Cherokee Deleware[sic] citizen and Susie Chamberlain a citizen by blood of the Creek Nation, are contained in schedule of minor

Applications for Enrollment of Creek Newborn
Act of 1905   Volume XI

citizens by blood of the Creek Nation, approved by the Secretary of the Interior, January 4, 1906, opposite Roll numbers 982 and 983.

                            Respectfully,
                                            Commissioner.

BIRTH AFFIDAVIT.

DEPARTMENT OF THE INTERIOR.
COMMISSION TO THE FIVE CIVILIZED TRIBES.

IN RE APPLICATION FOR ENROLLMENT, as a citizen of the Creek Nation, of Jesse May Huston, born on the 22 day of Jan, 1905

Name of Father: James Madison Huston   a citizen of the   U.S.   Nation.
Name of Mother: Lula F. Huston nee Barber   a citizen of the   Creek   Nation.
(Broken Arrow)
                                Postoffice   Mounds

AFFIDAVIT OF MOTHER.

UNITED STATES OF AMERICA, Indian Territory,
      Western   DISTRICT.

    I, Lula F. Huston nee Barber, on oath state that I am 19 years of age and a citizen by blood, of the Creek Nation; that I am the lawful wife of James Madison Huston, who is a citizen, by ------- of the U. S. Nation; that a female child was born to me on 22 day of Jan, 1905, that said child has been named Jesse May Huston, and ~~was living March 4, 1905~~. died Feb. 19-1905

                                          Lula F Huston

Witnesses To Mark:

    Subscribed and sworn to before me this 24 day of April, 1905.

(Seal)   Edw C Griesel
                                            Notary Public.

Applications for Enrollment of Creek Newborn
Act of 1905 Volume XI

AFFIDAVIT OF ATTENDING ~~PHYSICIAN~~ OR MID-WIFE.

UNITED STATES OF AMERICA, Indian Territory, }
    Western   DISTRICT.

I, Alice Barber, a Midwife, on oath state that I attended on Mrs. Lula F. Huston, wife of James Madison Huston on the 22 day of Jan, 1905; that there was born to her on said date a female child; that said child was living March 4, 1905, and is said to have been named Jesse May Huston

                         Her
                 Alice x Barber

Witnesses To Mark: mark
  { David Shelby
    Jesse McDermott

Subscribed and sworn to before me this 24 day of April, 1905.

(Seal)   Edw C Griesel
                               Notary Public.

NC 862   JLD
DEPARTMENT OF THE INTERIOR,
COMMISSIONER TO THE FIVE CIVILIZED TRIBES.

In the matter of the application for the enrollment of Jesse May Huston, deceased, as a citizen by blood of the Creek Nation.

....

STATEMENT AND ORDER.

The record in this case shows that on April 29, 1905, application was made, in affidavit form, for the enrollment of Jesse May Huston, deceased, as a citizen by blood of the Creek Nation, under the provisions of the Act of Congress approved March 3, 1905.

It appears from the affidavit filed in this matter that said Jesse May Huston, deceased, was born January 22, 1905, and died February 19, 1905.

The Act of Congress approved March 3, 1905, (33 Stats., 1048), provides:
"That the Commission to the Five Civilized Tribes is authorized for sixty days after the date of the approval of this act to receive and consider applications for enrollment, of children, <u>born subsequent to May twenty-fifth, nineteen hundred and one, and prior to March fourth, nineteen hundred and five, and living on said latter date, to citizens</u> of the Creek tribe of Indians whose enrollment has been approved by the Secretary of the Interior prior to the approval of this act; and to enroll and make allotments to such children."

It is, therefore, ordered that the application for the enrollment of Jesse May Huston, deceased, as a citizen by blood of the Creek Nation, be and the same is hereby dismissed.

Applications for Enrollment of Creek Newborn
Act of 1905   Volume XI

Tams Bixby Commissioner.

Muskogee, Indian Territory.
JAN 4 – 1907

BIRTH AFFIDAVIT.

DEPARTMENT OF THE INTERIOR.
COMMISSION TO THE FIVE CIVILIZED TRIBES.

IN RE APPLICATION FOR ENROLLMENT, as a citizen of the C R E E K - - - - - - - - - Nation, of Thomas Addison Huston , born on the first day of October , 1903

Name of Father: J.M. Huston   a citizen of the C R E E K[sic] Nation.
Name of Mother: Lula F. Huston - - - - - - - - -   a citizen of the C R E E K   Nation.
(Broken Arrow)   nee Barber
                                          Postoffice   Mounds, I.T.

AFFIDAVIT OF MOTHER.

Child Brought in
UNITED STATES OF AMERICA, Indian Territory,   5/24/05 - Gr.
     WESTERN   DISTRICT.

I, Lula F. Huston - - - - - - - - - - - - - - , on oath state that I am nineteen years of age and a citizen by Blood - - - , of the Creek   Nation; that I am the lawful wife of J. M. Huston - - - - - - - - - - - - - - , who is not a citizen   of the C R E E K - - - - - Nation; that a male   child was born to me on first - - - day of October - - - - - - , 1903 , that said child has been named   Thomas Adison[sic] Huston - - - - - - - - , and was living March 4, 1905.

Lula F Huston

Witnesses To Mark:

Subscribed and sworn to before me this 4th day of April - - - - , 1905.

B Barton
My Commission expires Feb. 21, 1907.   Notary Public.

AFFIDAVIT OF ATTENDING PHYSICIAN OR MID-WIFE.

UNITED STATES OF AMERICA, Indian Territory,
     WESTERN - - - - - -   DISTRICT.

I, M.D. Taylor - - - - - - - - - - - , a Physician - - - - - - , on oath state that I attended on Mrs. Lula F. Huston - - - - - - - - -, wife of J.M. Huston - - - - - - - - - on the first day of October - - - - - - , 1903 ; that there was born to her on said date a male

Applications for Enrollment of Creek Newborn
Act of 1905   Volume XI

child; that said child was living March 4, 1905, and is said to have been named Thomas Adison Huston

M.D. Taylor, M.D.

Witnesses To Mark:

{

    Subscribed and sworn to before me this 4th day of April - - - - , 1905.

                                      B Barton

My Commission expires Feb. 21, 1907.   Notary Public.

NC-863

MARRIAGE LICENSE.

UNITED STATES OF AMERICA,
    Indian Territory,   ss.   NO. 25
    Western District.

TO ANY PERSON AUTHORIZED BY LAW TO SOLEMNIZE MARRIAGE--GREETING:

    You are hereby commended[sic] to Solemnize the Rite and Publish the Banns of Matrimony between Mr. John W. Barber of Mounds , in the Indian Territory, aged 18 years, and Miss Cora Weatherly, of Mounds, Indian Territory in the Indian Territory, aged 19 years, according to law, and do you officially sign and return this License to the parties therein named.

    Witness my hand and official seal at Muskogee, Indian Territory, this 14 day of July, A. D. 1902.

    (SEAL)   R. P. HARRISON
                                                Clerk of the U.S. Court..
By R. A. Bayne, Deputy.

CERTIFICATE OF MARRIAGE.

	:	I, Rev. P. Johnson, a Minister of the
United States of America,	:	Gospel, do hereby certify that on the 16
Indian Territory,	: ss.	day of May, A. D. 1902, did duly and
Western District.	:	according to law as commanded in the
	:	foregoing License, solemnize the Rite

and Publish the Banns of Matrimony between the parties therein named.

Applications for Enrollment of Creek Newborn
Act of 1905   Volume XI

Witness my hand this 16 day of May, A. D. 1902.

My credentils[sic] are recorded in the office of the Clerk of the United States Court, Indian Territory, Western District, Book B, Page 126.

(signed) REV. P. JOHNSON,
a Minister of the Gospel.

CERTIFICATE OF RECORD.

United States of America,
    Indian Territory.   ss.
    Western District.

    I, Robert P. Harrison, Clerk of the United States Court in the Western District, Indian Territory, do hereby certify that the instrument hereto attached was filed for record in my office the 14 day of Aug. 1902, at ----M, and duly recorded in Book N, Marriage Record, Page 133.
    Witness my hand and seal of said Court at Muskogee, in said Territory this 14th day of Aug. A.D. 1902.

R.P. Harrison, Clerk
By J. L. Peacock, Deputy.

(SEAL)

Western Dist. Ind. Ter.
    FILED
  AUG 14, 1902
  R.P. HARRISON
Clerk U. S. Courts.

INDIAN TERRITORY, Western District.
    I, J. Y. Miller, a stenographer to the Commissioner to the Five Civilized Tribes, do hereby certify that the above and foregoing is a true and complete copy of its original.

JY Miller

Subscribed and sworn to before me
  this the 4th day of November,
    1905.

Edw C Griesel
Notary Public.

Applications for Enrollment of Creek Newborn
Act of 1905   Volume XI

BIRTH AFFIDAVIT.

DEPARTMENT OF THE INTERIOR.
COMMISSION TO THE FIVE CIVILIZED TRIBES.

IN RE APPLICATION FOR ENROLLMENT, as a citizen of the Creek Nation, of John Thomas Barber , born on the 30 day of April, 1903

Name of Father: John W. Barber   a citizen of the   Creek   Nation.
(Broken Arrow)
Name of Mother: Cora Barber   a citizen of the   Creek[sic]   Nation.

Postoffice   Mounds

AFFIDAVIT OF ~~MOTHER~~.   Father
Child Present

UNITED STATES OF AMERICA, Indian Territory,
Western   DISTRICT.

I, John W. Barber , on oath state that I am 21 years of age and a citizen by blood , of the Creek   Nation; that I am the lawful ~~wife~~ Husband of Cora Barber , who is a citizen, by ------- of the U. S. Nation; that a male   child was born to me on 30 day of April , 1903 , that said child has been named John Thomas Barber , and was living March 4, 1905.

                         His
                   John W x Barber

Witnesses To Mark: mark
    David Shelby
    Jesse McDermott

Subscribed and sworn to before me this 24 day of April , 1905.

(Seal)   Edw C Griesel
                                    Notary Public.

BIRTH AFFIDAVIT.

DEPARTMENT OF THE INTERIOR.
COMMISSION TO THE FIVE CIVILIZED TRIBES.

IN RE APPLICATION FOR ENROLLMENT, as a citizen of the Creek Nation, of John Thomas Barber , born on the 30 day of April, 1903

Name of Father: John W. Barber   a citizen of the   Creek   Nation.
(Broken Arrow)
Name of Mother: Cora Barber   a citizen of the   U. S.   Nation.

Applications for Enrollment of Creek Newborn
Act of 1905   Volume XI

Postoffice   Mounds I.T.

AFFIDAVIT OF MOTHER.   Child Present

UNITED STATES OF AMERICA, Indian Territory, ⎫
   Western   DISTRICT. ⎭

I, Cora Barber , on oath state that I am 21 years of age and a citizen by ------ , of the U.S. Nation; that I am the lawful wife of John W. Barber , who is a citizen, by blood of the Creek Nation; that a male child was born to me on 30 day of April , 1903 , that said child has been named John Thomas Barber , and was living March 4, 1905.

                              Cora Barber

Witnesses To Mark:
{

Subscribed and sworn to before me this 24 day of April , 1905.

                              Edw C Griesel
                              Notary Public.

AFFIDAVIT OF ATTENDING ~~PHYSICIAN~~ OR MID-WIFE.

UNITED STATES OF AMERICA, Indian Territory, ⎫
   Western   DISTRICT. ⎭

I, Alice A Barber , a Mid wife , on oath state that I attended on Mrs. Cora Barber , wife of John W. Barber on the 30 day of April , 1903; that there was born to her on said date a male child; that said child was living March 4, 1905, and is said to have been named John Thomas Barber   Her

                              Alice A. x Barber

Witnesses To Mark: mark
{ David Shelby
  Jesse McDermott

Subscribed and sworn to before me this 24 day of April , 1905.

                              Edw C Griesel
                              Notary Public.

Applications for Enrollment of Creek Newborn
Act of 1905   Volume XI

BIRTH AFFIDAVIT.

DEPARTMENT OF THE INTERIOR.
COMMISSION TO THE FIVE CIVILIZED TRIBES.

    IN RE APPLICATION FOR ENROLLMENT, as a citizen of the C R E E K - - - - - - - - Nation, of John Thomas Barber - - - - - - - - -, born on the 30th day of April - - - -, 1903

Name of Father: John W. Barber - - - - - - - - - - a citizen of the CR E E K - - Nation.
                                                non
Name of Mother: Cora Barber - - - - - - - - - - - a^citizen of the CR E E K - - Nation.

                                  Postoffice   Mounds I.T. - - - - - - - - - - -

AFFIDAVIT OF MOTHER.

UNITED STATES OF AMERICA, Indian Territory,
    W E S T E R N - - -   DISTRICT.

    I, Cora Barber - - - - - - - - - - - - - - -, on oath state that I am twenty one years of age and a non citizen ~~by~~ , of the C R E E K - - - - - - - Nation; that I am the lawful wife of John W. Barber - - - - - - - - - - - - - -, who is a citizen, by Blood - - - - - - of the C R E E K - - - - - - -- Nation; that a male - - child was born to me on 30th - - day of April - - - - - - - - - - , 1903 , that said child has been named John Thomas Barber - - - - - - - -, and was living March 4, 1905.

                                                  Mrs. Cora Barber

Witnesses To Mark:

    Subscribed and sworn to before me this 4th - - day of April - - - - - , 1905.

                                                  B Barton
My Commission expires Feb. 21, 1907.   Notary Public.

AFFIDAVIT OF ATTENDING ~~PHYSICIAN~~ OR MID-WIFE.

UNITED STATES OF AMERICA, Indian Territory,
    W E S T E R N   DISTRICT.

    I, M.D. Taylor - - - - - - - - - - - - - -- , a Physician - , on oath state that I attended on Mrs. Cora Barber - - - - - - - - - - -, wife of John W. Barber - - - - - - - - - on the 30th day of April - - - - - - - - , 1903; that there was born to her on said date a male child; that said child was living March 4, 1905, and is said to have been named John Thomas Barber

                                                M.D. Taylor, M.D.

Applications for Enrollment of Creek Newborn
Act of 1905 Volume XI

Witnesses To Mark:

{

Subscribed and sworn to before me this 4th day of April - - - - - , 1905.

B Barton

My Commission expires Feb. 21, 1907.   Notary Public.

REFER IN REPLY TO THE FOLLOWING:
NC-863.

DEPARTMENT OF THE INTERIOR,
COMMISSIONER TO THE FIVE CIVILIZED TRIBES.

Muskogee, Indian Territory, October 21, 1905.

R # 3414 John W Barber

Cora Barber,
   c/o John W. Barber,
      Mounds, Indian Territory.

Dear Madam:

    In the matter of the application for the enrollment of your minor child, John Thomas Barber, born April 30, 1903, as a citizen by blood of the Creek Nation, this office is unable to identify the alleged father of said child upon the final roll of citizens by blood of the Creek Nation. It is necessary that he be identified before the rights of your said child can be finally determined.

    You are, therefore, requested to state the name under which the father was enrolled, the names of his parents and other members of his family, the Creek Indian town to which he belongs and his roll number as the same appears upon his allotment certificate and deeds.

    You are advised that it will be necessary for you to furnish this office with evidence of your marriage to the father of the said John Thomas Barber. Such evidence may consist of either the original or a certified copy of your marriage license and certificate.

    Please give these matters your immediate attention.

               Respectfully,
               Tams Bixby   Commissioner.

Applications for Enrollment of Creek Newborn
Act of 1905   Volume XI

NC-863

Muskogee, Indian Territory, November 4, 1905.

John W. Barber,
    Mounds, Indian Territory.

Dear Sir:

    There is herewith enclosed your marriage license and certificate in the matter of the application for the enrollment of your minor child, John Thomas Barber, as a citizen by blood of the Creek Nation. A copy of said license and certificate has been made and filed with the record in the case.

                                  Respectfully,

                                                  Commissioner.

JYM-4-2

NF-864.

Muskogee, Indian Territory, November 8, 1905.

Kizzie Davis,
    Coweta, Indian Territory.

Dear Madam:

    In the matter of the application for the enrollment of your minor child, born April 2, 1904, it is stated in your affidavit, relative to the birth of said child, that her name is Kizzie Davis and in the affidavit of Hattie Sarty, the midwife who attended on you at the birth of said child, the name is given as Hattie Johnson Davis.

    There is enclosed herewith blank form of birth affidavit which you are requested to have executed, taking care to insert the correct name of said child, and when so executed return it to this office in the inclosed envelope.

                                  Respectfully,
                                  Tams Bixby
                                        Commissioner.

B C.
Env.

Applications for Enrollment of Creek Newborn
Act of 1905   Volume XI

BIRTH AFFIDAVIT.

DEPARTMENT OF THE INTERIOR.
COMMISSION TO THE FIVE CIVILIZED TRIBES.

IN RE APPLICATION FOR ENROLLMENT, as a citizen of the Creek Nation, of Hattie Johnson Davis, born on the 2nd day of April, 1904

Name of Father: Isaac Johnson	a citizen of the Creek	Nation.
Name of Mother: Kizzie Davis	a citizen of the Creek	Nation.

Postoffice   Coweta, Indian Territory.

AFFIDAVIT OF MOTHER.

UNITED STATES OF AMERICA, Indian Territory, ⎱
  Western   DISTRICT.   ⎰

I, Kizzie Davis, on oath state that I am 34 years of age and a citizen by birth, of the Creek Nation; that I am the lawful wife of (lived with Isaac Johnson as man and wife), who is a citizen, by birth of the Creek Nation; that a female child was born to me on 2nd day of April, 1904, that said child has been named Hattie Johnson David, and was living March 4, 1905.

                                                her
                                      Kizzie x Davis
Witnesses To Mark: mark
  ⎰ CE Hampton
  ⎱ M.J. Smith

Subscribed and sworn to before me this 23rd day of November, 1905.

                                      R. C. Allen
                                          Notary Public.

My commission expires March 15, 1908.

BIRTH AFFIDAVIT.

DEPARTMENT OF THE INTERIOR.
COMMISSION TO THE FIVE CIVILIZED TRIBES.

IN RE APPLICATION FOR ENROLLMENT, as a citizen of the Creek Nation, of Hattie Johnson Davis, born on the 2nd day of April, 1904

	Isaac Johnson	
Name of Father: Illegitimate child father was	a citizen of the Creek	Nation.
Name of Mother: Kizzie Davis	a citizen of the Creek	Nation.

Postoffice   Coweta, I.T.

Applications for Enrollment of Creek Newborn
Act of 1905   Volume XI

AFFIDAVIT OF MOTHER.

UNITED STATES OF AMERICA, Indian Territory, ⎫
   Western   DISTRICT. ⎬

    I, Kizzie Davis , on oath state that I am thirty ~~y~~ years of age and a citizen by blood , of the Creek   Nation; that I am ~~the lawful wife of (blank)~~ , who is a citizen, ~~by (blank) of the (blank)   Nation;~~ that an illegitimate female   child was born to me on 2nd day of April , 1904 , that said child has been named Kizzie Davis , and was living March 4, 1905.

                                                               her
Witnesses To Mark: Kizzie x Davis
   { Mary Reed   mark
   { Sanford Scott

    Subscribed and sworn to before me this 8 day of April , 1905.

                                              Bert J Beavers
                                                 Notary Public.
My commission expires Dec 19-1908

AFFIDAVIT OF ATTENDING PHYSICIAN OR MID-WIFE.

UNITED STATES OF AMERICA, Indian Territory, ⎫
   Western   DISTRICT. ⎬

    I, Hattie Sarty , a midwife , on oath state that I attended on Mrs. Kizzie Davis , ~~wife of (blank)~~ on the 2nd day of April , 1904 ; that there was born to her on said date illegitimate female child; that said child was living March 4, 1905, and is said to have been named Hattie Johnson Davis

                                               Hattie Sarty
Witnesses To Mark:
   { Mary Reed
   { Sanford Scott

    Subscribed and sworn to before me this 8 day of April , 1905.

                                              Bert J Beavers
                                               Notary Public.
My commission expires Dec 19-1908

Applications for Enrollment of Creek Newborn
Act of 1905   Volume XI

BIRTH AFFIDAVIT.
DEPARTMENT OF THE INTERIOR.
COMMISSION TO THE FIVE CIVILIZED TRIBES.

IN RE APPLICATION FOR ENROLLMENT, as a citizen of the Creek Nation, of Sillie May Turnham, born on the 30th day of July, 1902

Name of Father: Joe Turnham   a citizen of the United States Nation.
Name of Mother: Curley Turnham   a citizen of the Creek Nation.

Postoffice   Wagoner, Ind. Terr.

AFFIDAVIT OF MOTHER.

UNITED STATES OF AMERICA, Indian Territory,
    Western   DISTRICT.

I, Curley Turnham, on oath state that I am 25 years of age and a citizen by blood, of the Creek Nation; that I am the lawful wife of Joe Turnham, who is a citizen, by *(blank)* of the United States ~~Nation~~; that a female child was born to me on 30th day of July, 1902, that said child has been named Sillie May Turnham, and was living March 4, 1905.

           Curley Turnham

Witnesses To Mark:
{

Subscribed and sworn to before me this 22 day of April, 1905.

           Ross M. Simpson
           Notary Public.

AFFIDAVIT OF ATTENDING PHYSICIAN OR MID-WIFE.

UNITED STATES OF AMERICA, Indian Territory,
    Western   DISTRICT.

I, G. W. Ruble, a physician, on oath state that I attended on Mrs. Curley Turnham, wife of Joe Turnham on the 30$^{\underline{th}}$ day of July, 1902; that there was born to her on said date a female child; that said child was living March 4, 1905, and is said to have been named Sillie May Turnham

           G W Ruble

Witnesses To Mark:
{

Applications for Enrollment of Creek Newborn
Act of 1905   Volume XI

Subscribed and sworn to before me this 22 day of April , 1905.

           Ross M. Simpson
           Notary Public.

BIRTH AFFIDAVIT.

DEPARTMENT OF THE INTERIOR.
COMMISSION TO THE FIVE CIVILIZED TRIBES.

IN RE APPLICATION FOR ENROLLMENT, as a citizen of the Muskogee Nation, of Duard C. Douglas , born on the 7 day of Feb , 1904

Name of Father: Harry Douglas   a citizen of the United States Nation.
Name of Mother: Louie Mikey Douglas   a citizen of the Muskogee   Nation.

        Postoffice   Morse, I. T.

AFFIDAVIT OF MOTHER.

UNITED STATES OF AMERICA, Indian Territory,
  Western District[sic]   DISTRICT.

  I, Louie Mikey Douglas , on oath state that I am 31 years of age and a citizen by Blood , of the Muskogee Nation; that I am the lawful wife of Harry Douglas , who is a citizen, by *(blank)* of the United States ~~Nation~~; that a male child was born to me on 7 day of Feb , 1904 , that said child has been named Duard C. Douglas , and was living March 4, 1905.

          Louie Mikey Douglas

Witnesses To Mark:

  Subscribed and sworn to before me this 8 day of Apr , 1905.

My Commission Expires March 5th, 1908.   C. C. Eskridge
           Notary Public.

Applications for Enrollment of Creek Newborn
Act of 1905   Volume XI

AFFIDAVIT OF ATTENDING PHYSICIAN OR MID-WIFE.

UNITED STATES OF AMERICA, Indian Territory, }
    Western   DISTRICT.

    I, Silwar Mikey , a Midwife , on oath state that I attended on Mrs. Louie Mikey Douglas , wife of Harry Douglas on the 7 day of Feb , 1904 ; that there was born to her on said date a male child; that said child was living March 4, 1905, and is said to have been named Duard C. Douglas   her
                                  Silwar x Mikey
Witnesses To Mark: mark
 { J. G Bobbitt
   John W. Naines

    Subscribed and sworn to before me 8 day of Apr, 1905.

My Commission Expires March 5th, 1908.   C. C. Eskridge
                                            Notary Public.

BIRTH AFFIDAVIT.
DEPARTMENT OF THE INTERIOR.
COMMISSION TO THE FIVE CIVILIZED TRIBES.

    IN RE APPLICATION FOR ENROLLMENT, as a citizen of the Creek Nation, of Leola Hoffman, born on the Fourth day of October , 1904

Name of Father: Julius M Hoffman   a citizen of the United States Nation.
Name of Mother: Ella B Hoffman nee Boston   a citizen of the   Creek   Nation.

                        Postoffice   Muskogee Ind Ter

AFFIDAVIT OF MOTHER.

UNITED STATES OF AMERICA, Indian Territory, }
    Western   DISTRICT.

    I, Ella B Hoffman nee Boston , on oath state that I am Twenty years of age and a citizen by Blood , of the Creek Nation; that I am the lawful wife of Julius M Hoffman , who is a citizen, by *(blank)* of the United States Nation; that a Female

Applications for Enrollment of Creek Newborn
Act of 1905   Volume XI

child was born to me on Fourth day of October, 1904, that said child has been named Leola Hoffman, and was living March 4, 1905.

                                              Ella B Hoffman
Witnesses To Mark: nee Boston
{

    Subscribed and sworn to before me this 27th day of April, 1905.

My Commission   Thos A Jenkins
Expires December 26th 1907   Notary Public.

AFFIDAVIT OF ATTENDING PHYSICIAN OR MID-WIFE.

UNITED STATES OF AMERICA, Indian Territory, }
    Western   DISTRICT.

    I, Mrs Edith Seranton, a Mid-wife, on oath state that I attended on Mrs. Ella B Hoffman nee Boston, wife of Julius M Hoffman on the Fourth day of October, 1904; that there was born to her on said date a Female child; that said child was living March 4, 1905, and is said to have been named Leola Hoffman

                                            Mrs Edith Seranton
Witnesses To Mark:
{

    Subscribed and sworn to before me this 27th day of April, 1905.

My Commission   Thos A Jenkins
Expires December 26th 1907   Notary Public.

NC. 867.   I.S.N.
                        DEPARTMENT OF THE INTERIOR,
            COMMISSIONER TO THE FIVE CIVILIZED TRIBES.

    In the matter of the application for the enrollment of Leola Hoffman, as a citizen by blood of the Creek Nation.

                          STATEMENT AND ORDER.

    The record in this case shows that on April 29, 1905, application was made, in affidavit form, for the enrollment of Leola Hoffman, as a citizen by blood of the Creek Nation.

Applications for Enrollment of Creek Newborn
Act of 1905 Volume XI

The evidence shows that said Leola Hoffman is the minor child of Julius M. Hoffman, a citizen of the United States, and Ella B. Hoffman, nee Boston, identified under the name of Ella Boston as one of the applicants included in the Creek citizenship case of Josephine (Posey) Boston, et al., in which a decision, adverse to the applicants therein was rendered by the Commissioner to the Five Civilized Tribes on October 2, 1905, which said decision was affirmed by the Department March 6, 1906.

It is, therefore, ordered that there is no authority of law for the enrollment of said Leola Hoffman as a citizen by blood of the Creek Nation, and that the application for her enrollment as such should be and the same is hereby dismissed.

                                    Tams Bixby   Commissioner.

Muskogee, Indian Territory,
NOV 23 1906

DEPARTMENT OF THE INTERIOR,
COMMISSIONER TO THE FIVE CIVILIZED TRIBES.

Muskogee, Indian Territory, September 13, 1905.

Chief Clerk,
    Creek Enrollment Division
        General Office

Dear Sir:

In the matter of the application for the enrollment of Ella Boston Hoffman and Leola Hoffman for enrollment as citizens of the Creek Nation, you are advised that Creek Allotment Contests Nos. 881, 882 and 883 have been held open pending the determination of said applications.

As soon as these applications have been finally passed upon by the Honorable Secretary of the Interior you will advise the Allotment Contest Division so that these contests above referred to may be disposed of in the regular manner.

                                    Respectfully,
                                    Tams Bixby   Commissioner

Applications for Enrollment of Creek Newborn
Act of 1905   Volume XI

REFER IN REPLY TO THE FOLLOWING:
_____

DEPARTMENT OF THE INTERIOR,
COMMISSIONER TO THE FIVE CIVILIZED TRIBES.

Muskogee, Indian Territory, September 15, 1906.

Chief Clerk Creek Enrollment Division,
    General Office.

Dear Sir:-

    You are directed to advise the Creek Land Office whether or not application has been made for the enrollment of Ella Boston Hoffman and Leola Hoffman, as citizens by blood of the Creek Nation. If such applications have been filed, you will advise the status of the same.

                        Respectfully,
                        Tams Bixby   Commissioner.

N.C. 867

                    Muskogee, Indian Territory, November 24, 1906.

Ella B. Hoffman,
    Box 800,
        Muskogee, Indian Territory.

Dear Madam:

    There is herewith inclosed a copy of statement and order dismissing the application for the enrollment of your minor child Leola Hoffman as a citizen of the Creek Nation.

                        Respectfully,
                                  Commissioner.

Inc. CM-3-24.

N.C. 867

                    Muskogee, Indian Territory, November 24, 1906

Clerk in Charge,
    Creek Allotment Contest Division.

Dear Sir:

    You are hereby advised that on September 14, 1905, the Secretary of the Interior denied a motion for review in the matter of the application for the enrollment of

Applications for Enrollment of Creek Newborn
Act of 1905   Volume XI

Josephine Boston et al., in which Ella Boston now Ella Hoffman was one of the applicants, and that no further motion for review has been filed in same.

You are further advised that the application for the enrollment of Leola Hoffman, child of said Ella Hoffman, as a citizen of the Creek Nation has this day been dismissed and the parties in interest have been duly notified.

The application for enrollment as citizens of the Creek Nation of Josephine Boston et al. was denied by the Commissioner October 2, 1905, and his decision in same was approved by the Secretary of the Interior March 5, 1906.

Respectfully,
Commissioner.

BIRTH AFFIDAVIT.

DEPARTMENT OF THE INTERIOR.
COMMISSION TO THE FIVE CIVILIZED TRIBES.

IN RE APPLICATION FOR ENROLLMENT, as a citizen of the Creek Nation, of Joseph Mingo, born on the 5th day of January, 1902

Name of Father: Robert J. Mingo	a citizen of the Creek Nation.
Name of Mother: Irene Mingo	a citizen of the Creek Nation.

Postoffice   Wagoner, I.T.

AFFIDAVIT OF MOTHER.

UNITED STATES OF AMERICA, Indian Territory,
Western   DISTRICT.

I, Robert J. Mingo, on oath state that I am 27 years of age and a citizen by birth, of the Creek Nation; that I am the lawful husband of Irene Mingo, deceased, who is a citizen, by birth of the Creek Nation; that a male child was born to Irene Mingo on 5th day of January, 1902, that said child has been named Joseph Mingo, and was living March 4, 1905.

Robert J. Mingo

Witnesses To Mark:

Applications for Enrollment of Creek Newborn
Act of 1905   Volume XI

Subscribed and sworn to before me this 24th day of April, 1905.

R. C. Allen
Notary Public.

My commission expires Mch 15, 1908

AFFIDAVIT OF ATTENDING PHYSICIAN OR MID-WIFE.

UNITED STATES OF AMERICA, Indian Territory,
   Western   DISTRICT.

I, Hattie Atkins[sic], a midwife, on oath state that I attended on Mrs. Irene Mingo, wife of Robert J. Mingo on the 5th day of January, 1902; that there was born to her on said date a male child; that said child was living March 4, 1905, and is said to have been named Joseph Mingo

Hattie Adkins

Witnesses To Mark:
{

Subscribed and sworn to before me 25 day of April, 1905.

My Commission expires   R. W. Lumpkin
   Jany 13th 1909   Notary Public.

NC-868

Muskogee, Indian Territory, October 23, 1905.

Robert J. Mingo,
   Wagoner, Indian Territory.

Dear Sir:

In the matter of the application for the enrollment of your minor child, Joseph Mingo, born January 5, 1902, as a citizen by blood of the Creek Nation, it will be necessary for you to furnish this office the affidavits of two disinterested witnesses relative to the birth of said child. Said affidavits must set forth said child's name, the date of his birth, the names of his parents and whether or not he was living March 4, 1905.

You are also requested to fill out the inclosed death affidavit, giving the exact date of the death of your wife Irene Mingo, have the same executed and when so executed return it to this office in the inclosed envelope.

Respectfully,
D C Skaggs   Commissioner.
Env.

Applications for Enrollment of Creek Newborn
Act of 1905 Volume XI

C868

(Copy)

Wagoner, I. T. Oct 25, 05.

Daws[sic] Commission,
    Muscogee[sic], Ind. Ty.

Gents:

Did the Office receive my application of my minor child Joseph Mingo (New Born) or not? Please let me know at once. I sent the application by mail among the first. I have received no notice. It might be lost or misplaced some where.

Yours Truly
(signed)   ROBERT J. MINGO.
Wagoner.

N.C. 868

Muskogee, Indian Territory, October 28, 1905.

Robert J. Mingo,
    Wagoner, Indian Territory.

Dear Sir:

Receipt is acknowledged of your communication of October 25, 1905, in which you inquire as to the status of the matter of the application for the enrollment of your minor child, Joseph Mingo, as a citizen by blood of the Creek Nation.

In reply you are advised that on October 3, 1905, a letter was addressed to you at Wagoner, Indian Territory, setting forth in detail the evidence that was needed to complete the proof required by this office in said case.

Respectfully,
Commissioner.

Applications for Enrollment of Creek Newborn
Act of 1905   Volume XI

BIRTH AFFIDAVIT.

DEPARTMENT OF THE INTERIOR.
COMMISSION TO THE FIVE CIVILIZED TRIBES.

IN RE APPLICATION FOR ENROLLMENT, as a citizen of the CREEK Nation, of Joseph Mingo, born on the day of , 190 about 3 years ago

Name of Father: Robert Mingo a citizen of the Creek Nation.
Name of Mother: Irene " a citizen of the " Nation.

Postoffice   Wagoner I.T.

AFFIDAVIT OF ~~MOTHER~~.
Aunt

UNITED STATES OF AMERICA, Indian Territory, ⎫
WESTERN DISTRICT. ⎭

I, Lona Merrick , on oath state that I am 25 years of age and a citizen by blood, of the Creek Nation; that I am the lawful ~~wife~~ aunt of Joseph Mingo , ~~who is a citizen~~, by ~~(blank)~~ of the ~~(blank)~~ Nation; that a ~~(blank)~~ child ~~was born to me on~~ *(blank)* day of *(blank)* , 190--- , who was born about 3 years ago that said child has been named Joseph Mingo , and is now living.

Lona Merrick

Witnesses To Mark:
{

Subscribed and sworn to before me this 12" day of April , 1905.

Com expires Apr. 11, 1909.   Zera E Parrish

Notary Public.

AFFIDAVIT OF DISINTERESTED WITNESSES.

United States of America,
  Indian Territory,
  Western District.

We, the undersigned, on oath state that we are personally acquainted with Irene Mingo wife of Robert J Mingo ; and that there was born to her on or about the 6th day of January , 1902 , a Boy child; that said child was living March 5, 1905, and is said to have been named Joseph Mingo

Applications for Enrollment of Creek Newborn
Act of 1905   Volume XI

We further state that we have no interest in this case.

Cassie D Thompson
Frank F Thompson

(2) Witnesses to mark:
  J *(Illegible)*
  CG Wright

Subscribed and sworn to before me this 21 day of November 1905.

Com expires 1/2-08   Chester G. Wright
                                                     Notary Public.

HGH

REFER IN REPLY TO THE FOLLOWING:
NC-870.

DEPARTMENT OF THE INTERIOR,
COMMISSIONER TO THE FIVE CIVILIZED TRIBES.

Muskogee, Indian Territory, October 23, 1905.

Clemantine Berryhill,
    c/o George Franklin Berryhill,
        Stone Bluff, Indian Territory.

Dear Madam:

   In the matter of the application for the enrollment of your minor child, Sam Bob Berryhill, born September 23, 1902, as a citizen by blood of the Creek Nation, you are advised that it will be necessary for you to furnish this office with evidence of your marriage to George Franklin Berryhill, the father of said child, before his rights can be finally determined.

   Such evidence may consist of either the original or a certified copy of your marriage license and certificate.

Respectfully,
Tams Bixby   Commissioner.

Letter returned 12/6/05   Proof of marriage on Creek Card #4324
                          Correct - I.D.

Applications for Enrollment of Creek Newborn
Act of 1905   Volume XI

BIRTH AFFIDAVIT.

DEPARTMENT OF THE INTERIOR.
COMMISSION TO THE FIVE CIVILIZED TRIBES.

IN RE APPLICATION FOR ENROLLMENT, as a citizen of the Creek Nation, of Sam Bob Berryhill , born on the 23rd day of Sept , 1902

Name of Father: George Franklin Berryhill	a citizen of the	Creek	Nation.
Name of Mother: Clemantine Berryhill	a citizen of the		Nation.

Postoffice   Stone Bluff, I. T.

AFFIDAVIT OF MOTHER.

UNITED STATES OF AMERICA, Indian Territory, ⎫
    WESTERN   DISTRICT. ⎭

I, Clemantine Berryhill , on oath state that I am twenty-one years of age and a non citizen by *(blank)* , of the Creek   Nation; that I am the lawful wife of George Franklin Berryhill , who is a citizen, by blood of the Creek   Nation; that a   male child was born to me on 23rd day of Sept. , 1902, that said child has been named Sam Bob Berryhill , and is now living.

               her
            Clemantine x Berryhill
Witnesses To Mark: mark
 ⎧ H.M. Stillwell
 ⎩ Eli Combs

Subscribed and sworn to before me this   22nd day of April , 1905.

            EB Harris
            Notary Public.

AFFIDAVIT OF ATTENDING PHYSICIAN OR MID-WIFE.

UNITED STATES OF AMERICA, Indian Territory, ⎫
    Western   DISTRICT. ⎭

I, Arah Ann Berryhill , a mid-wife , on oath state that I attended on Mrs. Clemantine Berryhill , wife of George Franklin Berryhill on the 23rd day of Sept , 1902 ; that there was born to her on said date a male child; that said child is now living and is said to have been named   Sam Bob Berryhill

              her
          Arah Ann x Berryhill
            mark

Applications for Enrollment of Creek Newborn
Act of 1905   Volume XI

Witnesses To Mark:
{ H.M. Stillwell
  Eli Combs

Subscribed and sworn to before me this 22nd day of April, 1905.

EB Harris
Notary Public.

BIRTH AFFIDAVIT.

DEPARTMENT OF THE INTERIOR.
COMMISSION TO THE FIVE CIVILIZED TRIBES.

IN RE APPLICATION FOR ENROLLMENT, as a citizen of the Creek Nation, of Matilda Agatha Likowski, born on the 28th day of June, 1903

Name of Father: Frank . likowski[sic]	a citizen of the Non	(blank)	Nation.
Name of Mother: Senora . Likowski	a citizen of the	Creek	Nation.

Postoffice   Senora I. T.

AFFIDAVIT OF MOTHER.

UNITED STATES OF AMERICA, Indian Territory,
Western   DISTRICT.

I, Senora . Likowski , on oath state that I am Thirty Three years of age and a citizen by Blood , of the Creek Nation; that I am the lawful wife of Frank . Likowski, who is a non citizen, by x of the x x x Nation; that a Female child was born to me on 28th day of June , 1903 , that said child has been named Matilda Agatha Likowski , and Died October 10th 1904.

Senora Likowski

Witnesses To Mark:
{

Applications for Enrollment of Creek Newborn
Act of 1905   Volume XI

Subscribed and sworn to before me this 26th day of April , 1905.

MY COMMISSION EXPIRES JULY 13th, 1908   J W Fowler
                                                                            Notary Public.

AFFIDAVIT OF ATTENDING PHYSICIAN OR MID-WIFE.

UNITED STATES OF AMERICA, Indian Territory, ⎫
       Western   DISTRICT.   ⎭

I, Susan Willhite , a Midwife , on oath state that I attended on Mrs. Senora . Likowski , wife of Frank Likowski on the 28th day of June , 1903 ; that there was born to her on said date a Female child; that said child ~~was living March 4, 1905~~, Died October 10th 1904 and is said to have been named Matilda Agatha Likowski

                                                                    Susan Willhite
Witnesses To Mark:
{
Subscribed and sworn to before me this 26th day of April , 1905.

MY COMMISSION EXPIRES JULY 13th, 1908   J W Fowler
                                                                            Notary Public.

NC 872   JLD

DEPARTMENT OF THE INTERIOR,
COMMISSIONER TO THE FIVE CIVILIZED TRIBES.

In the matter of the application for the enrollment of Matilda Agatha Likowski, deceased, as a citizen by blood of the Creek Nation.

. . . .

STATEMENT AND ORDER.

The record in this case shows that on April 29, 1905, application was made, in affidavit form, for the enrollment of Matilda Agatha Likowski, deceased, as a citizen by blood of the Creek Nation, under the provisions of the Act of Congress approved March 3, 1905.

It appears from the affidavit filed in this matter that said Matilda Agatha Likowski, deceased, was born June 28, 1903, and died October 10, 1904.

The Act of Congress approved March 3, 1905, (33 Stats., 1048), provides:

"That the Commission to the Five Civilized Tribes is authorized for sixty days after the date of the approval of this act to receive and consider applications for enrollment, of children, <u>born subsequent to May twenty-fifth, nineteen hundred and one, and prior to March fourth, nineteen hundred and five, and living on said</u>

Applications for Enrollment of Creek Newborn
Act of 1905   Volume XI

latter date, to citizens of the Creek tribe of Indians whose enrollment has been approved by the Secretary of the Interior prior to the approval of this act; and to enroll and make allotments to such children."

It is, therefore, ordered that the application for the enrollment of said Mathilda Agatha Likowski, deceased, as a citizen by blood of the Creek Nation be, and the same is, hereby dismissed.

Tams Bixby Commissioner.

Muskogee, Indian Territory.
JAN 4 – 1907

BA 211.
DEPARTMENT OF THE INTERIOR,
COMMISSIONER TO THE FIVE CIVILIZED TRIBES.
MUSKOGEE, INDIAN TERRITORY, March 16, 1905.

-ooOoo-

In the matter of the application for the enrollment of George Elmer Haley as a citizen by blood of the Creek Nation.

WILLIAM DAVID HALEY, being duly sworn, testified as follows:

EXAMINATION BY COMMISSION:
Q What is your name? A William David Haley.
Q How old are you? A 25.
Q What is your postoffice address? A Boynton.
Q Have you a child named George Elmer Haley? A Yes, sir.
Q When was he born? A December 25, 1903.
Q Is he living? A Yes, sir.
Q What is the name of his mother? A Lena Haley, her name was Severe[sic].
Q Are you a citizen of the Creek Nation? A No, sir.
Q Are you a citizen of any Nation in Indian Territory? A No.
Q Is your wife a citizen of the Creek Nation? A Yes, sir.
Q And her name was Lena Severe before marriage? A Yes, sir.

Lena Severe is identified on Creek Indian Card, Field Number 133, and her name is contained in the partial list of citizens by blood of the Creek Nation, approved by the Secretary of the Interior March 13, 1902, Roll Number 482.

Q Is George Elmer Haley living? A Yes, sir.
Q Have you any other children born since May 25, 1901? A No, sir.

Applications for Enrollment of Creek Newborn
Act of 1905   Volume XI

Zera Ellen Parrish, being sworn on her oath states that as a stenographer to the Commission to the Five Civilized Tribes she reported the above case and that this is a full, true and correct transcript of her stenographic notes in same.

                            Zera Ellen Parrish

Subscribed and sworn to
before me this 18 day of March,
1905.   Edw C Griesel
                                          Notary Public.

BIRTH AFFIDAVIT.

DEPARTMENT OF THE INTERIOR,
COMMISSION TO THE FIVE CIVILIZED TRIBES.

IN RE Application for Enrollment, as a citizen of the Creek Nation, of George Elmer Haley, born on the 25th day of December, 1903

Name of Father: William D. Haley   a citizen of the United States ~~Nation~~.
Name of Mother: Lena Haley   a citizen of the   Creek   Nation.

                       Post-office: Boynton, I. T.

AFFIDAVIT OF MOTHER.

UNITED STATES OF AMERICA,
    INDIAN TERRITORY.
    Western   District.

I, Lena Haley, on oath state that I am 19 years of age and a citizen by blood, of the Creek Nation; that I am the lawful wife of William D. Haley, who is a citizen, by marriage of the Creek Nation; that a male child was born to me on 25th day of December, 1903, that said child has been named George Elmer Haley, and is now living.

                                          Lena Haley
WITNESSES TO MARK:
{

Subscribed and sworn to before me this 30 day of Aug, 1904.

                                      David A Lee
                                           NOTARY PUBLIC.

Applications for Enrollment of Creek Newborn
Act of 1905   Volume XI

AFFIDAVIT OF ATTENDING PHYSICIAN OR MID-WIFE.

UNITED STATES OF AMERICA,
   INDIAN TERRITORY.
   Western   District.

I, Samantha Steen , a midwife , on oath state that I attended on Mrs. Lena Haley, wife of William D. Haley on the 25th day of December , 1903 ; that there was born to her on said date a male child; that said child is now living and is said to have been named George Elmer Haley

                                       Samantha Steen

WITNESSES TO MARK:

Subscribed and sworn to before me this 30 day of   Aug, 1904.

                                       David A Lee
                                       NOTARY PUBLIC.

My Com Exp July -7 1906

BIRTH AFFIDAVIT.

DEPARTMENT OF THE INTERIOR.
COMMISSION TO THE FIVE CIVILIZED TRIBES.

IN RE APPLICATION FOR ENROLLMENT, as a citizen of the Creek Nation, of George Elmer Haley, born on the 25th day of December, 1903

                                     non

Name of Father: W. D. Haley   a citizen of the Creek   Nation.
Name of Mother: Lena Haley, nee Sevier   a citizen of the Creek   Nation.

                             Postoffice   Boynton, Ind. Ter.

AFFIDAVIT OF MOTHER.

UNITED STATES OF AMERICA, Indian Territory,
    Western   DISTRICT.

I, Lena Haley, nee Sevier , on oath state that I am   20 years of age and a citizen by Birth , of the Creek   Nation; that I am the lawful wife of W. D. Haley , ~~who is a citizen, by~~ *(blank)* of the *(blank)* Nation; that a male child was born to me on 25th day of December , 1903 , that said child has been named   George Elmer Haley , and was living March 4, 1905.

                                   Lena Haley

Applications for Enrollment of Creek Newborn
Act of 1905   Volume XI

Witnesses To Mark:
{ R.T. Potter
{ T.A. *(Illegible)*

Subscribed and sworn to before me this 26th day of April, 1905.

Harwood Keaton
Notary Public.

AFFIDAVIT OF ATTENDING PHYSICIAN OR MID-WIFE.

UNITED STATES OF AMERICA, Indian Territory,
   Western   DISTRICT.

I, Samantha Steen, a midwife, on oath state that I attended on Mrs. Lena Haley, nee Sevier, wife of W. D. Haley on the 25th day of December, 1903 ; that there was born to her on said date a male child; that said child was living March 4, 1905, and is said to have been named George Elmer Haley

Samantha Steen

Witnesses To Mark:
{ R.T. Potter
{ T.A. *(Illegible)*

Subscribed and sworn to before me this 26th day of April, 1905.

Harwood Keaton
Notary Public.

NC-874.

Muskogee, Indian Territory, October 23, 1905.

Nellie Berryhill,
    c/o Thomas J. Berryhill,
        Mounds, Indian Territory.

Dear Madam:

In the matter of the application for the enrollment of your minor children, Flora Edna Berryhill, born January 15, 1904, and May Bell Berryhill, born February 24, 1905, as citizens by blood of the Creek Nation, you are advised that it will be necessary for you

Applications for Enrollment of Creek Newborn
Act of 1905 Volume XI

to furnish this office with evidence of your marriage to Thomas J. Berryhill, the father of said children.

Such evidence may consist of either the original or a certified copy of your marriage license and certificate.

Respectfully,

Commissioner.

BIRTH AFFIDAVIT.

DEPARTMENT OF THE INTERIOR.
COMMISSION TO THE FIVE CIVILIZED TRIBES.

IN RE APPLICATION FOR ENROLLMENT, as a citizen of the Creek Nation, of Flora Edna Berryhill, born on the 15 day of Jan, 1904

Name of Father: Thos. J. Berryhill   a citizen of the   Creek   Nation.
(Broken Arrow)
Name of Mother: Nellie   "   a citizen of the   U.S.   ~~Nation~~.

Postoffice   Mounds I. Ter.

AFFIDAVIT OF MOTHER.   (Child Present)

UNITED STATES OF AMERICA, Indian Territory, ⎫
     Western   DISTRICT.   ⎬
                                           ⎭

     I, Nellie Berryhill, on oath state that I am 22 years of age and not a citizen ~~by~~ *(blank)*, of the Creek Nation; that I am the lawful wife of Thos. J. Berryhill, who is a citizen, by blood of the Creek Nation; that a female child was born to me on 15 day of Jan, 1904, that said child has been named Flora Edna Berryhill, and was living March 4, 1905.

                                            Nellie Berryhill

Witnesses To Mark:
{

     Subscribed and sworn to before me this 25" day of April, 1905.

(Seal)   J McDermott
                                        Notary Public.

Applications for Enrollment of Creek Newborn
Act of 1905   Volume XI

AFFIDAVIT OF ATTENDING PHYSICIAN OR MID-WIFE.

UNITED STATES OF AMERICA, Indian Territory, }
    Western   DISTRICT.

    I, Lizzie B. Berryhill , a midwife , on oath state that I attended on Mrs. Nellie Berryhill , wife of Thos J. Berryhill on or about the   15 day of Jan , 1904 ; that there was born to her on said date a female child; that said child was living March 4, 1905, and is said to have been named   Flora Edna Berryhill

                                her
                          Lizzie B x Berryhill
Witnesses To Mark: mark
  { Mrs Theodoria Berryhill
    Jesse McDermott

    Subscribed and sworn to before me this 26" day of April , 1905.

(Seal)   J McDermott
                                    Notary Public.

BIRTH AFFIDAVIT.

DEPARTMENT OF THE INTERIOR.
COMMISSION TO THE FIVE CIVILIZED TRIBES.

    IN RE APPLICATION FOR ENROLLMENT, as a citizen of the Creek Nation, of May Belle Berryhill , born on the   24 day of Feb , 1905

Name of Father: Thos. J. Berryhill   a citizen of the   Creek   Nation.
(Broken Arrow)
Name of Mother: Nellie   "   a citizen of the   U.S.   ~~Nation~~.

                      Postoffice   Mounds I. Ter.

AFFIDAVIT OF MOTHER.   (Child Present)

UNITED STATES OF AMERICA, Indian Territory, }
    Western   DISTRICT.

    I, Nellie Berryhill , on oath state that I am 22 years of age and not a citizen ~~by~~ (blank) , of the Creek Nation; that I am the lawful wife of Thos. J. Berryhill , who is a citizen, by blood of the Creek Nation; that a female child was born to me on 24" day of Feb , 1905 , that said child has been named May Belle Berryhill , and was living March 4, 1905.

                                Nellie Berryhill

Applications for Enrollment of Creek Newborn
Act of 1905   Volume XI

Witnesses To Mark:

{

Subscribed and sworn to before me this 25" day of April, 1905.

J McDermott
Notary Public.

AFFIDAVIT OF ATTENDING ~~PHYSICIAN~~ OR MID-WIFE.

UNITED STATES OF AMERICA, Indian Territory, }
Western   DISTRICT.

I, Lizzie B. Berryhill , a Mid wife , on oath state that I attended on Mrs. Nellie Berryhill , wife of Thos J. Berryhill on or about the 24 day of Feb , 1905 ; that there was born to her on said date a female child; that said child was living March 4, 1905, and is said to have been named May Belle Berryhill

             her
          Lizzie B x Berryhill
Witnesses To Mark: mark
{ Mrs Theodoria Berryhill
  Jesse McDermott

Subscribed and sworn to before me this 26" day of April, 1905.

J McDermott
Notary Public.

BIRTH AFFIDAVIT.
DEPARTMENT OF THE INTERIOR.
COMMISSION TO THE FIVE CIVILIZED TRIBES.

IN RE APPLICATION FOR ENROLLMENT, as a citizen of the (Muskogee) Creek Nation, of Clarance Ebert Kiefer , born on the 11th day of Feb , 1904

Name of Father: Smith Kiefer   not a citizen of the Creek Nation.
Name of Mother: Martha Lee Keifer[sic]   a citizen of the Creek Nation.
(Broken Arrow)
         Postoffice Mounds, Ind. Ter.

Applications for Enrollment of Creek Newborn
Act of 1905   Volume XI

AFFIDAVIT OF MOTHER.

UNITED STATES OF AMERICA, Indian Territory,
Western Judicial DISTRICT.

Child brought in
4/26/05

I, Martha Lee Keifer , on oath state that I am 38 years of age and a citizen by birth , of the (Muskogee) Creek   Nation; that I am the lawful wife of Smith Keifer , ~~who is a citizen, by~~ not a Citizen of the (Muskogee) Creek   Nation; that a male   child was born to me on 11th day of Feb , 1904 , that said child has been named Clarance Ebert Keifer , and was living March 4, 1905.

Martha Lee Kiefer

Witnesses To Mark:
{ (Seal)

Subscribed and sworn to before me this 26 day of April , 1905.

Edw C Griesel
Notary Public.

AFFIDAVIT OF ATTENDING PHYSICIAN OR MID-WIFE.

UNITED STATES OF AMERICA, Indian Territory,
Western Judicial DISTRICT.

I, Mary Murphy , a   mid wife , on oath state that I attended on Mrs. Martha Lee Keifer , wife of Smith Keifer on the 11th day of Feb , 1904 ; that there was born to her on said date a   male   child; that said child was living March 4, 1905, and is said to have been named Clarance Ebert Keifer

Mary Murphy

Witnesses To Mark:
{ Subscribed and sworn to before me 25th day of April, 1905.

My Commission Expires Aug 15th 190?.   B.H. Mills
Notary Public.

Applications for Enrollment of Creek Newborn
Act of 1905   Volume XI

NC-876
DEPARTMENT OF THE INTERIOR,
COMMISSIONER TO THE FIVE CIVILIZED TRIBES.

Muskogee, Indian Territory, November 1, 1905

In the matter of the application for the enrollment of Daniel and Bird Burgess as citizens by blood of the Creek Nation.

Susanna Burgess, being duly sworn, testified as follows (through Jesse McDermott, Official Interpreter):

EXAMINATION BY THE COMMISSIONER:
Q What is your name? A Susanna Burgess.
Q How old are you? A 27.
Q What is your postoffice address? A Schulter.
Q You made application for the enrollment of three newborn children, did you not, this Spring? A Yes sir.
Q What are their names? A One Bird, and one Daniel and Annie.
Q Are all of these children living? A One is dead.
Q Which one is dead? A Annie.
Q When did Annie die? A One year ago or two years ago. I don't know exactly just how long it has been since she died.
Q Did it die last year, two years ago or three years ago? A I think it is nearly three years.
Q When was Daniel born? A He was born on the 8th day of May.
Q What year? A He is over two years old now.
Q When was Bird born? A Born on the first day of January.
Q What year? A She is not a year old yet; will be next January.
Q Who is the father of these children? A This man here.
Q What is his name? A James.
Q You are a citizen of the Creek Nation, are you? A Yes sir.
Q Have you a record of the birth of these children? A Yes sir. The record is in the book that you have.

Witness here presents a record--memorandum book, in the middle of which is found a page upon which the following entries appear:
Daniel Burgess was born on 8th day of
   May, in the year of 1903
Birdie Burgess
   was born on the first day of January in the year 1905, on
Sunday.

Q We have an affidavit here on file, in which the mother and the midwife swore that this child was born the first day of January, 1904. This was made before Alex Posey while out in the field; is it correct? A At the time that I had the affidavit executed I told him

Applications for Enrollment of Creek Newborn
Act of 1905   Volume XI

just what I have stated here in my testimony; the mistake was made by the man who made out the affidavit, not mine.

Ulcy Randall, being duly sworn, testified as follows:

EXAMINATION BY THE COMMISSIONER:
Q What is your name? A Ulcy Randall.
Q How old are you? A I don't know; I am over 40.
Q What is you postoffice address? A Schulter.
Q Are you a citizen of the Creek Nation? A Yes sir.
Q Do you know Susan and James Burgess, the mother and father of Bird Burgess? A Yes sir.
Q Did you attend the mother at the birth of that child--Bird? A Yes sir.
Q When was Bird born? A She was born on the first day of January.
Q Of what year? A I don't know what year.
Q How old is that child now? A The child is not a year old yet.
Q You appeared before Alex Posey while he was out in the field and made affidavit that this child was born on the first day of January, 1904--is that correct? A No sir, that is a mistake. We told him that the child was born the first day of January, as we have stated in our testimony here.

INDIAN TERRITORY, Western District.

I, J. Y. Miller, a stenographer to the Commissioner to the Five Civilized Tribes, do hereby certify that the above and foregoing is a true and complete translation of my notes as same appear in my stenographic report of this case.

JY Miller

Sworn to and subscribed before me
this the 6th day of November,
1905.

(No Signature Given)
Notary Public.

BIRTH AFFIDAVIT.

DEPARTMENT OF THE INTERIOR.
COMMISSION TO THE FIVE CIVILIZED TRIBES.

IN RE APPLICATION FOR ENROLLMENT, as a citizen of the Creek Nation, of Annie Burgess, born on the 6 day of Feb , 1902 and died March 3, 1903

Name of Father: James Burgess   a citizen of the   Creek   Nation.
Big Springs Town
Name of Mother: Susanna Burgess   a citizen of the   Creek   Nation.
Cussehta Town

Postoffice   Schulter, Ind. Ter.

Applications for Enrollment of Creek Newborn
Act of 1905 Volume XI

AFFIDAVIT OF MOTHER.

UNITED STATES OF AMERICA, Indian Territory,
Western DISTRICT.

    I, Susanna Burgess , on oath state that I am 27 years of age and a citizen by blood , of the Creek Nation; that I am the lawful wife of James Burgess , who is a citizen, by blood of the Creek Nation; that a female child was born to me on 6 day of February , 1902 , that said child has been named Annie Burgess , and ~~was living March 4, 1905~~. died March 3, 1903

                                                             her
                                        Susanna x Burgess
Witnesses To Mark: mark
  { DC Skaggs
    Alex Posey

    Subscribed and sworn to before me this 10 day of April , 1905.

                                          Drennan C Skaggs
                                          Notary Public.

AFFIDAVIT OF ATTENDING PHYSICIAN OR MID-WIFE.

UNITED STATES OF AMERICA, Indian Territory,
Western DISTRICT.

                                                                my wife
    I, James Burgess , ~~a~~ , on oath state that I attended on^ Mrs. Susanna Burgess , ~~wife of~~ on the 6 day of Feb , 1902 ; that there was born to her on said date a female child; that said child ~~was living March 4, 1905~~ died March 3, 1903, and ~~is said to have been~~ was named Annie Burgess

                                          James Burgess
Witnesses To Mark:
  {
    Subscribed and sworn to before me this 10 day of April , 1905.

                                          Drennan C Skaggs
                                          Notary Public.

Applications for Enrollment of Creek Newborn
Act of 1905   Volume XI

NC 876   JLD
DEPARTMENT OF THE INTERIOR,
COMMISSIONER TO THE FIVE CIVILIZED TRIBES.

In the matter of the application for the enrollment of Annie Burgess, deceased, as a citizen by blood of the Creek Nation.

....

STATEMENT AND ORDER.

The record in this case shows that on April 13, 1905, application was made, in affidavit form, supplemented by sworn testimony taken November 1, 1905, for the enrollment of Annie Burgess, deceased, as a citizen by blood of the Creek Nation, under the provisions of the Act of Congress approved March 3, 1905.

It appears from the affidavit filed in this matter that said Anne Burgess, deceased, was born February 6, 1902, and died March 3, 1903.

The Act of Congress approved March 3, 1905, (33 Stats., 1048), provides:

"That the Commission to the Five Civilized Tribes is authorized for sixty days after the date of the approval of this act to receive and consider applications for enrollment, of children, <u>born subsequent to May twenty-fifth, nineteen hundred and one, and prior to March fourth, nineteen hundred and five, and living on said latter date,</u> to citizens of the Creek tribe of Indians whose enrollment has been approved by the Secretary of the Interior prior to the approval of this act; and to enroll and make allotments to such children."

It is, therefore, ordered that the application for the enrollment of said Annie Burgess, deceased, as a citizen by blood of the Creek Nation be, and the same is, hereby dismissed.

Tams Bixby   Commissioner.

Muskogee, Indian Territory.
JAN 15 1907

COPY.

BIRTH AFFIDAVIT.

DEPARTMENT OF THE INTERIOR.
COMMISSION TO THE FIVE CIVILIZED TRIBES.

IN RE APPLICATION FOR ENROLLMENT, as a citizen of the Creek Nation, of Bird Burgess, born on the 1 day of Jan, 1905.

Name of Father: James Burgess	a citizen of the Creek	Nation.
Name of Mother: Susanna Burgess	a citizen of the Creek	Nation.

Postoffice   Schulter, I.T.

Applications for Enrollment of Creek Newborn
Act of 1905   Volume XI

AFFIDAVIT OF MOTHER.

UNITED STATES OF AMERICA, Indian Territory, ⎫   Child Present
   Western   DISTRICT.   ⎭

    I, Susanna Burgess , on oath state that I am 27 years of age and a citizen by blood , of the Creek Nation; that I am the lawful wife of James Burgess , who is a citizen, by blood of the Creek Nation; that a male child was born to me on 1st day of January , 1905 , that said child has been named Bird Burgess , and was living March 4, 1905.

                                                 her
                                    Susanna x Burgess
Witnesses To Mark: mark
  ⎰ Edw C Griesel
  ⎱ Jesse McDermott

    Subscribed and sworn to before me this 1st day of Nov. , 1905.

                                      J McDermott
                                      Notary Public.

AFFIDAVIT OF ATTENDING ~~PHYSICIAN~~ OR MID-WIFE.

UNITED STATES OF AMERICA, Indian Territory, ⎫
   Western   DISTRICT.   ⎭

    I, Ulcey Randall , a midwife , on oath state that I attended on Mrs. Susanna Burgess , wife of James Burgess on the 1st day of January , 1905 ; that there was born to her on said date a *(blank)* child; that said child was living March 4, 1905, and is said to have been named Bird Burgess   her
                                    Ulcey x Randall
                                        mark

Witnesses To Mark:
  ⎰ Edw C Griesel
  ⎱ Jesse McDermott

    Subscribed and sworn to before me 1st day of January, 1905.

                                      J McDermott
                                      Notary Public.

Applications for Enrollment of Creek Newborn
Act of 1905   Volume XI

BIRTH AFFIDAVIT.

DEPARTMENT OF THE INTERIOR.
COMMISSION TO THE FIVE CIVILIZED TRIBES.

IN RE APPLICATION FOR ENROLLMENT, as a citizen of the Creek Nation, of Bird Burgess, born on the 1 day of Jan , 1904

Name of Father: James Burgess   a citizen of the   Creek   Nation.
Big Springs Town
Name of Mother: Susanna Burgess   a citizen of the   Creek   Nation.
Cussehta Town

                  Postoffice   Schulter, Ind. Ter.

AFFIDAVIT OF MOTHER.

UNITED STATES OF AMERICA, Indian Territory, }   Child is present
   Western   DISTRICT.

    I, Susanna Burgess , on oath state that I am 27 years of age and a citizen by blood , of the Creek Nation; that I am the lawful wife of James Burgess , who is a citizen, by blood of the Creek Nation; that a male child was born to me on 1 day of January , 1904 , that said child has been named Bird Burgess , and was living March 4, 1905.
                                            her
                             Susanna x Burgess
Witnesses To Mark: mark
  { Alex Posey
    DC Skaggs

    Subscribed and sworn to before me this 10 day of April , 1905.

                                  Drennan C Skaggs
                                  Notary Public.

AFFIDAVIT OF ATTENDING ~~PHYSICIAN~~ OR MID-WIFE.

UNITED STATES OF AMERICA, Indian Territory, }
   Western   DISTRICT.

    I, Ulcy Randall , a midwife , on oath state that I attended on Mrs. Susanna Burgess , wife of James Burgess on the 1 day of January , 1904 ; that there was born to her on said date a male child; that said child was living March 4, 1905, and is said to have been named Bird Burgess   her
                               Ulcy x Randall
                                  mark

Applications for Enrollment of Creek Newborn
Act of 1905   Volume XI

Witnesses To Mark:
{ Alex Posey
  DC Skaggs

Subscribed and sworn to before me this 10 day of April, 1905.

Drennan C Skaggs
Notary Public.

BIRTH AFFIDAVIT.

DEPARTMENT OF THE INTERIOR.
COMMISSION TO THE FIVE CIVILIZED TRIBES.

IN RE APPLICATION FOR ENROLLMENT, as a citizen of the Creek Nation, of Daniel Burgess, born on the 8 day of May, 1903

Name of Father: James Burgess   a citizen of the   Creek   Nation.
Big Springs Town
Name of Mother: Susanna Burgess   a citizen of the   Creek   Nation.
Cussehta Town
                              Postoffice   Schulter, Ind. Ter.

AFFIDAVIT OF MOTHER.

UNITED STATES OF AMERICA, Indian Territory, } Child is present
      Western   DISTRICT.

I, Susanna Burgess, on oath state that I am 27 years of age and a citizen by blood, of the Creek Nation; that I am the lawful wife of James Burgess, who is a citizen, by blood of the Creek Nation; that a male child was born to me on 8 day of May, 1903, that said child has been named Daniel Burgess, and was living March 4, 1905.

                              her
                    Susanna x Burgess
                              mark

Witnesses To Mark:
{ Alex Posey
  DC Skaggs

Subscribed and sworn to before me this 10 day of April, 1905.

Drennan C Skaggs
Notary Public.

Applications for Enrollment of Creek Newborn
Act of 1905   Volume XI

AFFIDAVIT OF ATTENDING PHYSICIAN OR MID-WIFE.

UNITED STATES OF AMERICA, Indian Territory,
Western DISTRICT.

I, Ulcy Randall , a midwife , on oath state that I attended on Mrs. Susanna Burgess , wife of James Burgess on the 8 day of May , 1903 ; that there was born to her on said date a male child; that said child was living March 4, 1905, and is said to have been named Daniel Burgess

her
Ulcy x Randall
mark

Witnesses To Mark:
{ Alex Posey
  DC Skaggs

Subscribed and sworn to before me this 10 day of April , 1905.

Drennan C Skaggs
Notary Public.

NC-876.

Muskogee, Indian Territory, October 23, 1905.

Susanna Burgess,
  c/o James Burgess,
    Schulter, Indian Territory.

Dear Madam:

In the matter of the application for the enrollment of your minor children, Daniel Burgess and Bird Burgess, as citizens by blood of the Creek Nation you are hereby notified to appear before this office within fifteen days from date with the midwife, who attended at the birth of said children, and at least one other witness who knows the date of their birth for the purpose of being examined under oath.

You are also requested to bring with you any record or note of the birth of said children which you may have.

Respectfully,

Commissioner.

Applications for Enrollment of Creek Newborn
Act of 1905   Volume XI

Nc 876.

Muskogee, Indian Territory, January 17, 1907.

Susanna Burgess,
    c/o James Burgess,
        Schulter, Indian Territory.

Dear Madam:

    There is herewith enclosed one copy of the Statement and Order of the Commissioner to the Five Civilized Tribes, dated January 15, 1907, dismissing the application made by you for the enrollment of your minor child, Annie Burgess, as a citizen by blood of the Creek Nation.

                Respectfully,
                              Commissioner.

LM-78.

BIRTH AFFIDAVIT.

DEPARTMENT OF THE INTERIOR.
COMMISSION TO THE FIVE CIVILIZED TRIBES.

IN RE APPLICATION FOR ENROLLMENT, as a citizen of the Creek Nation, of Ladossa Fredor Boone, born on the 13 day of May, 1904

Name of Father: Imy R Boone	a citizen of the Creek	Nation.
Hitchitee	non citizen	
Name of Mother: Belle Boone (nee Hogan)	a citizen of the ~~Cre~~	Nation.

                Postoffice   Eufaula, I. T.

Applications for Enrollment of Creek Newborn
Act of 1905 Volume XI

AFFIDAVIT OF MOTHER.

UNITED STATES OF AMERICA, Indian Territory, }
Western DISTRICT.

I, Imy R Boone , on oath state that I am 25 years of age and a citizen by blood , of the Creek Nation; that I am the lawful ~~wife~~ husband of Belle Boone , who is a citizen, ~~by blood of the Cr~~ United States Nation; that a female child was born to ~~me~~ her on 13 day of May , 1904 , that said child has been named Ladossa Fredor Boone , and was living March 4, 1905.

Imy R. Boone

Witnesses To Mark:
{

Subscribed and sworn to before me this 16 day of Sept , 1905.

Drennan C Skaggs
Notary Public.

BIRTH AFFIDAVIT.

DEPARTMENT OF THE INTERIOR.
COMMISSION TO THE FIVE CIVILIZED TRIBES.

IN RE APPLICATION FOR ENROLLMENT, as a citizen of the Creek Nation, of Ladossa Fredre Boone, born on the 13th day of May , 1904

Name of Father: Imy R Boone   a citizen of the Creek Nation.
Name of Mother: Mrs Imy R. Boone   a citizen of the United States Nation.

Postoffice   Eufaula, Ind. Ter.

AFFIDAVIT OF MOTHER.

UNITED STATES OF AMERICA, Indian Territory, }
Western DISTRICT.

I, Mrs Imy R. Boone , on oath state that I am 22 years of age and a citizen by *(blank)* , of the United States ~~Nation~~; that I am the lawful wife of Imy R. Boone , who is a citizen, by blood of the Cr eek Nation; that a Female child was born to me on 13th day of May , 1904 , that said child has been named Ladossa Fredre Boone , and was living March 4, 1905.

Mrs Imy R Boone

Witnesses To Mark:
{

Applications for Enrollment of Creek Newborn
Act of 1905 Volume XI

Subscribed and sworn to before me this 27th day of April, 1905.

JB Morrow
Notary Public.

My Commission Expires July 1, 1906.

AFFIDAVIT OF ATTENDING PHYSICIAN OR MID-WIFE.

UNITED STATES OF AMERICA, Indian Territory,
Western DISTRICT.

I, Jennie Patton as mid wife   we
I, J.A. Settle, a Doctor, on oath state that I attended on Mrs. Imy R Boone, wife of Imy R Boone on the 13th day of May, 1904; that there was born to her on said date a Female child; that said child was living March 4, 1905, and is said to have been named Ladossa Fredre Boone

Dr. J.A. Settle
Jennie Patton

Witnesses To Mark:
 D. H. Patton
 F.P. Patton

Subscribed and sworn to before me 24 day of April, 1905.

Ray E. Sutton
Notary Public.

MY COMMISSION EXPIRES MARCH 7, 1907.

BIRTH AFFIDAVIT.
DEPARTMENT OF THE INTERIOR.
COMMISSION TO THE FIVE CIVILIZED TRIBES.

IN RE APPLICATION FOR ENROLLMENT, as a citizen of the Creek Nation, of Lucile Taylor, born on the 24th day of February, 1905

Name of Father: William Taylor   a non citizen   (colored)   ~~Nation.~~
Name of Mother: Rose Taylor   a citizen of the   Creek   Nation.

Postoffice   Coweta Ind. Ter.

Applications for Enrollment of Creek Newborn
Act of 1905   Volume XI

AFFIDAVIT OF MOTHER.

UNITED STATES OF AMERICA, Indian Territory, ⎱
   Western   DISTRICT. ⎰

    I, Rose Taylor , on oath state that I am thirty four years of age and a citizen by birth , of the Creek   Nation; that I am the lawful wife of William Taylor , ~~who is a citizen, by~~ *(blank)* ~~of the~~ a non-citizen ~~Nation~~; that a female child was born to me on 24th day of February , 1905 , that said child has been named Lucile Taylor , and was living March 4, 1905.

                                        Rosa[sic] Taylor

Witnesses To Mark:
⎰
⎱

    Subscribed and sworn to before me this 27 day of April , 1905.

My Commission   R. W. Lumpkin
expires Jany 13th 1909   Notary Public.

AFFIDAVIT OF ATTENDING PHYSICIAN OR MID-WIFE.

UNITED STATES OF AMERICA, Indian Territory, ⎱
   Western   DISTRICT. ⎰

    I, Amanda Woodward , a midwife , on oath state that I attended on Mrs. Rose Taylor , wife of William Taylor on the 24th day of February , 1905 ; that there was born to her on said date a female child; that said child was living March 4, 1905, and is said to have been named Lucile Taylor   her

                                  Amanda x Woodward
Witnesses To Mark: mark
  ⎰ C.C. Hullquist
  ⎱ Jackson McIntosh

    Subscribed and sworn to before me this 27 day of April , 1905.

My Commission   R. W. Lumpkin
expires Jany 13th 1909   Notary Public.

Applications for Enrollment of Creek Newborn
Act of 1905   Volume XI

N.C. 879.

DEPARTMENT OF THE INTERIOR,
COMMISSIONER TO THE FIVE CIVILIZED TRIBES.
Muskogee, Indian Territory, March 7, 1906.

In the matter of the application for the enrollment of Tullie McNac as a citizen by blood of the Creek Nation.

WICEY McNAC, being duly sworn, testified as follows through Jesse McDermott official interpreter.

Q What is your name? A My name at present is Wicey McNac but I am enrolled as Wicey Johnson.
Q There was filed in the office of the Commissioner April 29, 1905, an affidavit in the matter of the birth of one Tullie McNac are you the mother of that child? A Yes, sir.
Q What is your post office address? A Senora.
Q How old are you? A I don't know how old I am but I am past twenty.
Q Is that child living? A Yes, sir.
Q What is the name of your mother? A Mollie Hope.
Q What is the name of your father? A Henry Hope.

Witness if identified on Creek card field No. 138 opposite roll No. 511

Q Were you at one time married to a man named Fred Johnson? A Yes, sir.
Q Is he living or dead? A He is living.
Q Have you separated from him? A We are separated now.
Q Have you since married another man? A Yes, sir.
Q What is the name of your present husband? A Philip McNac.
Q Is he the father of your child Tullie McNac? A Yes, sir.

I, Anna Garrigues, on oath state that the above and foregoing is a true and correct transcript of my stenographic notes as taken in said cause on said date.

Anna Garrigues

Subscribed and sworn to before me
this 16 day of March 1906.

J McDermott
Notary Public.

Applications for Enrollment of Creek Newborn
Act of 1905 Volume XI

BIRTH AFFIDAVIT.

DEPARTMENT OF THE INTERIOR.
COMMISSION TO THE FIVE CIVILIZED TRIBES.

IN RE APPLICATION FOR ENROLLMENT, as a citizen of the Creek Nation, of Tullie McNac, born on the 14th day of March, 1904

Name of Father: Phillip McNac   a citizen of the   Creek   Nation.
Name of Mother: Wicy McNac   a citizen of the   Creek   Nation.

Postoffice   Senora, Ind. Ter.

AFFIDAVIT OF MOTHER.

UNITED STATES OF AMERICA, Indian Territory, }   Child is present
   Western Judicial   DISTRICT.

I, Wicy McNac, on oath state that I am 29 years of age and a citizen by blood, of the Creek Nation; that I am the lawful wife of Phillip McNac, who is a citizen, by blood of the Creek Nation; that a male child was born to me on 14th day of March, 1904, that said child has been named Tullie McNac, and was living March 4, 1905.

                     her
                 x Wicy McNac
Witnesses To Mark: mark
   { John Pemberton   Henryetta I.T.
   { J H Osborne   Henryetta I.T.

Subscribed and sworn to before me this 28th day of April, 1905.

                M. G. Clarke
M.G.Clarke   Notary Public.

AFFIDAVIT OF ATTENDING PHYSICIAN OR MID-WIFE.

UNITED STATES OF AMERICA, Indian Territory, }
   Western Judicial   DISTRICT.

I, Kizzie Scott, a woman, on oath state that I attended on Mrs. Wicy McNac, wife of Phillip McNac on the 14th day of March, 1904; that there was born to her on said date a male child; that said child was living March 4, 1905, and is said to have been named Tullie McNac   her
                 x Kizzie McNac
Witnesses To Mark: mark
   { John Pemberton   Henryetta I.T.
   { J H Osborne   Henryetta I.T.

Applications for Enrollment of Creek Newborn
Act of 1905   Volume XI

Subscribed and sworn to before me this 28th day of April, 1905.

M.G.Clarke
M. G. Clarke
Notary Public.

N.C. 879

Muskogee, Indian Territory, October 19, 1905.

Wicey McNac,
    Care Phillip McNac,
        Senora, Indian Territory.

Dear Madam:

    In the matter of the application for the enrollment of your minor child, Tullie McNac, born March 14, 1904, as a citizen by blood of the Creek Nation, this office is unable to identify you upon the final roll of citizens by blood of the Creek Nation. It is necessary that you be so identified before the rights of said Tullie McNac can be finally determined.

    You are, therefore requested to advise this office as to your maiden name, the names of your parents, the Creek Indian Town to which you belong, and your roll number as the same appears on your deeds and allotment certificate.

Respectfully,

Commissioner.

NC-879

Muskogee, Indian Territory, December 15, 1905.

Wicey McNac,
    Care of Phillip McNac,
        Senora, Indian Territory.

Dear Madam:

    In the matter of the application for the enrollment of your minor child, Tullie McNac, born March 14, 1904, as a citizen by blood of the Creek Nation, you are advised that this Office is unable to identify you on its final rolls of citizens of the Creek Nation.

    You are requested to write this Office at an early date, giving your maiden name, the names of your parents and other members of your family, the Creek Indian Town to which you belong, and, if possible, your roll number as same appear[sic] on your allotment certificate or deeds to land in the Creek Nation.

Applications for Enrollment of Creek Newborn
Act of 1905   Volume XI

Respectfully,
Commissioner.

(The letter below typed as given.)

NC 879

Senora, I. T., Dec. 30th, 1905.

Mr. Bixby,
    Muskogee, I. T.

Dear Sir

    I have your letter of the 19th of Oct. My maiden name or the name I was enrooled By is Wicey Johnson But now McNack   Henry Hope is my Father I belong to Okfuskee Town

    I havent the Deed To My land with me And cant Send The no of it But Will Later if you Demand it.

Resp yours,

    In answer to #879 for enrooling Tullie McNack Born on 14" of March 1904.

Signed   Wicey McNack
or Johnson.

BIRTH AFFIDAVIT.

DEPARTMENT OF THE INTERIOR.
COMMISSION TO THE FIVE CIVILIZED TRIBES.

IN RE APPLICATION FOR ENROLLMENT, as a citizen of the C R E E K - - - - - - - - Nation, of Earl Berryhill - - - - - - - - - - - - , born on the 8th day of April - - - - - -, 1903

Name of Father: Theodore Berryhill - - - - - - -   a citizen of the C R E E K - - Nation.
(Broken Arrow)   non
Name of Mother: Rilla Berryhill - - - - - - - - - -   a^citizen of the C R E E K - - Nation.

Postoffice   Sapulpa, I.T.

Applications for Enrollment of Creek Newborn
Act of 1905 Volume XI

AFFIDAVIT OF MOTHER.

UNITED STATES OF AMERICA, Indian Territory, }
Western - - - - - - - - - DISTRICT.

Child Brought in
5/26/05 - Gr.

    I, Rilla Berryhill - - - - - - - - - - - - - - , on oath state that I am Twenty seven years of age and a non citizen ~~by~~, of the C R E E K- - - - - - - - - - - - - -   Nation; that I am the lawful wife of Theodore Berryhill - - - - - - - - - , who is a citizen, by Blood -- -- of the C R E E K - - - - - - - - - - - - Nation; that a male ---- child was born to me on 8th - - - - day of April - - - - - - - - , 1903 , that said child has been named Earl Berryhill - - - - - - - - - - - - - , and was living March 4, 1905.

                                          Rilla Berryhill

Witnesses To Mark:
{

    Subscribed and sworn to before me this 26 day of April , 1905.

    (Seal)   Edw C Griesel
                                                Notary Public.

AFFIDAVIT OF ATTENDING PHYSICIAN OR MID-WIFE.

UNITED STATES OF AMERICA, Indian Territory, }
Western - - - - - - - - - DISTRICT.

    I, M.D. Taylor - - - - - - - - - - - - - - - - - , a Physician - - - , on oath state that I attended on Mrs. Rilla Berryhill - - - -- - - -- , wife of Theodore Berryhill - - - - - - - on the eighth day of April - - - - - - , 1903 ; that there was born to her on said date a male child; that said child was living March 4, 1905, and is said to have been named Earl Berryhill

                                          M.D. Taylor, M.D.

Witnesses To Mark:
{

    Subscribed and sworn to before me 24th day of April - - - - - -, 1905.

                                          B Barton

My Commission expires Feb. 21, 1907.   Notary Public.

Applications for Enrollment of Creek Newborn
Act of 1905   Volume XI

BIRTH AFFIDAVIT.

DEPARTMENT OF THE INTERIOR.
COMMISSION TO THE FIVE CIVILIZED TRIBES.

IN RE APPLICATION FOR ENROLLMENT, as a citizen of the Creek Nation, of Ves Berryhill, born on the 23 day of July, 1901

Name of Father: Theodore Berryhill   a citizen of the   Creek   Nation.
(Broken Arrow)
Name of Mother: Rilla   "   a citizen of the   U.S.   Nation.

Postoffice   Sapulpa

AFFIDAVIT OF MOTHER.   Child Present

UNITED STATES OF AMERICA, Indian Territory,
   Western   DISTRICT.

I, Rilla Berryhill, on oath state that I am 27 years of age and a citizen by -----, of the Creek Nation; that I am the lawful wife of Theodore Berryhill, who is a citizen, by blood of the Creek Nation; that a male child was born to me on 23 day of July, 1901, that said child has been named Ves Berryhill, and was living March 4, 1905.

                                        Rilla Berryhill
Witnesses To Mark:
{

Subscribed and sworn to before me this 26 day of April, 1905.

(Seal)   Edw C Griesel
                                        Notary Public.

AFFIDAVIT OF ~~ATTENDING PHYSICIAN OR MID-WIFE~~.
                            Father

UNITED STATES OF AMERICA, Indian Territory,
   Western   DISTRICT.

I, Theodore Berryhill, ~~a (blank)~~, on oath state that I attended on Mrs. Rilla Berryhill my, wife ~~of (blank)~~ on the 23 day of July, 1901; that there was born to her on said date a male child; that said child was living March 4, 1905, and is said to have been named Ves Berryhill

                                        Theodore Berryhill
Witnesses To Mark:
{

Applications for Enrollment of Creek Newborn
Act of 1905   Volume XI

Subscribed and sworn to before me this 26 day of April, 1905.

(Seal)   Edw C Griesel
   Notary Public.

AFFIDAVIT OF ATTENDING PHYSICIAN OR MID-WIFE.

UNITED STATES OF AMERICA,
   INDIAN TERRITORY.
(blank)   District.

   we
We, Maggie Self and Anna Ford , a *(blank)* , on oath state that I attended on Mrs. Rilla Berryhill , wife of Theodore Berryhill on the 23^d day of July , 1901 ; that there was born to her on said date a Male child; that said child is now living and is said to have been named Ves Berryhill

   Maggie Self
WITNESSES TO MARK: Annie Ford
{

Subscribed and sworn to before me this 8" *day of* November , *1905*.

My Commission Expires July 8th. 1906.   John M. Weeks
   NOTARY PUBLIC.

AFFIDAVIT.

WESTERN DISTRICT.   I
   I
INDIAN TERRITORY.   I SS   Asst Midwife
   I
U.   S.   A.   I

Persoanally[sic] appeared before me a Notary Public in and for the above District, Mrs Susan Brown, to me well known and after being by me duly sworn according to law deposes says that she was present when Mrs Rilla Berryhill gave birth to a male child on the 23rd, day of July, 1901 that said child is said to have been named Ves Berryhill.

   Susan Brown

Subscribed and sworn to before me this 24th day of April, 1905.

   B Barton
My Commission expires Feb. 21, 1907.   Notary Public.

Applications for Enrollment of Creek Newborn
Act of 1905   Volume XI

CERTIFICAT E Record[sic]

United States of America,	)
	)
Indian Territory	)
	)
I[sic] Judicial Division.	) S S.
	)
	)

    I Joseph W. Phillips Clerk of the United States Court in the Indian Territory do hereby certify that the the[sic] instrument hereto attached was filed for record in my Office the 8 day of Dec, 1894 at __M; and duly recorded in Book D Marriage Record, Page 192

    Witness my hand and seal of said Court at Muskogee in said Territory this the 12 day of Dec, 1894

                                J. W. Phillips Clerk

By J. W. Dodson Deputy.

I John M. Weeks a Notary Public within and for the western District of the Indian Territory do hereby certify that the foregoing instrument is a true and exact Copy of the original.

Witness my hand and seal of Office in Sapulpa I. T. this the 8th day Nov. 1905.

                                              John M. Weeks
My commission expires July 8th 1906.   Notary Public.

(The below Marriage License and Certificate typed as given.)

MARRIAGE LICENS.

United States of America,	)	
	)	
Indian Territory	)	
	)	
First Judicial Division.	)	
	)	No 797.

                                  To any person Authorized by law to Solemn ze Marriages Greeting:

    YOU ARE HEREBY COMMANDED to solemnize the rite and publish the Bans of Matrimony between Mr Theo Berryhill of Chaska in the B. aged 20 years and

Applications for Enrollment of Creek Newborn
Act of 1905 Volume XI

Miss Rilla Wilson of Chaska in the B aged 17 years, according to law, and do you officially sign and return this License to the parties therein named.

Witness my hand and Official Seal this the 30th day of Nov. A. D. 1894

J. W. Phillips
By J. S. Dodson Deputy.   Clerk of the U. S. Court

CERTIFICATE OF MARRIAGE.

United States of America,)
)
Indian Territory   ) S S.
)
First Judicial Division.   )   I J. R. ROwell a minister of the Gospel
)
)

DO HEREBY CERTIFY, That on the 6th day of December 1894 I did duly and according to law as commanded in the foregoing Licens, solemnize the Rite and publish the Banns of Matrimony between the parties therein named.

Witness my hand this the 6 day of December 1894.

My credentials are recorded in the Office of the Clerk of the United States Court, Indian Territory, First Judicial Division, Book A, Page 189

Elder J. R. Rowell a minister of the Gospel.

N.C. 880

Muskogee, Indian Territory, October 19, 1905.

Rilla Berryhill,
    Care Theodore Berryhill,
        Sapulpa, Indian Territory.

Dear Madam:

In the matter of the application for the enrollment of your minor children, Ves Berryhill, born July 23, 1901, and Earl Berryhill, born April 8, 1903, as citizens by blood of the Creek Nation, this office desires proof of your marriage to Theodore Berryhill, the alleged father of said children. Said proof may consist of either the original or a certified copy of your marriage license and certificate.

Applications for Enrollment of Creek Newborn
Act of 1905   Volume XI

The affidavit of the midwife relative to the birth of said Ves Berryhill is insufficient inasmuch as she fails to state whether or not said Ves Berryhill was living on March 4, 1905.

Form of affidavit for the midwife, which has been properly filled out, is herewith enclosed and if the same correctly states the facts in the case, you are requested to have it executed and return to this office in the enclosed envelope.

This matter should receive your prompt attention.

                Respectfully,

                              Commissioner.

AC-1

NC-881

                          Muskogee, Indian Territory, October 6, 1905.

Harry Beaver,
    Okmulgee, Indian Territory.

Dear Sir:

There is on file in this Office an affidavit relative to the birth of your minor child, Wilson Beaver. It is stated in said affidavit that you and Louisa Beaver (deceased), the mother of said child, are citizens of the Creek Nation.

This Office is unable to identify you or said Louisa Beaver on its rolls of citizens of the Creek Nation. You are requested to write this Office at an early date giving said Louisa Beaver's maiden name, the names of your and her parents, the Creek Indian Town to which each of you belongs, and, if possible, your respective roll numbers as same appear on your deeds to land in the Creek Nation.

This matter should receive your prompt attention.

                Respectfully,

                              Commissioner.

Applications for Enrollment of Creek Newborn
Act of 1905   Volume XI

NC 881

Muskogee, Indian Territory, October 19, 1905.

Harry Beaver,
Okmulgee, Indian Territory.

Dear Sir:

In the matter of the application for the enrollment of application for the enrollment of your minor child, Wilson Beaver, born December 27, 1902, as a citizen by blood of the Creek Nation; it is stated in your affidavit filed in said case that Louisa Beaver, the mother of said child is dead.

It will be necessary for you to furnish this office in lieu of the affidavit of said Louisa Beaver, deceased, the affidavits of two disinterested witnesses relative to the birth of said Wilson Beaver. Said affidavits must set forth said child's name, the date of his birth, the names of his parents and whether or not he was living on March 4, 1905.

You are further advised that this office is unable to identify the said Louisa Beaver, deceased, on its final roll of citizens by blood of the Creek Nation.

You are requested to write this office at an early date giving the maiden name of said Louisa Beaver, deceased, the names of your and her parents, the Creek Indian town to which each of you belongs, and if possible your respective roll numbers as same appear on your deeds and allotment certificates.

This matter should receive your prompt attention.

Respectfully,

Commissioner.

(Copy)

NC-881

Okmulgee, I. T.
Oct. 21, '05.

Dawes Commission
   To The Five Civilized Tribes
   Muskogee, I. T.

Sir: Your letter #N.C. 881 relative to the birth affidavit of Wilson Beaver is duly received, and in reply will say that Louisa Beaver and Louisa Marsey are same person, which you will find on the Cessetah Roll as Louisa Marsey and Harry Beaver as Halleyamson on the Arbeka Talledega Roll.

Applications for Enrollment of Creek Newborn
Act of 1905   Volume XI

   I hope you will find no trouble to get the name straight.

I am

        Very Truly,
          (signed)   E. E. HARDRIDGE.

N.C. 881

        Muskogee, Indian Territory, October 30, 1905.

Harry Beaver,
  Care E.E. Hardridge,
    Okmulgee, Indian Territory.

Dear Sir:

   Receipt if acknowledged of your communication of October 21, 1905, in the matter of the application for the enrollment of your minor child, Wilson Beaver, born December 27, 1902, as a citizen by blood of the Creek Nation.

   The information contained in said letter is sufficient to enable this office to identify you and Louisa Beaver, the mother of said child, on the final roll of citizens by blood of the Creek Nation.

   Your attention is called to the letter of this office of October 19, 1905, and you are again advised that it will be necessary for you to furnish this office, in lieu of the affidavit of said Louisa Beaver, deceased, with the affidavits of two disinterested witnesses relative to the birth of said Wilson beaver[sic]. Said affidavits must set forth said child's name, the date of his birth, the names of his parents and whether or not he was living on March 4, 1905.

   This matter should receive your immediate attention.

        Respectfully,
           Commissioner.

Indian Territory)
) SS
Western District)

   We, the undersigned, on oath state that we are personally acquainted with Louisa Beaver (deceased)   wife of   Harry Beaver ; and that on or about the 27 day of December , 1902, a   male   child was born to them and has been named   Wilson Beaver ; and that said child was living March 4, 1905.

   We further state that we have no interest in the above case.

Applications for Enrollment of Creek Newborn
Act of 1905   Volume XI

                                          Moses Asbury
                                                    her
                                        Sallie x Asbury
Witnesses to mark: mark
Alex Posey
B. W. Christian

Subscribed and sworn to before me this 16 day of Mch 1906.

                                          Alex Posey
                                                  Notary Public.

BIRTH AFFIDAVIT.

DEPARTMENT OF THE INTERIOR.
COMMISSION TO THE FIVE CIVILIZED TRIBES.

IN RE APPLICATION FOR ENROLLMENT, as a citizen of the Creek Nation, of Wilson Beaver, born on the 27 day of December, 1902

Name of Father: Harry Beaver   a citizen of the   Creek   Nation.
Taladega Town
Name of Mother: Louisa Beaver   a citizen of the   Creek   Nation.
Cussehta Town
                            Postoffice   Okmulgee, I.T

                                  father
AFFIDAVIT OF ~~MOTHER~~.

UNITED STATES OF AMERICA, Indian Territory,   Child present.
    Western   DISTRICT.

     I, Harry Beaver, on oath state that I am 29 years of age and a citizen by blood, of the Creek Nation; that I ~~am~~ was the lawful ~~wife~~ husband of Louisa Beaver, deceased, who ~~is~~ was a citizen, by blood of the Creek Nation; that a male child was born to ~~me~~ her on 27 day of December, 1902, that said child has been named Wilson Beaver, and was living March 4, 1905. That the mother Louisa Beaver, died Jan 13, 1905.

                                          Harry Beaver
Witnesses To Mark:

Applications for Enrollment of Creek Newborn
Act of 1905   Volume XI

Subscribed and sworn to before me this 10 day of April, 1905.

                                   Drennan C Skaggs
                                   Notary Public.

AFFIDAVIT OF ATTENDING PHYSICIAN OR MID-WIFE.

UNITED STATES OF AMERICA, Indian Territory, }
    Western   DISTRICT.

    I, Nicey Scott , a mid-wife , on oath state that I attended on Mrs. Louisa Beaver, wife of Harry Beaver on the 27 day of December , 1902 ; that there was born to her on said date a male child; that said child was living March 4, 1905, and is said to have been named Wilson Beaver

                                     her
                              Nicey x Scott
Witnesses To Mark: mark
  { DC Skaggs
    Alex Posey

Subscribed and sworn to before me this 10 day of April, 1905.

                                   Drennan C Skaggs
                                   Notary Public.

N.C. 882.

                              Muskogee, Indian Territory, October 19, 1905.

Nellie Canard,
     Care James Canard,
         Okmulgee, Indian Territory.

Dear Madam:

    In the matter of the application for the enrollment of your minor child, Cilla Canard, born November 12, 1904, as a citizen by blood of the Creek Nation, it is necessary that you should furnish this office with the affidavit of the midwife who attended on you at the birth of said child.

Applications for Enrollment of Creek Newborn
Act of 1905   Volume XI

In the event that there was no midwife or physician in attendance when said child was born, it will be necessary for you to furnish this office with the affidavits of two disinterested witnesses relative to her birth. Said affidavits must set forth said child's name, the date of her birth, the names of her parents and whether or not she was living on March 4, 1905.

                        Respectfully,

                                    Commissioner.

NC-882

                      Muskogee, Indian Territory, December 16, 1905.

Nellie Canard,
    Care of James Canard,
        Okmulgee, Indian Territory.

Dear Madam:

In the matter of the application for the enrollment of your minor child, Cilla Canard, born November 12, 1904, as a citizen by blood of the Creek Nation, you are again advised that it will be necessary for you to furnish this Office with the affidavit of the physician or midwife who attended at the birth of said child. A blank for that purpose is herewith enclosed. In the event there was no physician or midwife in attendance when said child was born, it will be necessary for you to furnish this Office with the affidavits of two disinterested persons relative to said child's birth, and a blank for that purpose is herewith enclosed.

                        Respectfully,

                                    Commissioner.

1 B A
Dis

BIRTH AFFIDAVIT.

DEPARTMENT OF THE INTERIOR.
COMMISSION TO THE FIVE CIVILIZED TRIBES.

IN RE APPLICATION FOR ENROLLMENT, as a citizen of the Creek Nation, of Cilla Canard, born on the 12" day of Nov. , 1904

Name of Father: James Kanard[sic] Cusseta[sic]	a citizen of the	Creek	Nation.
Name of Mother: Mellie[sic] Kanard Cussehta	a citizen of the	Creek	Nation.

                        Postoffice   Okmulgee, I.T.

Applications for Enrollment of Creek Newborn
Act of 1905   Volume XI

AFFIDAVIT OF MOTHER.

UNITED STATES OF AMERICA, Indian Territory,
Western   DISTRICT.

I, James Kanard , on oath state that I am about 33 years of age and a citizen by blood , of the Creek Nation; that I ~~am~~ was the lawful ~~wife~~ husband of Nellie Kanard , who is a citizen, by blood of the Creek Nation; that a female child was born to ~~me~~ her on the 12" day of Nevember[sic]   , 1904 , that said child has been named Cilla Kanard , and was living March 4, 1905.

James Kanard

Witnesses To Mark:

Subscribed and sworn to before me this 8" day of March, 1906.

Drennan C Skaggs
Notary Public.

Indian Territory)
) SS
Western District)

We, the undersigned, on oath state that we are personally acquainted with Nellie Canard   wife of   James Kanard[sic]   ; and that on or about the 12" day of Nov. , 1904, a female   child was born to them and has been named Cilla Canard ; and that said child was living March 4, 1905.

We further state that we have no interest in the above case.

Moses Asbury

Joe Grayson

Witnesses to mark:

Subscribed and sworn to before me this 7 day of March 1906.

Drennan C Skaggs
Notary Public.

Applications for Enrollment of Creek Newborn
Act of 1905 Volume XI

BIRTH AFFIDAVIT.

DEPARTMENT OF THE INTERIOR.
COMMISSION TO THE FIVE CIVILIZED TRIBES.

IN RE APPLICATION FOR ENROLLMENT, as a citizen of the Creek Nation, of Cilla Canard, born on the 12 day of Nov., 1904

Name of Father: James Canard   a citizen of the   Creek   Nation.
Cusseta Town
Name of Mother: Nellie Canard (nee Davis)   a citizen of the   Creek   Nation.
Cussehta Town
                        Postoffice   Okmulgee, Ind. Ter.

AFFIDAVIT OF MOTHER.

UNITED STATES OF AMERICA, Indian Territory, }
       Western   DISTRICT.   }   Child is present

I, Nellie Canard , on oath state that I am 28 years of age and a citizen by blood , of the Creek Nation; that I am the lawful wife of James Canard , who is a citizen, by blood of the Creek Nation; that a female child was born to me on 12 day of November , 1904 , that said child has been named Cilla Canard , and was living March 4, 1905.

                                        Nellie Kanard
Witnesses To Mark:
 { Alex Posey
 { DC Skaggs

Subscribed and sworn to before me this 10 day of April , 1905.

                                        Drennan C Skaggs
                                           Notary Public.

AFFIDAVIT OF ATTENDING PHYSICIAN OR MID-WIFE.

UNITED STATES OF AMERICA, Indian Territory, }
       Western   DISTRICT.   }

                                                           my wife
I, James Canard , a ~~(blank)~~ , on oath state that I attended on ^ Mrs. Nellie Canard , ~~wife of~~ *(blank)* on the 12 day of Nov. , 1904 ; that there was born to her on said date a female child; that said child was living March 4, 1905, and is said to have been named Cilla Canard

                                        James Canard
Witnesses To Mark:
 {
 {

Applications for Enrollment of Creek Newborn
Act of 1905 Volume XI

Subscribed and sworn to before me this 10 day of April, 1905.

          Drennan C Skaggs
          Notary Public.

2221 B.

DEPARTMENT OF THE INTERIOR,
COMMISSION TO THE FIVE CIVILIZED TRIBES.
April 25, 1905, Sapulpa, Ind. Ter.

In the matter of the application for the enrollment of William McKinley Clayton, as a citizen by blood of the Creek Nation.

Mrs. J. O. Hereford, being duly sworn, by E.C. Griesel, a Notary Public, testified as follows:

By Commission:
Q What is your name? A Mrs. J.O. Hereford.
Q What is your age? A 47.
Q What is your post office address? A Sapulpa.
Q Do you know a child by the name of William McKinley Clayton? A Yes I did, he has been nick named Bud.
Q Do you know when that child was born? A I do not.
Q Have you any means of arriving at the date of the birth of that child? A Yes. I have a rental contract, dated January 1, 1903, and I know that that child was born prior to that.
Q Who is the mother of that child? A Della Clayton.
Q Who is the father? A Charlie Clayton.
--------------------oOo--------------------

JOHN F. EGAN, being duly sworn by E.C. Griesel, a Notary Public, testified as follows:

By Commission:
Q What is your name? A John F. Egan.
Q What is your age? A 44.
Q What is your post office? A Sapulpa.
Q Do you know a child by the name of William McKinley Clayton? A I know a baby Clayton who was nicknamed Bud.
Q Have you any means of arriving at the date of the birth of that child? A Yes.

Applications for Enrollment of Creek Newborn
Act of 1905   Volume XI

Q What is it? A I drew up a rental contract between the mother of the child and J.O. Hereford in the year, 1903, January 1st, and Mrs. Clayton had the child, for it there was at that time a baby in her arms.
Q So you saw the child on the first day of January, 1903? A Yes sir.
Q About how old was the child at that time? A About a month old.
Q Have you seen that child frequently since that time? A Yes sir.
Q Who is the mother of this child? A Della Harry, I call her mother Mollie, known as Jacobs later on.
Q You identify the child present then as the child of Della and Charlie Clayton? A Yes sir.
Q And that the child was born prior to January 1, 1903, and living on the 4th day of March, 1905? A Yes sir.
Q How long have you known the mother of this child? A 11 years.
Q Do you know the father? A Yes.
Q Are they reputable people? A Yes sir.
Q You have no interest in this matter, have you? A No sir.

E.C. Griesel, being duly sworn, on his oath, states that the above and foregoing is a true and correct transcript of his stenographic notes as taken in said cause on said date.

Edw C Griesel

Subscribed and sworn to before me this 5 day of May, 1905.

Zera E Parrish
Notary Public.

2273 B.

DEPARTMENT OF THE INTERIOR,
COMMISSION TO THE FIVE CIVILIZED TRIBES.
SAPULPA, I.T. APRIL 25, 1905.

In the matter of the application for the enrollment of Ernest Clayton, as a citizen by blood of the Creek Nation.

Annie Pettigrew, being duly sworn, by E.C. Griesel, a Notary Public, testified as follows:

By Commission:
Q What is your name? A Annie Pettigrew.
Q What is your age? A 25.
Q What is your post office? A Sapulpa.
Q Are you a citizen of the Creek Nation? A No sir.
Q Q[sic] Do you know a child by the name of Ernest Clayton? A I knew such a child.
Q Who were the parents of that child? A Charlie and Della Clayton.

Applications for Enrollment of Creek Newborn
Act of 1905   Volume XI

Q When was that child born? A Born on the 2nd day of March, 1905.
Q On what day of the week was that child born? A On Thursday morning between 10 and 11 o'clock.
Q Were you present at the birth of that child? A I was not present just then but was about 2 or 300 yards away.
Q How soon after the birth of the child did you see the mother? A I sent down within 24 hours.
Q How long did you stay there? A I stayed there night and day until the mother died. The mother died on Friday morning and was buried on Saturday afternoon.
Q Where you present at her death? A I was right there and was looking right in her face when her breath left her.
Q Was the child living at this time? A Yes.
Q Is the child living now? A No sir.
Q When did the child die? A 21st of March, 1905. At 2 in the morning. I was the only one there.
Q You are willing to swear that this child was born on the 2nd day of March and died on the 31st day of March, all in the year 1905? A Yes sir.
Q Are you related to her in anyway? A No, sir no relation. I lived in one of their places.
Q Was there a doctor in attendance on the child and mother? A The Dr. was there to see the mother. He saw the child.
Q What was the Dr's name? A Dr. Plumstead.

------------------oOo--------------

Dr. M.E. Plumstead, being duly sworn, by E.C. Griesel, a Notary Public, testified as follows:

By Commission:
Q What is your name? A Dr. M.E. Plumstead.
Q How old are you? A 32.
Q What is your post office address? A Sapulpa.
Q Were you in attendance during the illness of Mrs. Della Clayton? A Yes sir.
Q When did you first visit Mrs. Clayton? A It was on Friday the 2nd day of March.
Q Did she have a baby then? A Yes.
Q Do you know the name of that child? A No sir.
Q How old did that child seemed to be to you? A Must have been a week or ten days old from the looks of the child.
Q Who was the father of that child? A I don't know.
Q Who was said to be the father? A Charlie Clayton.
Q When did the mother die? A I don't know exactly, but I attended her about a week before she died.
Q Do you know when the child died? A No sir.
Q What was the cause of the death of the mother? A The predisposing cause was septic fever or child fever as a result of giving birth and the treatment given her. The indications were that the child had been born a week or more before you were called into see the mother? A Yes.

Applications for Enrollment of Creek Newborn
Act of 1905   Volume XI

Q You saw the child? A Yes sir. One indication was an unbellical[sic] or naval cord which was completely healed showing that it was several days old. These cords usually come off in four or five days.
Q Did you not visit this child professionally? A No sir; I looked the child over when I was attending the mother.

--------------oOo--------------

E.C. Griesel, being duly sworn, on oath, states that the above and foregoing is a true and correct transcript of her[sic] stenographic notes as taken in said proceedings on said date.

Edw C Griesel

Subscribed and sworn to before me this 5 day of May, 1905.

Zera E. Parrish
Notary Public.

BIRTH AFFIDAVIT.
DEPARTMENT OF THE INTERIOR.
COMMISSION TO THE FIVE CIVILIZED TRIBES.

IN RE APPLICATION FOR ENROLLMENT, as a citizen of the Creek Nation, of Ernest Clayton, born on the 2 day of March, 1905

Name of Father: Charlie Clayton   a citizen of the   U.S.   Nation.
Name of Mother: Della Jacobs Clayton (dec)   a citizen of the   Creek   Nation.
(Tuskegee)
                                Postoffice   Sapulpa

AFFIDAVIT OF ~~MOTHER~~. Father

UNITED STATES OF AMERICA, Indian Territory,
    Western   DISTRICT.

I, Charlie Clayton, on oath state that I am 23 years of age and a citizen by----, of the U. S. Nation; that I am the lawful ~~wife~~ Husband of Della Jacobs Clayton (dec), who is a citizen, by blood of the Creek Nation; that a male child was born to ~~me~~ my wife on 2 day of March , 1905 , that said child has been named Ernest Clayton , and ~~was living March 4, 1905~~. died March 30, 1905

Charlie Clayton

Witnesses To Mark:

Applications for Enrollment of Creek Newborn
Act of 1905   Volume XI

Subscribed and sworn to before me this 25 day of April, 1905.

(Seal)   Edw C Griesel
Notary Public.

AFFIDAVIT OF ATTENDING PHYSICIAN OR MID-WIFE.

UNITED STATES OF AMERICA, Indian Territory,
Western   **DISTRICT.**

I, Alice Vann , a Mid-wife , on oath state that I attended on Mrs. Della Jacobs Clayton , wife of Charlie Clayton on the ----- ~~day~~ during first wk of[sic] of March , 1905 ; that there was born to her on said date a male child; that said child was living March 4, 1905, & died Mar 31st of March 1905[sic] and is said to have been named Ernest Clayton

Alice Vann

Witnesses To Mark:
{

Subscribed and sworn to before me this 25 day of April, 1905.

(Seal)   Edw C Griesel
Notary Public.

BIRTH AFFIDAVIT.
DEPARTMENT OF THE INTERIOR.
COMMISSION TO THE FIVE CIVILIZED TRIBES.

IN RE APPLICATION FOR ENROLLMENT, as a citizen of the Creek Nation, of William McKinley Clayton , born on the ----- day of Dec , 1902

Name of Father: Charlie Clayton   a citizen of the   U.S.   Nation.
Name of Mother: Della Jacobs Clayton (dec)   a citizen of the   Creek   Nation.
(Tuskegee)

Postoffice   Sapulpa

Applications for Enrollment of Creek Newborn
Act of 1905   Volume XI

AFFIDAVIT OF ~~MOTHER~~. Father

UNITED STATES OF AMERICA, Indian Territory, }   Child Present
Western   DISTRICT.

I,   Charlie Clayton , on oath state that I am 23 years of age and a citizen by----, of the U. S. Nation; that I am the lawful ~~wife~~ Husband of Della Jacobs Clayton , who is a citizen, by blood of the Creek Nation; that a male   child was born to me on ----- day of Dec , 1902 , that said child has been named William McKinley Clayton , and was living March 4, 1905.

Charlie Clayton

Witnesses To Mark:
{

Subscribed and sworn to before me this 25 day of April, 1905.

(Seal)   Edw C Griesel
                                    Notary Public.

AFFIDAVIT OF ATTENDING PHYSICIAN OR MID-WIFE.

UNITED STATES OF AMERICA, Indian Territory, }
.... DISTRICT.

I, ..., a ...., on oath state that I attended on Mrs. ...., wife of .... on the .... day of ...., 1.......; that there was born to her on said date a .... child; that said child is now living and is said to have been named
....

Midwife now demented

Witnesses To Mark: testimony of witnesses taken
{

Subscribed and sworn to before me this .... day of ...., 1........ .

                                    Notary Public.

Applications for Enrollment of Creek Newborn
Act of 1905   Volume XI

HGH

REFER IN REPLY TO THE FOLLOWING:
NC
884

DEPARTMENT OF THE INTERIOR,
COMMISSIONER TO THE FIVE CIVILIZED TRIBES.

Muskogee, Indian Territory, October 19, 1905.

Lucy Davis,
    Care Alex Davis,
        Okemah, Indian Territory.

Dear Madam:

    In the matter of the application for the enrollment of your minor child, Nicey Davis, born December 10, 1903, as a citizen by blood of the Creek Nation, this office desires the affidavit of the midwife or physician in attendance at the birth of said child and blank for that purpose is enclosed herewith.

    In the event that there was no physician or midwife in attendance when said child was born, it will be necessary for you to furnish this office with the affidavits of two disinterested witnesses relative to her birth. Said affidavits must set forth said child's name, the date of her birth, the names of her parents and whether or not she was living on March 4, 1905.

                Respectfully,
                      Tams Bixby   Commissioner.

B C-Env.

NC-884

Muskogee, Indian Territory, December 16, 1905.

Lucy Davis,
    Care of Alex Davis,
        Okemah, Indian Territory.

Dear Madam:

    In the matter of the application for the enrollment of your minor child, Nicey Davis, born December 10, 1903, as a citizen by blood of the Creek Nation, you are advised that this Office requires the affidavit of the attending physician or midwife at said child's birth, and a blank for that purpose is herewith enclosed. In the event there was no physician or midwife in attendance when said child was born, it will be necessary for you to secure the affidavits of two disinterested witnesses relative to its birth, and a blank for that purpose is herewith enclosed.

    You are further advised that this Office is unable to identify you on its rolls of citizens of the Creek Nation. You are requested to write this Office at an early date,

Applications for Enrollment of Creek Newborn
Act of 1905   Volume XI

giving your maiden name, the names of your parents and other members of your family, the Creek Indian Town to which you belong, and, if possible, your name and roll number as same appear on your allotment certificate or deeds to land in the Creek Nation.

This matter should receive your immediate attention.

Respectfully,

Commissioner.

1 B A
Dis

Okmulgee, Ind. Ter.
Feb. 26, 1906.

To the Hon. Dawes Commission,
        Muskogee, I.T.

Gentlemen:

In compliance with your request of 12/10-05 I herewith hand you the affidavits of disinterested witnesses.

There was no midwife attended me. This matter would have been attended to sooner, but the letter was sent to Okemah instead of Okmulgee. I only received it a few days ago.

Hoping this will fill all of the requirements, I beg to remain.

Yours truly,
Lucy Davis (Nee Asbury)

P.S.
    My maiden name was Lucy Asbury.
    "   Father   "   is Mose Asbury of Coweta, I.T.

_____ District
Indian Territory   SS

We, the undersigned, on oath state that we are personally acquainted with   Lucy Davis, nee Asbury   wife of   Alex Davis   ; and that on or about the 10 day of Dec. , 1901, a   Female   child was born to them and has been named   Nicey Davis   ; and that said child was living March 4, 1905.

We further state that we have no interest in the above case.

Applications for Enrollment of Creek Newborn
Act of 1905   Volume XI

                          Walter W Morton

                          Joe Grayson

Witness to mark:

_____
_____
_____
_____

Subscribed and sworn to before me this 26 day of Feb 1906

                          Wm P Morton

My Com Ex July 23-06   Notary Public.

BIRTH AFFIDAVIT.

DEPARTMENT OF THE INTERIOR.
COMMISSION TO THE FIVE CIVILIZED TRIBES.

    IN RE APPLICATION FOR ENROLLMENT, as a citizen of the Creek Nation, of Nicey Davis, born on the 10 day of Dec , 1903

Name of Father: Alex Davis   a citizen of the   Creek   Nation.
Tulwa Thlosso Town
Name of Mother: Lucy Davis   a citizen of the   Creek   Nation.
Coweta Town

                    Postoffice   Okmulgee, Ind. Ter.

AFFIDAVIT OF MOTHER.

UNITED STATES OF AMERICA, Indian Territory,
    Western   **DISTRICT.**   Child is present

    I, Lucy Davis , on oath state that I am about 26 years of age and a citizen by blood , of the Creek Nation; that I am the lawful wife of Alex Davis , who is a citizen, by blood of the Creek Nation; that a female child was born to me on 10 day of December , 1903 , that said child has been named Nicey Davis , and was living March 4, 1905.

                          Lucy Davis

Witnesses To Mark:

Applications for Enrollment of Creek Newborn
Act of 1905 Volume XI

Subscribed and sworn to before me this 10 day of April, 1905.

Drennan C Skaggs
Notary Public.

AFFIDAVIT OF ATTENDING PHYSICIAN OR MID-WIFE.

UNITED STATES OF AMERICA, Indian Territory,⎫
    Western   DISTRICT. ⎭

my wife
    I, Alex Davis, a (blank), on oath state that I attended on ^ Mrs. Lucy Davis, wife of *(blank)* on the 10 day of December, 1903; that there was born to her on said date a female child; that said child was living March 4, 1905, and is said to have been named Nicey Davis

Alex Davis

Witnesses To Mark:
{

Subscribed and sworn to before me this 10 day of April, 1905.

Drennan C Skaggs
Notary Public.

BIRTH AFFIDAVIT.

DEPARTMENT OF THE INTERIOR.
COMMISSION TO THE FIVE CIVILIZED TRIBES.

    IN RE APPLICATION FOR ENROLLMENT, as a citizen of the Creek Nation, of Mary Davis, born on the 17 day of Nov, 1902 and died July 22, 1904

Name of Father: Alex Davis   a citizen of the   Creek   Nation.
Tulwa Thlosso Town
Name of Mother: Lucy Davis   a citizen of the   Creek   Nation.
Coweta Town
                      Postoffice   Okmulgee, Ind. Ter.

AFFIDAVIT OF MOTHER.

UNITED STATES OF AMERICA, Indian Territory,⎫
    Western   DISTRICT. ⎭

    I, Lucy Davis, on oath state that I am about 26 years of age and a citizen by blood, of the Creek Nation; that I am the lawful wife of Alex Davis, who is a citizen, by blood of the Creek Nation; that a female child was born to me on 17

Applications for Enrollment of Creek Newborn
Act of 1905   Volume XI

day of November , 1902 , that said child has been named Mary Davis , and ~~was living March 4, 1905~~. died July 22, 1904

Lucy Davis

Witnesses To Mark:

{

Subscribed and sworn to before me this 10 day of April , 1905.

Drennan C Skaggs
Notary Public.

AFFIDAVIT OF ATTENDING PHYSICIAN OR MID-WIFE.

UNITED STATES OF AMERICA, Indian Territory,
  Western   DISTRICT.

                                                      my wife

I, Alex Davis , ~~a (blank)~~ , on oath state that I attended on ^ Mrs. Lucy Davis , ~~wife of~~ (blank) on the 17 day of November , 1902 ; that there was born to her on said date a female child; that said child ~~was living March 4, 1905~~, and ~~is said to have been~~ named Mary Davis   died July 22, 1904
was

Alex Davis

Witnesses To Mark:

{

Subscribed and sworn to before me this 10 day of April , 1905.

Drennan C Skaggs
Notary Public.

NC 884   JLD

DEPARTMENT OF THE INTERIOR,
COMMISSIONER TO THE FIVE CIVILIZED TRIBES.

    In the matter of the application for the enrollment of Mary Davis, deceased, as a citizen by blood of the Creek Nation.

. . . .

STATEMENT AND ORDER.

    The record in this case shows that on April 13, 1905, application was made, in affidavit form, for the enrollment of Mary Davis, deceased, as a citizen by blood of the Creek Nation, under the provisions of the act of Congress approved March 3, 1905.

    It appears from the affidavit filed in this matter that said Mary Davis, deceased, was born November 17, 1902, and died July 22, 1904.

Applications for Enrollment of Creek Newborn
Act of 1905   Volume XI

The Act of Congress approved March 3, 1905, (33 Stats., 1048), provides:
"That the Commission to the Five Civilized Tribes is authorized for sixty days after the date of the approval of this act to receive and consider applications for enrollment, of children, <u>born subsequent to May twenty-fifth, nineteen hundred and one, and prior to March fourth, nineteen hundred and five, and living on said latter date,</u> to citizens of the Creek tribe of Indians whose enrollment has been approved by the Secretary of the Interior prior to the approval of this act; and to enroll and make allotments to such children."

It is, therefore, ordered that the application for the enrollment of , deceased, as a citizen by blood of the Creek Nation be, and the same is, hereby dismissed.

Tams Bixby   Commissioner.

Muskogee, Indian Territory.
JAN 4 – 1907

BA-1914-B

DEPARTMENT OF THE INTERIOR,
COMMISSION TO THE FIVE CIVILIZED TRIBES.

Muskogee, Indian Territory, May 1, 1905.

In the matter of the application for the enrollment of Beulah Doyle as a citizen by blood of the Creek Nation.

Nimrod L. Doyle, being duly sworn, testified as follows:

EXAMINATION BY THE COMMISSION:
Q What is your name? Nimrod L. Doyle.
Q What is your age? A 57 last December.
Q What is your postoffice? A Muskogee.
Q Did you know John N. Doyle? A That is my son; my oldest son.
Q Was he married to a woman named Rhoda Doyle? A No sir.
Q Is John N. Doyle living? A No sir. He is dead.
Q How long has he been dead? A Died last March a year ago--about that time. I think it was in March. Died at Okmulgee.
Q Was he married to anyone at the time of his death? A Married to Minnie Bowie.
Q Is she living? A I don't know whether she is living or not. She was the last accounts I heard from her; she went to Colorado.
Q Do you know a woman that calls herself Rhoda Doyle? A Yes sir.
Q Did you son ever live with her? A Yes sir.

Applications for Enrollment of Creek Newborn
Act of 1905 Volume XI

Q Did he live with her during the year 1901 that you know of? A 1902, in July, was the first time I ever knew that they were living together.
Q Are you sure they never lived together before? A Not that I know anything about.
Q Did she have a child by him? A I don't know. She says it was his; it was his child; they were living together part of the time.
Q She says she[sic] was born the 29th day of May, 1902; you say he didn't commence to live with her until July, 1902? A Yes sir.
Q This child was born two months before that? A Lived with her three years--until July--before he died--in March; it would have been three years in July;
Q Died last year, did he? A Yes sir.
Q That makes it July, 1902, that he commenced to live with her--is that correct? A (?)
Q He died in 1904? A Yes sir.
Q Do you know this child, Beulah, that she says is his? A Yes sir
Q You think that is his child? A I have no right to say that it was not his child; it might have been. I think it was.
Q Did he live with her continuously or did she have other men too? A He lived with her first from July to January, and left and went to Texas and stayed there during the fall and summer--about eight months; he was called back and took her to Texas and lived with her until he died.
Q They were never married? A He told me they were not.

INDIAN TERRITORY, Western District.
    I, J. Y. Miller, a stenographer to the Commission to the Five Civilized Tribes, do hereby certify that the above and foregoing is a true and complete translation of my notes as same appear in my stenographic report of this case.

                          JY Miller

Sworn to and subscribed before me
   this the 2 day of May, 1905.

                          Zera E Parrish
                              Notary Public.

NC-885
DEPARTMENT OF THE INTERIOR,
COMMISSIONER TO THE FIVE CIVILIZED TRIBES.

Muskogee, Indian Territory, October 31, 1905.

    In the matter of the application for the enrollment of application for the enrollment of Beulah Doyle as a citizen by blood of the Creek Nation.

    Rhoda Doyle, being duly sworn, testified as follows:

EXAMINATION BY THE COMMISSIONER:
Q What is your name? Rhoda Doyle.
Q How old are you? A I am 31 years old.

Applications for Enrollment of Creek Newborn
Act of 1905   Volume XI

Q What is your postoffice address? A Stroud, Oklahoma.
Q You have previously made application for the enrollment of your minor child, Beulah Doyle, as a Creek citizen? A Yes sir.
Q Is this your child? A Yes sir.
Q When was Beulah born? A The 29th day of May, 1902.
Q Who is the father of this child? A John N. Doyle.
Q Is the child living? A Yes, the child is here.

John N. Doyle, the father of said child, is identified on Creek Indian card, field No. 1117, and his name is included in the list of citizens by blood of the Creek Nation approved by the Department March 13, 1902, opposite Roll No. 3609.

Q Were you lawfully married to John N. Doyle? A Yes sir.
Q When were you married to him? A 1901.
Q What day and the month? A 8th day of July.
Q Where were you married? A Stroud, Oklahoma.
Q Who performed the ceremony? A A. E. Foster.
Q Is he a minister? A He was a notary public.
Q Is your husband living? A No sir, he is dead.
Q When did he die? A March, 1904.
Q You have your marriage certificate with you? A Yes, I have certificate.

Witness here presents a certificate of marriage.

Q Did you live with your husband up to the time of his death? A He was gone from home eleven months.
Q Where did he die? A In Okmulgee. He was in Texas and came back here, went back to Texas, lived eighteen months and came back to Okmulgee and died.
Q Do you know Timrod L. Doyle? A Yes sir.
Q Any relation to you? A Mr. Doyle's father.
Q Do you know if your husband ever lived or married anyone else? A Not that I know. I heard that he was married.
Q Do you know the name of that party? A No sir, I don't know. I heard that he was married twice, I believe.
Q Had he been lawfully divorced from the other women? A I couldn't tell you; he said he had.
Q If Limrod[sic] L. Doyle stated that you were never married to John N. Doyle, would his statement be correct? A I couldn't tell you. We were married--whether it was lawfully, we were married; that's is[sic] the certificate.
Q Did you have a license to get married? A Yes, he got the license; he showed me the license he got.
Q How long did you live with him as his lawful wife? A I lived with him six months, went to Texas gone eleven months and come back home in November; he lived until next February.
Q Was this child born after you were lawfully married to him? A Yes sir.
Q While you were living with him? A No sir, he was in Texas at the time of her birth. Joe Nobles came down there in June, after Mr. Doyle's death in February, and told me

Applications for Enrollment of Creek Newborn
Act of 1905   Volume XI

that Nimrod[sic] L. Doyle said if I would give him fifty dollars that he would relinquish his claim that he had on those forty acres of the John Doyle's homestead and I would give Mr. Nobles the marriage certificate and he never would bother me any more, but he told his son and his son's wife that if I did not give him that money, he would get it some way, and he again was bragging to them and his wife that he was going to do everything to keep me from filing for this baby. I never said anything more to him and tried to get more money out of me afterwards.
Q You have custody of this child, have you? A Yes sir, I can get any amount of witnesses that it is John Doyle's child.

Eliza Lawrence, being duly sworn, testified as follows:

EXAMINATION BY THE COMMISSIONER:
Q What is your name? A Eliza Lawrence.
Q How old are you? A 46.
Q What is your postoffice address? A Okmulgee.
Q Were you present at the birth of Beulah Doyle? A Yes sir
Q Who is the mother of that child? A Rhoda Doyle.
Q Who is the father of that child? A John Doyle.
Q When was this child, Beulah Doyle, born? A May 29.
Q What year? A 1902 or 1903, I can't. I never paid attention.
Q How old will it be in May of next year? A Four years old.
Q This is the child, is it? (pointing to the child). A Yes sir.
Q Was any one present at the birth of this child? A Me and the doctor and another lady, I don't know the name; she lives there close.
Q Who was the doctor in attendance? A Dr. W. C. Mitchener.
Q You have forgotten the name of that other woman? a Yes--it is Emma (prompted by the mother of the child: Emma Scott.

INDIAN TERRITORY, Western District.
I, J. Y. Miller, a stenographer to the Commissioner to the Five Civilized Tribes, do hereby certify that the above and foregoing is a true and complete translation of my notes as same appear in my stenographic report of this case.

JY Miller

Subscribed and sworn to before me
this the 4th day of November,
1905.

Edw C Griesel
Notary Public.

Applications for Enrollment of Creek Newborn
Act of 1905   Volume XI

BIRTH AFFIDAVIT.
DEPARTMENT OF THE INTERIOR.
COMMISSION TO THE FIVE CIVILIZED TRIBES.

IN RE APPLICATION FOR ENROLLMENT, as a citizen of the Creek Nation, of Beulah Doyle , born on the 29 day of May , 1902

Name of Father: John N. Doyle   a citizen of the   Creek   Nation.
Coweta Town
Name of Mother: Rhoda Doyle   a citizen of the United States Nation.

Postoffice   Stroud, Okla. Terr.

AFFIDAVIT OF MOTHER.

UNITED STATES OF AMERICA, Indian Territory,
   Western   **DISTRICT.**

I, Rhoda Doyle , on oath state that I am 31 years of age and a citizen by ----- , of the United States Nation; that I am the lawful wife of John N. Doyle , who is a citizen, by blood of the Creek Nation; that a female child was born to me on 29 day of May , 1902 , that said child has been named Beulah Doyle , and was living March 4, 1905.

Rhoda Doyle

Witnesses To Mark:
{

Subscribed and sworn to before me this 10 day of April , 1905.

Drennan C Skaggs
Notary Public.

AFFIDAVIT OF ATTENDING PHYSICIAN OR MID-WIFE.

UNITED STATES OF AMERICA, Indian Territory,
   Western   **DISTRICT.**

I, W. C. Mitchener , a physician , on oath state that I attended on Mrs. Rhoda Doyle , wife of John N. Doyle on the 29 day of May , 1902 ; that there was born to her on said date a female child; that said child was living March 4, 1905, and is said to have been named Beulah Doyle

W. C. Mitchener

Witnesses To Mark:
{

Applications for Enrollment of Creek Newborn
Act of 1905   Volume XI

Subscribed and sworn to before me this 10 day of April, 1905.

                              Drennan C Skaggs
                              Notary Public.

NC-885

THIS CERTIFICATE OF MARRIAGE

certifies that

She will do him good and not evil all the days of her life. Prov. XXXI--12	RHODA BURRUS and JOHN N. DOYLE were by me united in	Husbands, love your wives, even as Christ also loved the Church and gave Himself for it. Eph. V--25

HOLY MATRIMONY

According to the Ordinance of God and the Laws of the State of Oklahoma at Stroud on the 8 day of July in the year of our Lord One Thousand Eight Hundred and 1901.

    Witnesses   Signed by E. A. FOSTER.

        A. W. Jones

INDIAN TERRITORY,   :   I, J. Y. Miller, a stenographer to the
Western District   :   Commissioner to the Five Civilized
                                  :   Tribes, do hereby certify that the above
and foregoing is a true and complete copy of its original.

                              JY Miller

Sworn to and subscribed before me
   this the 31st day of October,
   1905.

                              J McDermott
                              Notary Public.

Applications for Enrollment of Creek Newborn
Act of 1905   Volume XI

NC 885

Muskogee, Indian Territory, October 19, 1905.

Rhoda Doyle,
    Stroud, Oklahoma Territory.

Dear Madam:

    In the matter of the application for the enrollment of your minor child, Beulah Doyle, born May 29, 1902, as a citizen by blood of the Creek Nation, you are requested to furnish this office with evidence of marriage of yourself and John N. Doyle, the alleged father of said child. Said evidence may consist of either the original or a certified copy of your marriage license and certificate.

    In the event that you were not married to said John N. Doyle, who it appears is now dead, you are notified to appear before this office within fifteen days from the date hereof, with the midwife or physician who attended at the birth of said child and at least two other witnesses who know the exact date of the birth of said Beulah Doyle and whether or not said John N. Doyle was in fact the father of said Beulah Doyle.

                      Respectfully,

                                (No Signature Given.)

N.C. 885

Muskogee, Indian Territory, November 2, 1905.

Rhoda Doyle,
    Stroud, Oklahoma Territory.

Dear Madam:

    There is herewith returned to you certificate of your marriage to John N. Doyle, a copy of which has been made and filed with the papers in the matter of the application for the enrollment of your minor child, Beulah Doyle.

                      Respectfully,
                                    Commissioner.

AG-10

Applications for Enrollment of Creek Newborn
Act of 1905   Volume XI

Payments- Creek
Equalization.
John N. Doyle,
dec'd C3609,
9/11/16 OCH-TKK ENCLO.

Sept. 11, 1916.

    Alex Johnston, Probate Attorney,
        Okmulgee, Oklahoma.

Dear Mr. Johnston:

    There is $32 due to equalize the allotment of the decedent above named. His father, Nimrod P. Doyle, lives at Morris, Oklahoma. A few days ago Mr. Doyle was in the office and stated that his son John N. Doyle has a daughter living, enroll-as Beulah Doyle opposite New Born Creek Roll No. 989.

    It was gathered from conversation with Mr. Doyle that his son and Rhoda Doyle, the mother of said Beulah Doyle, lived together at intervals for two or three years as husband and wife and regarded one another as such, but that formal license to wed was not obtained nor was a ceremony performed.

    It was further stated that a suit involving the title to the land was tried at Okmulgee, Oklahoma. You are requested to examine the record in this case for the purpose of determining whether or not the court held that a common-law marriage existed between said John N. Doyle and Rhoda Doyle. Mr. Nimrod P. Doyle was requested to call upon you and render any assistance in his power, and he agreed to do so.

    Form for proof of heirship is herewith. Kindly have the same executed as soon as the facts are available. If this child Beulah is legitimate she will receive the amount due to equalize her father's allotment, otherwise she will not. Kindly see, therefore, that the proof of heirship recites the necessary facts.

                    Sincerely,

                    Superintendent for the
                    Five Civilized Tribes.

Applications for Enrollment of Creek Newborn
Act of 1905   Volume XI

OFFICE OF
PROBATE ATTORNEY.
Payments-Creek.
Equilization[sic].
John N. Doyle, decd.
C3609.
9-11-16-OCH-TKK-Enclo.

AJ-SMD-12

RECEIVED
SUPT. 5 CIVIC TRIBES
DEC 14 1916
No.   119484

Department of the Interior

United States Indian Service

Five Civilized Tribes

Okmulgee, Oklahoma.
December 12th, 1916.

Dear Mr. Parker:

Replying to your letter relative to the above subject, I beg leave to state that you do not inform me the title of the suit you refer to, which you state was "Tried at Okmulgee, Oklahoma." It would necessitate a search of the entire chain of title to discover the title of this litigation before I could investigate the files and learn the result of such suit.

I wish you would kindly advise me the title of the cause, whereupon I will be glad to give this matter a thorough investigation.

I have written Mr. Nimrod P. Doyle for this information, also.

Very truly yours,
Alex Johnston
United States Probate Attorney.

Hon. Gabe E. Parker, Supt.,
Five Civilized Tribes,
Muskogee, Oklahoma.

Payments
O. C. H.- MBS
1- 8- 17

John N. Doyle, deceased,
Creek, N. 3609.

January 8, 1917.

Mr. Alex Johnson,
    Probate Attorney,
        Okmulgee, Oklahoma.

Applications for Enrollment of Creek Newborn
Act of 1905   Volume XI

Dear Mr. Johnson:

Replying to your letter of the 12th ultimo, you are advised that the office is not informed of the style of the suit tried at Okmulgee, Indian Territory involving title to the allotment of John M. Doyle, deceased.

Just prior to the time request was made of you to assist in the preparation of proof of heirship in this case, the father of said deceased allottee appeared at the office and stated that title to this land was at one time in suit at Okmulgee. Mr. Doyle said he would call upon you at Okmulgee and assist in every way he could in this matter. About three weeks ago he again appeared at this office and made inquiry concerning this case and at that time he agreed to call upon you.

Reference is made to letter addressed to you relative to this subject on September 11, 1916, which contains a recital of the information in possession of this office in regard to this matter.

Sincerely yours,

Superintendent for the Five Civilized Tribes.

BIRTH AFFIDAVIT.

DEPARTMENT OF THE INTERIOR.
COMMISSION TO THE FIVE CIVILIZED TRIBES.

IN RE APPLICATION FOR ENROLLMENT, as a citizen of the C R E E K - - - - - - - - - Nation, of Lum Berryhill - - - - - - - - - -, born on the 10th day of October - -, 1901

Name of Father: William Berryhill - - - - - - - -   a citizen of the C R E E K ---Nation.
(Broken Arrow)   non
Name of Mother: Alice Berryhill - - - - - - - -   ^ citizen of the C R E E K ---Nation.

Postoffice   Mounds, Indian Territory - - - - -

Applications for Enrollment of Creek Newborn
Act of 1905   Volume XI

AFFIDAVIT OF MOTHER.

UNITED STATES OF AMERICA, Indian Territory, }
   Western - - - - - - - - DISTRICT.

      I, Alice Berryhill - - - - - - - - - - - - - - - - - , on oath state that I am   Twenty Four years of age and a non citizen by - - - - - - - - , of the Creek - - - - - - - - - - -   Nation; that I am the lawful wife of William Berryhill - - - - - - - - - - , who is a citizen, by Blood - - - of the C R E E K - - - - - -   Nation; that a Male   child was born to me on   tenth - - - day of October - - - - - - - - - , 1901 , that said child has been named Lum Berryhill - - - - , and was living March 4, 1905.

                                                    Alice Berryhill

Witnesses To Mark:
{

      Subscribed and sworn to before me this 24th day of April - - - - -, 1905.

                                                    B Barton

My Commission expires Feb. 21, 1907.   Notary Public.

AFFIDAVIT OF ATTENDING PHYSICIAN OR MID-WIFE.

UNITED STATES OF AMERICA, Indian Territory, }
   Western - - - - -   DISTRICT.
                           Mid wife
      I,   Maggie Self , a   ~~Physician~~ - - - , on oath state that I attended on Mrs. Alice Berryhill - - - - - - - - , wife of William Berryhill - - - - - - - on the tenth day of October - - - - - - , 1901 ; that there was born to her on said date a male child; that said child was living March 4, 1905, and is said to have been named Lum Berryhill - - - - - - - -

                                                 Maggie Self

Witnesses To Mark:
{

      Subscribed and sworn to before me 26 day of April, 1905.

     (Seal)   Edw C Griesel
                                                    Notary Public.

Applications for Enrollment of Creek Newborn
Act of 1905   Volume XI

BIRTH AFFIDAVIT.
DEPARTMENT OF THE INTERIOR.
COMMISSION TO THE FIVE CIVILIZED TRIBES.

IN RE APPLICATION FOR ENROLLMENT, as a citizen of the C R E E K - - - - - - - - - Nation, of Archie Berryhill - - - - - - - - - -, born on the 24th day of January - -, 1904

Name of Father: William Berryhill - - - - - - - -   a citizen of the C R E E K ---Nation.
(Broken Arrow)   non
Name of Mother: Alice Berryhill - - - - - - - - -   ^ citizen of the C R E E K ---Nation.

Postoffice   Mounds, Indian Territory - - - - -

AFFIDAVIT OF MOTHER.
                                                Child Brought in
UNITED STATES OF AMERICA, Indian Territory, ⎫   5/26/05
   Western - - - - -   DISTRICT. ⎭

I, Alice Berryhill - - - - - - - - - - - - - - - - - , on oath state that I am Twenty Four years of age and a non citizen by - - - - - - -, of the Creek - - - - - - --- - -   Nation; that I am the lawful wife of William Berryhill - - - - - - - - - , who is a citizen, by Blood - - - of the C R E E K - - - - - -   Nation; that a Male   child was born to me on   24th - - - day of January - - - - - - , 1904 , that said child has been named Archie Berryhill - - - -, and was living March 4, 1905.
                                          Alice Berryhill
Witnesses To Mark:
{

Subscribed and sworn to before me this 24th day of April - - - - -, 1905.

                                B Barton
My Commission expires Feb. 21, 1907.   Notary Public.

AFFIDAVIT OF ATTENDING PHYSICIAN OR MID-WIFE.

UNITED STATES OF AMERICA, Indian Territory, ⎫
   Western - - - - -   DISTRICT. ⎭

I, M.D. Taylor - - - - - - - - - - , a Physician - - - , on oath state that I attended on Mrs. Alice Berryhill - - - - - - - - - , wife of William Berryhill - - - - - - - on the 24th day of January - - - - - - , 1904 ; that there was born to her on said date a male child; that said child was living March 4, 1905, and is said to have been named Archie Berryhill - - - - - - -
                                    M. D. Taylor, M.D.

Applications for Enrollment of Creek Newborn
Act of 1905 Volume XI

Witnesses To Mark:

{

    Subscribed and sworn to before me this 24th day of April - - - - -, 1905.

                                              B Barton

My Commission expires Feb. 21, 1907.   Notary Public.

CERTIFICATE OF RECORD.

United States of America,
    Indian Territory,   ss.
    Northern District.

    I, JAMES A. WINSTON, Clerk of the United States Court in the Northern District, Indian Territory, do hereby certify that the instrument hereto attached was filed for record in my office the 9 day of November, 1897, at . . . . M, and duly recorded Book F, Marriage Record, Page 190
    Witness my hand and seal of said Court at Vinita Muscogee[sic], in said Territory, this 11 day of November, A. D. 1897.

                                        JAS. A. WINSTON, Clerk.

INDIAN TERRITORY, Western District.	I, J. Y. Miller, a stenographer to the Commissioner to the Five Civilized Tribes, do hereby certify that the above

and foregoing is a true and complete copy of its original.

                                              JY Miller

Sworn to and subscribed before me
    this the 1st day of November,
    1905.

                                              J McDermott
                                              Notary Public.

NC-886

MARRIAGE LICENSE.

United States of America,
    Indian Territory,   ss.   NO. 391.
    Northern District.

TO ANY PERSON AUTHORIZED BY LAW TO SOLEMNIZE MARRIAGE--GREETING:

Applications for Enrollment of Creek Newborn
Act of 1905   Volume XI

You are hereby commanded to solemnize the Rite and publish the Banns of Matrimony between Mr. William Berryhill of Sapulpa, in the Indian Territory, aged 25 years, and Miss Alice Self, of Sapulpa, in the Indian Territory, aged 18 years, according to law, and do you officially sign and return this License to the parties therein named.
do you officially sign and return this License to the parties therein named.

Witness my hand and official seal at Vinita, Indian Territory, this 21st day of July, A. D. 1897.

(signed)   JAS. A. WINSTON,

(SEAL)   Clerk of the U.S. Court.

By J. C. Anderson,
    Deputy.

CERTIFICATE OF MARRIAGE.

United States of America,
   Indian Territory,   ss.
   Northern District.

I, P. Jonson, a Minister of the Gospel, do hereby certify that on the 24 day of July, A.D. 1897, I did duly and according to law as commanded in the foregoing Licnse, solemnize the Rite and publish the Banns of Matrimony between the parties therein named.
Witness my hand this 24 day of July, A. D. 1897.
My credentials are recorded in the office of the Clerk of the United States Court, Indian Territory, Northern District, Book B, Page 126.

(signed)   P. Jonson,
a Minister of the Gospel.

FILED
NOV 9 1897
JAS. A. WINSTON, Clerk.

(The below Affidavit typed as given.)

    AFFIDAVIT IN/ENROLLMENT OF MINOR.LUM BERRYHILL, ARCHIE BERRYHILL.

Hon.Tams Bixby,Commissioner,
                  Muskogee, I.T.

Dear Sirs:-

    The undersigned,William Berryhill, states that he is the father of Lum Berryhill, and Archie Berryhill,minors whose application for enrollment is on file, N.C. 886,Lum

Applications for Enrollment of Creek Newborn
Act of 1905   Volume XI

Berryhill was born October, 10th.1901,and Archie Berryhill,born January 24th.1904, and are both living now.
I am a citizen of the Creek Nation,Roll Number, 2511,and my other two children, are enrolled,Joseph F.Berryhill,Roll No., 2512.and Nevada Berryhill,Roll No. 2513.My deeds and theirs have been delivered and were approved,Jan.27.1903.
I was married to Alice Self, by P. Johnson,A Minister of the Gospel,near Mounds I.T. on July 24th.1897,as appears from the Original Certificate,herewith enclosed. My father is G.W.Berryhill,mother,Arie Berryhill,I belonged to Broken Arrow Town.

Attest to his mark: his
   JL Mars   William x Berryhill
   James J Mars   mark

United States of America,)
)
Western District of,   )
Indian Territory.   )

        William Berryhill, of lawful age,being by me first duly sworn,upon his oath according to law,says,that he has heard read over the foregoing statement of facts,and that same is true and correct.

Attest to his mark: his
   JL Mars   William x Berryhill
   James J Mars   mark
Subscribed and sworn to before me this 28th.day of October, 1905.

                                        James J. Mars
                                        Notary Public,Western District of Ind. Ter.

                                                                                J.D.

                                                             Cr-BA-2291-B
                                                            Cr-BA-2292-B
N C 886
                              Muskogee, Indian Territory, May 1, 1905.

Mrs. Alice Berryhill,
   Care of William Berryhill,
      Broken Arrow, Indian Territory.   now Mounds I.T.

Dear Madam:

        The Commission acknowledges receipt of affidavits executed by you relative to the birth of your minor children, Archie and Lum Berryhill. It is stated in said affidavits

Applications for Enrollment of Creek Newborn
Act of 1905   Volume XI

that the name of the father of these children is William Berryhill, a citizen by blood of the Creek Nation.

As there are several persons named William Berryhill on the approved rolls of citizens by blood of the Creek Nation, it is impossible to identify the father of said children without further information. You are accordingly requested to advise the Commission as to the roll number of said William Berryhill as the same appears on his deeds or allotment certificate.

Respectfully,

Chairman.

NC-886

Muskogee, Indian Territory, October 6, 1905.

Mrs. Alice Berryhill,
    Care of William Berryhill,
        Mounds, Indian Territory.

Dear Madam:

There are on file in this Office affidavits relative to the birth of your minor children, Archie and Lum Berryhill. It is states in said affidavits that the name of the father of these children is William Berryhill, a citizen by blood of the Creek Nation.

As there are several persons named William Berryhill on the approved rolls of citizens by blood of the Creek Nation, it is impossible to identify the father of said children without further information. You are accordingly requested to advise this Office as to the roll number of said William Berryhill as the same appears on his deeds or allotment certificate.

Respectfully,

Commissioner.

N.C. 886

Muskogee, Indian Territory, October 19, 1905.

Mrs. Alice Berryhill,
    Care William Berryhill,
        Mounds, Indian Territory.

Dear Madam:

In the matter of the application for the enrollment of your minor children, Lum Berryhill, born October 10, 1901, and Archie Berryhill, born January 24, 1904, you are again advised that inasmuch as there are several persons named William Berryhill on the approved rolls of citizens by blood of the Creek Nation, it is impossible to identify the

Applications for Enrollment of Creek Newborn
Act of 1905 Volume XI

father of said children without further information. You are accordingly requested to advise this office as to the names of the parents of said William Berryhill, the Creek Indian town to which he belongs, his roll number as the same appears on his deeds and allotment certificate, and if any children of said William Berryhill have been enrolled as citizens of the Creek Nation, you are requested to state the names of said children.

You are further advised that this office desires evidence of your marriage to said William Berryhill; said evidence may consist of either the original or a certified copy of your marriage license and certificate.

Respectfully,

Commissioner.

NC-886

Muskogee, Indian Territory, November 2, 1905.

William Berryhill,
Sapulpa, Indian Territory.

Dear Sir:

In accordance with your request, there is herewith enclosed marriage license filed by you in the matter of the application for the enrollment of your minor children, Lum and Archie Berryhill, as citizens by blood of the Creek Nation.

A copy of said license has been made and filed with the papers in the case.

Respectfully,

Commissioner.

JYM-2-2

Applications for Enrollment of Creek Newborn
Act of 1905 Volume XI

BIRTH AFFIDAVIT.
DEPARTMENT OF THE INTERIOR.
COMMISSION TO THE FIVE CIVILIZED TRIBES.

IN RE APPLICATION FOR ENROLLMENT, as a citizen of the Creek Nation, of Lucy Marshall, born on the 15th day of July, 1904

Name of Father: Phillip Marshall   a citizen of the   Creek   Nation.
Name of Mother: Lizie Marshall   a citizen of the   Creek   Nation.

               Postoffice   Okmulgee, Indian Territory

AFFIDAVIT OF ATTENDING PHYSICIAN OR MID-WIFE.

UNITED STATES OF AMERICA, Indian Territory,
Western Judicial   **DISTRICT.**

     I, Phillip Marshall, Husband of Lizie Marshall, on oath state that I attended on Mrs. Lizie Marshall, my wife, who is now dead, on the 15th day of July, 1904 ; that there was born to her on said date a Female child; that said child was ~~living March 4, 1905, and is said to have been~~ named Lucy Marshall, and died on December 5th, 1904

                                    his
                             Phillip x Marshall
Witnesses To Mark: mark
   { George C Beidleman
   { J.H. Winston

     Subscribed and sworn to before me 22nd day of April, 1905.

                              George C Beidleman
My Commission Expires April 27th, 1908.   Notary Public.

NC 887   JLD
DEPARTMENT OF THE INTERIOR,
COMMISSIONER TO THE FIVE CIVILIZED TRIBES.

     In the matter of the application for the enrollment of Lucy Marshall, deceased, as a citizen by blood of the Creek Nation.

                . . . .

STATEMENT AND ORDER.

     The record in this case shows that on April 29, 1905, application was made, in

Applications for Enrollment of Creek Newborn
Act of 1905   Volume XI

affidavit form, for the enrollment of Lucy Marshall, deceased, as a citizen by blood of the Creek Nation, under the provisions of the Act of Congress approved March 3, 1905.

It appears from the affidavit filed in this matter that said Lucy Marshall, deceased, was born July 15, 1904, and died December 5, 1904.

The Act of Congress approved March 3, 1905, (33 Stats., 1048), provides:

"That the Commission to the Five Civilized Tribes is authorized for sixty days after the date of the approval of this act to receive and consider applications for enrollment, of children, <u>born subsequent to May twenty-fifth, nineteen hundred and one, and prior to March fourth, nineteen hundred and five, and living on said latter date</u>, to citizens of the Creek tribe of Indians whose enrollment has been approved by the Secretary of the Interior prior to the approval of this act; and to enroll and make allotments to such children."

It is, therefore, ordered that the application for the enrollment of said Lucy Marshall, deceased, as a citizen by blood of the Creek Nation be, and the same is, hereby dismissed.

Tams Bixby Commissioner.

Muskogee, Indian Territory.
JAN 4 – 1907

N.C. 888

Muskogee, Indian Territory, October 19, 1905.

Sallie Bird,
    Care Moses Bird,
        Okmulgee, Indian Territory.

Dear Madam:

In the matter of the application for the enrollment of your minor child, Kizzie Bird, born December 3, 1904, as a citizen by blood of the Creek Nation, this office desires the affidavit of the midwife or physician in attendance at the birth of said child and a blank for that purpose is enclosed herewith.

In the event that there was no physician or midwife in attendance when said child was born, it will be necessary for you to furnish this office with the affidavits of two disinterested witnesses relative to her birth. Said affidavits must set forth the name of said child, the date of her birth, the names of her parents and whether or not she was living on March 4, 1905.

Respectfully,

B C   Commissioner.
Env.

Applications for Enrollment of Creek Newborn
Act of 1905   Volume XI

BIRTH AFFIDAVIT.

DEPARTMENT OF THE INTERIOR.
COMMISSION TO THE FIVE CIVILIZED TRIBES.

    IN RE APPLICATION FOR ENROLLMENT, as a citizen of the Creek Nation, of Kizzie Fuswa (or Bird), born on the 3 day of Dec, 1904

Name of Father: Mose Fuswa (or Bird)   a citizen of the   Creek   Nation.
(Illegible) Town
Name of Mother: Sally Fuswa (or Bird)   a citizen of the   Creek   Nation.
Thlop Thlocco Town
                  Postoffice   Okmulgee, Ind. Ter.

AFFIDAVIT OF MOTHER.

UNITED STATES OF AMERICA, Indian Territory,   Child is present
    Western   DISTRICT.

    I, Sally Fuswa (or Bird), on oath state that I am about 40 years of age and a citizen by blood, of the Creek Nation; that I am the lawful wife of Mose Fuswa (or Bird), who is a citizen, by blood of the Creek Nation; that a female child was born to me on 3 day of December, 1904, that said child has been named Kizzie Fuswa (or Bird), and was living March 4, 1905.
                            her
                    Sally x Fuswa (or Bird)
Witnesses To Mark: mark
 { Alex Posey
  DC Skaggs

    Subscribed and sworn to before me this 10 day of April, 1905.

                          Drennan C Skaggs
                            Notary Public.

AFFIDAVIT OF ATTENDING PHYSICIAN OR MID-WIFE.

UNITED STATES OF AMERICA, Indian Territory,
    Western   DISTRICT.

                                    my wife
    I, Mose Fuswa (or Bird), a~~ (blank)~~, on oath state that I attended on ^ Mrs. Sally Fuswa (or Bird), ~~wife of~~ *(blank)* on the 3 day of Dec, 1904; that there was born to her on said date a female child; that said child was living March 4, 1905, and is said to have been named Kizzie Fuswa (or Bird)

Applications for Enrollment of Creek Newborn
Act of 1905   Volume XI

Witnesses To Mark:
{ Alex Posey
  DC Skaggs

his
Mose x Fuswa (or Bird)
mark

Subscribed and sworn to before me this 10 day of April , 1905.

Drennan C Skaggs
Notary Public.

BIRTH AFFIDAVIT.
DEPARTMENT OF THE INTERIOR.
COMMISSION TO THE FIVE CIVILIZED TRIBES.

IN RE APPLICATION FOR ENROLLMENT, as a citizen of the Creek Nation, of Kizzie Bird , born on the 3" day of December , 1904

Name of Father: Moses Bird   a citizen of the   Creek   Nation.
Name of Mother: Sallie Bird   a citizen of the   Creek   Nation.

Postoffice   Sharp, I.T.

AFFIDAVIT OF MOTHER.

UNITED STATES OF AMERICA, Indian Territory,
   Western   DISTRICT.

I, Sallie Bird , on oath state that I am about 40 years of age and a citizen by Blood , of the Creek Nation; that I am the lawful wife of Moses Bird , who is a citizen, by Blood of the Creek Nation; that a Female child was born to me on 3" day of December , 1904 , that said child has been named Kizzie Bird , and is now living.   his[sic]
                              Sallie Bird x
Witnesses To Mark: mark
{ Isom Peters
  Stella Haynes

Subscribed and sworn to before me this 30 day of October , 1905.

Wm P Morton
Notary Public.

My Com. Expires July 23-1906

167

Applications for Enrollment of Creek Newborn
Act of 1905   Volume XI

AFFIDAVIT OF ATTENDING PHYSICIAN OR MID-WIFE.

UNITED STATES OF AMERICA, Indian Territory,
Western   DISTRICT.

    I, Maggie Harjo, a mid-wife, on oath state that I attended on Mrs. Sallie Bird, wife of Moses Bird on the 3rd day of December, 1904; that there was born to her on said date a Female child; that said child is now living and is said to have been named Kizzie Bird

                                       her
                          Maggie Harjo x
Witnesses To Mark: mark
   { *(Name Illegible)*
     J. T. Busey

    Subscribed and sworn to before me this 27" day of Oct, 1905.

                                B B Chitwood
                                Notary Public.

UNITED STATES OF AMERICA)
    Indian Territory   (ss.
WESTERN JUDICIAL DISTRICT)

    Pleasant Berryhill and James Kanard, being first duly sworn, on their oath say; that they are well acquainted with Martha Gibson daughter of Joseph Gibson and Hettie Gibson; that said Martha Gibson was born July 26th, 1904, and is et living; that both the parents of the said Martha Gibson are citizens of the Creek Nation, and that these affiants are not related to the said Martha Gibson, or in any way interested in her enrollment as a citizen of the Creek Nation. And further deponents say not.

                              Pleasant Berryhill

                              James Kanard

Subscribed and sworn to before me this 8th, day of December, 1905.

                              W C McAdoo
                              Notary Public.
My commission expires on the 23 day of Apr, 1907

Applications for Enrollment of Creek Newborn
Act of 1905 Volume XI

BIRTH AFFIDAVIT.

DEPARTMENT OF THE INTERIOR.
COMMISSION TO THE FIVE CIVILIZED TRIBES.

IN RE APPLICATION FOR ENROLLMENT, as a citizen of the Creek Nation, of Martha Gibson, born on the 26 day of July, 1904

Name of Father: Joseph Gibson	a citizen of the	Creek	Nation.
Name of Mother: Hattie[sic] Gibson	a citizen of the	Creek	Nation.

Postoffice   Okmulgee I.T.

AFFIDAVIT OF MOTHER.

UNITED STATES OF AMERICA, Indian Territory,
   Western   DISTRICT.

I, Hattie Gibson, on oath state that I am (31) years of age and a citizen by blood, of the Creek Nation; that I am the lawful wife of Joseph Gibson, who is a citizen, by blood of the Creek Nation; that a Female child was born to me on 26" day of July, 1904, that said child has been named Martha Gibson, and is now living.

Hettie Gibson

Witnesses To Mark:
   { Sarah Chamblen
   { Maggie Dearsaw

Subscribed and sworn to before me this 23rd day of Oct, 1905.

Samuel J Checote
Notary Public.
Com Exp Nov 6-1906

BIRTH AFFIDAVIT.

DEPARTMENT OF THE INTERIOR.
COMMISSION TO THE FIVE CIVILIZED TRIBES.

IN RE APPLICATION FOR ENROLLMENT, as a citizen of the Creek Nation, of Mottie Gibson, born on the 20 day of July, 1904

Name of Father: Joseph Gibson Coweta Town	a citizen of the	Creek	Nation.
Name of Mother: Hettie Gibson Coweta Town	a citizen of the	Creek	Nation.

Applications for Enrollment of Creek Newborn
Act of 1905 Volume XI

Postoffice   Okmulgee, I.T.

AFFIDAVIT OF MOTHER.

UNITED STATES OF AMERICA, Indian Territory,　}
　Western　　　DISTRICT.

I, Hettie Gibson , on oath state that I am 31 years of age and a citizen by blood, of the Creek Nation; that I am the lawful wife of Joseph Gibson , who is a citizen, by blood of the Creek Nation; that a female child was born to me on 20 day of July, 1904 , that said child has been named Mottie Gibson , and was living March 4, 1905.

　　　　　　　　　　　　　　Hettie Gipson[sic]

Witnesses To Mark:
{

Subscribed and sworn to before me this 10 day of April , 1905.

　　　　　　　　　　　　　　Drennan C Skaggs
　　　　　　　　　　　　　　Notary Public.

AFFIDAVIT OF ATTENDING PHYSICIAN OR MID-WIFE.

UNITED STATES OF AMERICA, Indian Territory,　}
　Western　　　DISTRICT.

　　　　　　　　　　　　　　　　　　　　　　my wife
I, Joseph Gibson , a~~ (blank)~~ , on oath state that I attended on ^ Mrs. Hettie Gibson , ~~wife of~~ *(blank)* on the 20 day of July , 1904 ; that there was born to her on said date a female child; that said child was living March 4, 1905, and is said to have been named Mottie Gibson

　　　　　　　　　　　　　　Joseph Gibson

Witnesses To Mark:
{

Subscribed and sworn to before me this 10 day of April, 1905.

　　　　　　　　　　　　　　Drennan C Skaggs
　　　　　　　　　　　　　　Notary Public.

Applications for Enrollment of Creek Newborn
Act of 1905   Volume XI

N.C. 889

Muskogee, Indian Territory, October 6, 1905.

Joseph Gibson,
   Okmulgee, Indian Territory.

Dear Sir:

In the matter of the application for the enrollment of your minor child, Mattie[sic] Gibson, as a citizen by blood of the Creek Nation, this office is unable to identify your wife, Hettie Gibson on its roll of Creek citizens.

You are requested to state her maiden name, the names of her parents, the Creek Indian town to which she belongs, and, if possible, the roll number which appears on her deeds to land in the Creek Nation.

Respectfully,

Commissioner.

Okmulgee, I.T.   Oct. 7, 1905.

Hon. Tams Bixby,
   Muskogee, I.T.

Dear Sir:

Replying to yours of the 6th inst. "N.C.889" I will say that the maiden name of my wife was Hettie Checote, she was married before our marriage and her name then was Hattie Derisaw, and under this name I think she took her allotment. Her father was Samuel Checote, she is a member of Coweta town, and the roll number which appears on her deed is 1488.

I trust by this you will be able to identify my minor child Mattie Gibson.

Yours very truly,
his
Joseph x Gibson
mark

Wit to mark
   E.T. Noble

Applications for Enrollment of Creek Newborn
Act of 1905   Volume XI

N.C. 889

Muskogee, Indian Territory, October 19, 1905.

Hettie Gibson,
    Care Joseph Gibson,
        Okmulgee, Indian Territory.

Dear Madam:

    In the matter of the application for the enrollment of your minor child, Mattie Gibson, born July 20, 1904, as a citizen by blood of the Creek Nation, this office desires affidavit of the midwife or physician in attendance at the birth of said child and a blank for that purpose is enclosed herewith.

    In the event that there was no physician or midwife in attendance when said child was born, it will be necessary for you to furnish this office with the affidavits of two disinterested witnesses relative to her birth. Said affidavits must set forth the name of said child, the date of her birth, the names of her parents and whether or not she was living on March 4, 1905.

                      Respectfully,

BC-Env.   Commissioner.

C889

Okmulgee, I. T. Oct. 23rd, 1905.

Commission to the Fife[sic] Civilized Tribes.
    Muscogee[sic] I. T.

Gentlemen:

    The date in your letter in regards to our birth of child is not correct, it was 26, and not the 20" of July.

    Also the name of the child is Martha, and not (Mattie) so we make this affidavit, as stated in the forgoing[sic] affidavit for enrollment. But we never had no mid wife or a Doctor.

    Therefore we hope this enclosed affidavit will be found satisfactory we remain

                Yours Truly

            (signed)   JOSEPH GIBSON.
            (signed)   HETTIE GIBSON.

Applications for Enrollment of Creek Newborn
Act of 1905   Volume XI

BD-889

Muskogee, Indian Territory, October 27, 1905.

Hettie Gibson,
 Care of Joseph Gibson,
  Okmulgee, Indian Territory.

Dear Madam:

Receipt is acknowledged of your communication of October 23, 1905, enclosing your affidavit in the matter of the application for the enrollment of your minor child, Martha Gibson, born July 26, 1904, as a citizen by blood of the Creek Nation. You state that there was no physician or midwife in attendance at the birth of said child.

In reply you are again advised that, as there was no physician or midwife in attendance when said child was born, it will be necessary for you to furnish this Office with the affidavits of two disinterested witnesses relative to her birth. Said affidavits must set forth the name of said child, the date of her birth, the names of her parents and whether or not she was living on March 4, 1905.

This matter should receive your immediate attention.

Respectfully,

Commissioner.

N.C. 890.
DEPARTMENT OF THE INTERIOR,
COMMISSIONER TO THE FIVE CIVILIZED TRIBES.
Muskogee, Indian Territory, February 26, 1906.

In the matter of the application for the enrollment of Tom Sevier an Lena Sevier as citizens by blood of the Creek Nation.

MARCH THOMPSON, being duly sworn testified as follows through Alex Posey official interpreter.

Q What is your name? A March Thompson.
Q What is your age? A About sixty two.
Q What is your post office address? A Burney.

Applications for Enrollment of Creek Newborn
Act of 1905   Volume XI

Q We have on file in this office affidavits in the matter of the birth of Tom and Lena Sevier, are you elated to these children? A They are the children of my brother's daughter.
Q What was the name of your brother? A Soto Thompson.
Q What is the name of his daughter who is the mother of these children A Amanda Thompson, now Sevier.
Q What was the name of her husband? A Lewis Sevier.
Q Are Amanda and Lewis living? A Yes, sir.
Q Living together as man and wife? A Yes, sir.
Q Are these children Tom and Lena living? A Yes, sir.

Amanda Sevier is identified as Amanda Thompson on Creek Indian card field No. 2207 opposite roll No. 6734.

Q What Creek town did Amanda Sevier belong to? A Tokpofka.
Q Is her daughter Lucy living? A No, sir the child is dead.
Q What is the post office address of Lewis and Amanda? A Burney.

The affidavits now on file in this office in the matter of the birth of Tom and Lena Sevier are insufficient inasmuch as they are not signed by affidavits of two disinterested witnesses and you are requested to secure the affidavits of two disinterested witnesses and blank forms will be given you for that purpose. These blanks should be filled out and sent in as soon as possible.

I, Anna Garrigues, on oath state that the above and foregoing is a true and correct transcript of my stenographic notes as taken in said cause on said date.

                                        Anna Garrigues

Subscribed and sworn to before me
this 28 day of February 1906.

                                        J McDermott
                                        Notary Public.

Western District
Indian Territory, SS,

      We The Undersigned on oath state that we are personaly[sic] aquinted[sic] with Amanda Thompson   Wife of   Lewis Sevier   and that on or about the   24th   day of June 1902 a   male   child was born to them and had been named,   Tom Sevier   that said child was living March 4, 1905.

      We further state that we have no interest in the above case.

Applications for Enrollment of Creek Newborn
Act of 1905   Volume XI

Witness to mark.

_____
E A Fowler
C. L. Fowler
_____

Willie Hope
Her
Mind x Hope
mark

Subscribed and sworn to before me
this the 23rd day of February 1906.
My Commission Expires July 13th 1908.

J.W. Fowler
Notary Public.

_____

BIRTH AFFIDAVIT.

DEPARTMENT OF THE INTERIOR.
COMMISSION TO THE FIVE CIVILIZED TRIBES.

_____

IN RE APPLICATION FOR ENROLLMENT, as a citizen of the Creek Nation, of Tom Sevier, born on the 24 day of June, 1902

Name of Father: Lewis Sevier	a citizen of the	Creek Nation.
Name of Mother: Amanda Sevier	a citizen of the	Creek Nation.

Postoffice   Burney I.T.

_____

AFFIDAVIT OF MOTHER.

UNITED STATES OF AMERICA, Indian Territory, ⎫
Western   DISTRICT.   ⎬

I, Amanda Sevier, on oath state that I am 24 years of age and a citizen by Blood, of the Creek Nation; that I am the lawful wife of Lewis Sevier, who is a citizen, by Blood of the Creek Nation; that a male child was born to me on 24 day of June, 1902, that said child has been named Tom Sevier, and was living March 4, 1905.

Amanda Sevier

Witnesses To Mark:
{

Subscribed and sworn to before me this 24 day of April, 1905.

Joseph C. Morton
Notary Public.

My Commission Expires Feb 29th 1908

_____

Applications for Enrollment of Creek Newborn
Act of 1905   Volume XI

AFFIDAVIT OF ATTENDING PHYSICIAN OR MID-WIFE.

UNITED STATES OF AMERICA, Indian Territory,
.... DISTRICT.

  I, ..., a ...., on oath state that I attended on Mrs. ...., wife of .... on the .... day of ...., 1......; that there was born to her on said date a .... child; that said child is now living and is said to have been named ....

     She states to me that She had no midwife

             ....

Witnesses To Mark: or Doctor But was alone

{ ....
 ....

  Subscribed and sworn to before me this .... day of ...., 1........

            Joseph C Morton
            Notary Public.

Western District
Indian Territory, SS,

  We The Undersigned on oath state that we are personaly[sic] aquinted[sic] with Amanda Thompson   Wife of   Lewis Sevier   and that on or about the   27   day of January   1904 a   Female   child was born to them and had been named,   Lena Sevier that said child was living March 4, 1905.

  We further state that we have no interest in the above case.

Witness to mark.

            Willie Hope
_____
            Her
E A Fowler   Mind x Hope
C. L. Fowler   mark

Subscribed and sworn to before me
this the 23rd day of February 1906.
My Commission Expires July 13th 1908.

            J.W. Fowler
            Notary Public.

Applications for Enrollment of Creek Newborn
Act of 1905 Volume XI

BIRTH AFFIDAVIT.

DEPARTMENT OF THE INTERIOR.
COMMISSION TO THE FIVE CIVILIZED TRIBES.

IN RE APPLICATION FOR ENROLLMENT, as a citizen of the Creek Nation, of Lena Sevier, born on the 27 day of January, 1904

Name of Father: Lewis Sevier	a citizen of the Creek	Nation.
Name of Mother: Amanda Sevier	a citizen of the Creek	Nation.

Postoffice Burney I.T.

AFFIDAVIT OF MOTHER.

UNITED STATES OF AMERICA, Indian Territory,
Western DISTRICT.

I, Amanda Sevier, on oath state that I am 24 years of age and a citizen by Blood, of the Creek Nation; that I am the lawful wife of Lewis Seviere[sic], who is a citizen, by Blood of the Creek Nation; that a Female child was born to me on the 27 day of January, 1904, that said child has been named Lena Sevier, and was living March 4, 1905.

Amanda Sevier

Witnesses To Mark:

Subscribed and sworn to before me this 26 day of April, 1905.

Joseph C. Morton
Notary Public.

My Commission Expires Feb 29=1908

AFFIDAVIT OF ATTENDING PHYSICIAN OR MID-WIFE.

UNITED STATES OF AMERICA, Indian Territory,
.... DISTRICT.

I, ..., a ...., on oath state that I attended on Mrs. ...., wife of .... on the .... day of ...., 1.......; that there was born to her on said date a .... child; that said child is now living and is said to have been named

She also states that She was alone at the

Witnesses To Mark: above mentioned date

Applications for Enrollment of Creek Newborn
Act of 1905   Volume XI

Subscribed and sworn to before me this .... day of ...., 1........

Joseph C Morton
Notary Public.

N.C._____

DEPARTMENT OF THE INTERIOR,
COMMISSIONER TO THE FIVE CIVILIZED TRIBES.
BURNEY, I. T., AUGUST 24, 1906.

In the matter of the application for the enrollment of two unnamed minor children of Louis Sevier and Amanda Thompson, as citizens by blood of the Creek Nation.

AMANDA SEVIER, being duly sworn, testified as follows:

Through Alex Posey, Official Interpreter.

BY THE COMMISSIONER:

Q What is your name? A Amanda Sevier.
Q How old are you? A About 26.
Q What is your postoffice address? A Burney.
Q Are you a citizen of the Creek Nation? A Yes sir.
Q To what Creek town do you belong? A Tokpafka[sic].
Q What was your maiden name? A Amanda Thompson.
Q Who are your parents? A Sotto and Nancy Thompson; both are dead.
Q To what Creek towns did you parents belong? A My father belonged to Tuluathlocco and my mother belonged to Tokpafka[sic].
Q Are you married? A Yes sir.
Q To whom? A Louis Sevier.
Q Are you lawfully married to him? A Yes sir.
Q To what Creek town does Louis Sevier belong? A Tulsa Canadian town?[sic]
Q Application has been made to the Commissioner for the enrolment of two minor children of yours. Have you such children? A Yes sir.
Q Have you made application for their enrolment? A Yes sir.
Q What are their names? A Solomon and Lena Sevier.
Q How old is Solomon? A Four years old.
Q How old is Lena? A Two years old. The Postmaster at Hitchita fixed up the papers for me, and sent them in to the Commissioner for me. I received notice from the Commissioner afterwards that certain witness were necessary as to the birth of the children and I had a Notary Public at Senora fix out some more papers for me about the children. I have not since heard from the Commissioner. I have had another child born to me since.
Q What is the child's name? A Willie. He was born December 5, 1905.

Applications for Enrollment of Creek Newborn
Act of 1905   Volume XI

Q Have you made application for the enrollment of Willie? A No sir, I heard that application was being made for the enrollment of children this year, but I made no attempt to have the child enrolled, having no opportunity to appear in person before the Commissioner.
Q Why did not your husband make application for the child? A He belongs to the Snake Faction and was opposed to having the child enrolled, but the family has enough land to spare the child a few acres if it has lost its rights.

James B. Myers, being first duly sworn, states, that as stenographer to the Commissioner to the Five Civilized Tribes, he recorded the testimony in the foregoing proceedings, and that the above is a true, and correct transcript of his stenographic notes thereof.

James B Myers

Subscribed and sworn to before me this 30 day of August, 1906.

Alex Posey
Notary Public.

N.C. 890

Muskogee, Indian Territory, October 6, 1905.

Lewis Sevier,
    Burney, Indian Territory.

Dear Sir:

In the matter of the application for the enrollment of your minor children, Tom and Lena Sevier, as citizens by blood of the Creek Nation, this office is unable to identify your wife, Amanda Sevier, on its roll of Creek citizens.

You are requested to state her maiden name, the names of her parents, the Creek Indian town to which she belongs, and, if possible, the roll number which appears on her deeds to land in the Creek Nation.

Respectfully,
Commissioner.

Applications for Enrollment of Creek Newborn
Act of 1905   Volume XI

N.C. 890

Muskogee, Indian Territory, October 19, 1905.

Amanda Sevier,
    Care Lewis Sevier,
        Burney, Indian Territory.

Dear Madam:

    In the matter of the application for the enrollment of your minor children, Tom Sevier, born June 24, 1902, and Lena Sevier, born January 27, 1904, this office is unable to identify you on its roll of citizens by blood of the Creek Nation; you are requested to state your maiden name, the names of your parents, the Creek Indian town to which you belong, and, if possible, numbers which appear on your deeds and allotment certificate.

    You are further advised that this office desires the affidavits of two disinterested witnesses relative to the birth of each of said children. Said affidavits must set forth the names of said children, the date of their birth, the names of their parents and whether or not they were living on March 4, 1905.

                     Respectfully,
                                Commissioner.

NC-890

Muskogee, Indian Territory, December 16, 1905.

Amanda Sevier,
    Care of Joseph J. Morton,
        Hitchita, Indian Territory.

Dear Madam:

    In the matter of the application for the enrollment of your minor children, Tom Sevier, born June 24, 1902, and Lena Sevier, born January 27, 1904, as citizens by blood of the Creek Nation, this Office is unable to identify you on its final rolls of citizens by blood of the Creek Nation. It is necessary that you should be so identified before the right to enrollment of said children can be determined.

    You are requested to write this Office at an early date, giving your maiden name, the names of your parents and other members of your family, the Creek Indian Town to which you belong, and, if possible, your name and roll number as same appear on your allotment certificate or deeds to land in the Creek Nation.

    You are also requested to furnish this Office with the affidavits of two disinterested persons relative to the birth of your said children, and blanks for that purpose are herewith enclosed.

Applications for Enrollment of Creek Newborn
Act of 1905 Volume XI

These matters should receive your prompt attention.

Respectfully,

Commissioner.

2 Dis

REFER IN REPLY TO THE FOLLOWING:
N.C. ____

DEPARTMENT OF THE INTERIOR,
COMMISSIONER TO THE FIVE CIVILIZED TRIBES.

Calvin, Indian Territory, August 31, 1906.

Commissioner to the Five Civilized Tribes,
Muskogee, Indian Territory.

Sir:

There is inclosed herewith the testimony of Amanda Sevier, taken by the Creek Field Party August 24, 1906, in the matter of the application for the enrollment of two unnamed minor children of Louis Sevier and Amanda Thompson, as citizens by blood of the Creek Nation.

Respectfully,

Alex Posey
In Charge,
Creek Field Party.

JBM

DEPARTMENT OF THE INTERIOR,
COMMISSION TO THE FIVE CIVILIZED TRIBES.

Okmulgee, Indian Territory I. T., April 10, 1905.

In the matter of the application for the enrollment of Sarah Grayson as a citizen by blood of the Creek Nation.

BETTIE ADAMS, being duly sworn, testified as follows:

BY COMMISSION:
Q What is your name? A Bettie Adams.

Applications for Enrollment of Creek Newborn
Act of 1905 Volume XI

Q How old are you? A Thirty-two.
Q To what town do you belong? A Okmulgee.
Q Are you a citizen of the Creek Nation? A Yes, sir.
Q To what town do you belong? A Ketchapataka.
Q Do you make application for the enrollment of your minor child, Sarah Grayson, as a citizen of the Creek Nation? A Yes, sir.
Q Who is the father of that child? A George Grayson.
Q Is he your lawful husband? A No, sir.
Q Were you ever married? A No, sir.
Q Did you ever live together as man and wife? A No, sir.
Q Is he a citizen of the Creek Nation? A Yes, sir.
Q To what town does he belong? A North Fork Colored.
Q Does he acknowledge Sarah as his own? A Yes, sir
Q Does he contribute towards the support of the child? A No, sir, he never has bought it anything.

---oooOOOooo---

I, D. C. Skaggs, on oath state that the above and foregoing is a full and true transcript of my stenographic notes as taken in said cause on said date.

D. C. Skaggs

Subscribed and sworn to before me this 24 day of July, 1905.

J. McDermott
Notary Public.

BIRTH AFFIDAVIT.
DEPARTMENT OF THE INTERIOR.
COMMISSION TO THE FIVE CIVILIZED TRIBES.

IN RE APPLICATION FOR ENROLLMENT, as a citizen of the Creek Nation, of Sarah Grayson , born on the 28 day of Sept , 1902

Name of Father: George Grayson   a citizen of the   Creek   Nation.
North Fork Col. Town
Name of Mother: Bettie Adams   a citizen of the   Creek   Nation.
Ketchapatcha Town
                        Postoffice   Okmulgee, Ind. Ter.

Applications for Enrollment of Creek Newborn
Act of 1905 Volume XI

AFFIDAVIT OF MOTHER.

UNITED STATES OF AMERICA, Indian Territory, }
   Western   DISTRICT.   Child is present

    I, Bettie Adams , on oath state that I am about 38 years of age and a citizen by blood , of the Creek Nation; that I am not the lawful wife of George Grayson , who is a citizen, by blood of the Creek Nation; that a female child was born to me on 28 day of September , 1902 , that said child has been named Sarah Grayson , and was living March 4, 1905.

                                                          her
Witnesses To Mark: Bettie x Adams
  { Alex Posey   mark
  { DC Skaggs

    Subscribed and sworn to before me this 10 day of April , 1905.

                                         Drennan C Skaggs
                                         Notary Public.

AFFIDAVIT OF ATTENDING PHYSICIAN OR MID-WIFE.

UNITED STATES OF AMERICA, Indian Territory, }
   Western   DISTRICT.

                                                                                    iss
    I, Mahaley Adams , a midwife , on oath state that I attended on M~~rs~~. Bettie Adams , ~~wife of~~ (blank) ~~on the (blank) day of (blank)~~ , 1~~90~~ ; that there was born to her on said date a female child; that said child was living March 4, 1905, and is said to have been named Sarah Grayson

                                                 her
Witnesses To Mark: Mahaley x Adams
  { Alex Posey   mark
  { DC Skaggs

    Subscribed and sworn to before me 10 day of April, 1905.

                                         Drennan C Skaggs
                                         Notary Public.

Applications for Enrollment of Creek Newborn
Act of 1905   Volume XI

(The letter below typed as given.)

NC-891
NC-973

OKMULGEE, I. T. 11/17,05.

Hon Tams Bixby,
      Commissioner.

in reply to your letter one is Bettie Adams child name Sarah Grayson and Mary Adams child name Pleses Tobler I got all home I am gardien of the holden I want to field for thouse childem
very yours Respectfully
                    (signed)   T. J. Adams,

                              ans soon

NC-891
NC-973

                              Muskogee, Indian Territory, November 24, 1905.

T. J. Adams,
      Okmulgee, Indian Territory.

Dear Sir:

      Receipt is acknowledged of your letter of November 17, 1905, relative to the status of the application for the enrollment of Sarah Grayson and Pleasant Tobler as citizens by blood of the Creek Nation.

      In reply you are advised that the matter of the enrollment of said Sarah Grayson is pending before the Secretary of the Interior, and that of Pleasant Tobler is pending before this Office, and that when final action is had in same, the parties in interest will be duly notified with regard to filing.

                              Respectfully,
                                                Acting Commissioner.

Applications for Enrollment of Creek Newborn
Act of 1905   Volume XI

(The letter below typed as given.)

N.C. 892

Muskogee, Indian Territory, October 6, 1905.

Willie Gray,
    Henryetta, Indian Territory.

Dear Sir:

    In the matter of the application for the enrollment of your minor children, Fannie and Susie Gray, as citizens by blood of the Creek Nation, this office is unable to identiry your wife, Millie Gray, on its roll of Creek citizens.

    You are requested to state her maiden name, the names of her parents, the Creek Indian town to which she belongs, and, if possible, the roll number which appears on her deeds to land in the Creek Nation.

                                Respectfully,
                                              Commissioner.

N.C. 892

                                          Henryetta I T
                                          Octo 10 05

Mr. Tams Bixby
    Muskogee, I T

Dear Sir

    You requested me to send parents[sic] names of this children Millie Checotah first afterward she married and now she is Millie Gray, she belongs to Cussetah town and this children and I also belongs to Cusseetah Town.

                                    Yours truly
                                    Willie Gray

Applications for Enrollment of Creek Newborn
Act of 1905   Volume XI

BIRTH AFFIDAVIT.

DEPARTMENT OF THE INTERIOR.
COMMISSION TO THE FIVE CIVILIZED TRIBES.

IN RE APPLICATION FOR ENROLLMENT, as a citizen of the Creek Nation, of Susie Gray, born on the 15 day of March, 1904

Name of Father: Willie Gray   a citizen of the   Creek   Nation.
Cussehta Town
Name of Mother: Millie Gray   a citizen of the   Creek   Nation.
Cussehta Town

Postoffice   Henryetta, Ind. Terr.

Child present

AFFIDAVIT OF MOTHER.

UNITED STATES OF AMERICA, Indian Territory, }
    Western   DISTRICT.

I, Millie Gray, on oath state that I am about 35 years of age and a citizen by blood, of the Creek Nation; that I am the lawful wife of Willie Gray, who is a citizen, by blood of the Creek Nation; that a female child was born to me on 15 day of March, 1904, that said child has been named Susie Gray, and was living March 4, 1905.

                                                her
                                    Millie x Gray
Witnesses To Mark: mark
{ DC Skaggs
{ Alex Posey

Subscribed and sworn to before me this 10 day of April, 1905.

                                    Drennan C Skaggs
                                        Notary Public.

AFFIDAVIT OF ATTENDING PHYSICIAN OR MID-WIFE.

UNITED STATES OF AMERICA, Indian Territory, }
    Western   DISTRICT.

I, Melissa Wiley, a mid-wife, on oath state that I attended on Mrs. Millie Gray, wife of Willie Gray on or about the 15 day of March, 1904 ; that there was born to her on said date a female child; that said child was living March 4, 1905, and is said to have been named Susie Gray

                                             her
                                    Mellissa[sic] x Wiley
                                          mark

Applications for Enrollment of Creek Newborn
Act of 1905   Volume XI

Witnesses To Mark:
{ DC Skaggs
{ Alex Posey

    Subscribed and sworn to before me 10 day of April, 1905.

                                 Drennan C Skaggs
                                 Notary Public.

BIRTH AFFIDAVIT.

DEPARTMENT OF THE INTERIOR.
COMMISSION TO THE FIVE CIVILIZED TRIBES.

IN RE APPLICATION FOR ENROLLMENT, as a citizen of the Creek Nation, of Fannie Gray, born on the 15 day of September, 1901

Name of Father: Willie Gray   a citizen of the   Creek   Nation.
Cussehta Town
Name of Mother: Millie Gray   a citizen of the   Creek   Nation.
Cussehta Town

                    Postoffice   Henryetta, I. T.

                                  Child present.

AFFIDAVIT OF MOTHER.

UNITED STATES OF AMERICA, Indian Territory, }
    Western   DISTRICT. }

    I, Millie Gray, on oath state that I am 35 years of age and a citizen by blood, of the Creek Nation; that I am the lawful wife of Willie Gray, who is a citizen, by blood of the Creek Nation; that a female child was born to me on 15 day of September, 1901, that said child has been named Fannie Gray, and was living March 4, 1905.

                                          her
                                  Millie x Gray

Witnesses To Mark: mark
{ DC Skaggs
{ Alex Posey

    Subscribed and sworn to before me this 10 day of April, 1905.

                                 Drennan C Skaggs
                                 Notary Public.

Applications for Enrollment of Creek Newborn
Act of 1905 Volume XI

AFFIDAVIT OF ATTENDING PHYSICIAN OR MID-WIFE.

UNITED STATES OF AMERICA, Indian Territory,
Western DISTRICT.

I, Mulley Scott, a mid-wife, on oath state that I attended on Mrs. Millie Gray, wife of Willie Gray on or about the 15 day of September, 1901; that there was born to her on said date a female child; that said child was living March 4, 1905, and is said to have been named Fannie Gray

her
Mulley x Scott
mark

Witnesses To Mark:
{ DC Skaggs
{ Alex Posey

Subscribed and sworn to before me 10 day of April, 1905.

Drennan C Skaggs
Notary Public.

BIRTH AFFIDAVIT.

DEPARTMENT OF THE INTERIOR.
COMMISSION TO THE FIVE CIVILIZED TRIBES.

IN RE APPLICATION FOR ENROLLMENT, as a citizen of the Creek Nation, of Charlie S Berryhill, born on the 21 day of April, 1902

Name of Father: Columbus Berryhill   a citizen of the   Creek   Nation.
Name of Mother: Emma Berryhill   a citizen of the   Creek   Nation.

Postoffice   Stonebluff I T

AFFIDAVIT OF MOTHER.

UNITED STATES OF AMERICA, Indian Territory,
Western DISTRICT.

I, Emma Berryhill, on oath state that I am 38 years of age and a citizen by Blood, of the Creek Nation; that I am the lawful wife of Columbus Berryhill, who

Applications for Enrollment of Creek Newborn
Act of 1905   Volume XI

is a citizen, by Blood of the Creek Nation; that a male child was born to me on 21 day of April, 1902, that said child has been named Charlie S Berryhill, and was living March 4, 1905.

Emma Berryhill

Witnesses To Mark:
{

Subscribed and sworn to before me this 26th day of April, 1905.

Ralph Dresback
Notary Public.

AFFIDAVIT OF ATTENDING PHYSICIAN OR MID-WIFE.

UNITED STATES OF AMERICA, Indian Territory,
Western   DISTRICT.

I, Mrs. A A Berryhill, a mid-wife, on oath state that I attended on Mrs. Emma Berryhill, wife of Columbus Berryhill on the 21 day of April, 1902; that there was born to her on said date a male child; that said child was living March 4, 1905, and is said to have been named Charlie S Berryhill   her
                                                                                  Mrs A A x Berryhill
Witnesses To Mark: mark
  { C O Arnold
    N.C. Dresback

Subscribed and sworn to before me this 26th day of April, 1905.

Ralph Dresback
Notary Public.

BIRTH AFFIDAVIT.

DEPARTMENT OF THE INTERIOR.
COMMISSION TO THE FIVE CIVILIZED TRIBES.

IN RE APPLICATION FOR ENROLLMENT, as a citizen of the Creek Nation, of Emma C Berryhill, born on the 24 day of Sep, 1904

Name of Father: Columbus Berryhill   a citizen of the   Creek   Nation.
Name of Mother: Emma Berryhill   a citizen of the   Creek   Nation.

Postoffice   Stonebluff I T

Applications for Enrollment of Creek Newborn
Act of 1905   Volume XI

AFFIDAVIT OF MOTHER.

UNITED STATES OF AMERICA, Indian Territory,
Western   DISTRICT.

I, Emma Berryhill, on oath state that I am 38 years of age and a citizen by Blood, of the Creek Nation; that I am the lawful wife of Columbus Berryhill, who is a citizen, by Blood of the Creek Nation; that a female child was born to me on 24 day of September, 1904, that said child has been named Emma C Berryhill, and was living March 4, 1905.

             Emma Berryhill

Witnesses To Mark:

Subscribed and sworn to before me this 26 day of April, 1905.

             Ralph Dresback
             Notary Public.

AFFIDAVIT OF ATTENDING PHYSICIAN OR MID-WIFE.

UNITED STATES OF AMERICA, Indian Territory,
Western   DISTRICT.

I, Mrs. A A Berryhill, a mid-wife, on oath state that I attended on Mrs. Emma Berryhill, wife of Columbus Berryhill on the 24 day of September, 1904; that there was born to her on said date a female child; that said child was living March 4, 1905, and is said to have been named Emma C Berryhill

             her
          (Mrs) A A x Berryhill

Witnesses To Mark: mark
 CO Arnold
 N.C. Dresback

Subscribed and sworn to before me this 26th day of April, 1905.

             Ralph Dresback
             Notary Public.

Applications for Enrollment of Creek Newborn
Act of 1905 Volume XI

United States of America)
Indian Territory) ss.
Western District.)

I, S. J. Logan of Brush Hill postoffice, Indian Territory, and I, Siah Gray, of Fame post office, Indian Territory, being first duly sworn does each for himself depose and say, that he is well acquainted with R. W. Huckaby and Elcy Huckaby his wife, and that a female child was born to me on day of , 190, that said child has been named , and was living March 4, 1905. was born to said R. W. Huckaby and Elcy Huckaby on or about the 29th day of March 1903, which said child is now living and is known as Ora May Huckaby.

S. J. Logan

Siah Gray

Subscribed and sworn to before me this 23rd day of October, 1905.

Fred H. Smith
Notary Public.
My Commission expires March 12th 1907.

BIRTH AFFIDAVIT.

DEPARTMENT OF THE INTERIOR.
COMMISSION TO THE FIVE CIVILIZED TRIBES.

IN RE APPLICATION FOR ENROLLMENT, as a citizen of the Creek Nation, of Randolph Huckaby, born on the 7 day of Dec. , 1904 and died Dec. 8, 1904

Name of Father: R.W. Huckaby a citizen of the United States ~~Nation~~.
Name of Mother: Elcy Huckaby a citizen of the Creek Nation.
Arbaka Deep Fork Town
Postoffice Okmulgee, Ind. Ter.

AFFIDAVIT OF MOTHER.

UNITED STATES OF AMERICA, Indian Territory, }
Western DISTRICT.

I, Elcy Huckaby , on oath state that I am 33 years of age and a citizen by blood, of the Creek Nation; that I am the lawful wife of R. W. Huckaby , who is a citizen, ~~by~~ *(blank)* of the United States Nation; that a male child was born to me on 7 day of December , 1904 , that said child ~~has been~~ was named Randolph Huckaby , and ~~was living March 4, 1905~~. died Dec. 8, 1904.

191

Applications for Enrollment of Creek Newborn
Act of 1905   Volume XI

Witnesses To Mark:
{

Elcy Huckaby

Subscribed and sworn to before me this 10 day of April, 1905.

Drennan C Skaggs
Notary Public.

AFFIDAVIT OF ATTENDING PHYSICIAN OR MID-WIFE.

UNITED STATES OF AMERICA, Indian Territory,
  Western   DISTRICT.   }

my wife
I, R. W. Huckaby, ~~a (blank)~~, on oath state that I attended on ^ Mrs. *(blank)*, ~~wife of~~ *(blank)* on the 7 day of December, 1904; that there was born to her on said date a male child; that said child ~~was living March 4, 1905~~, and ~~is said to have been~~ was named Randolph Huckaby   died Dec 8, 1904

R W Huckaby

Witnesses To Mark:
{

Subscribed and sworn to before me this 10 day of April, 1905.

Drennan C Skaggs
Notary Public.

NC 894   JLD
DEPARTMENT OF THE INTERIOR,
COMMISSIONER TO THE FIVE CIVILIZED TRIBES.

In the matter of the application for the enrollment of Randolph Huckaby, deceased, as a citizen by blood of the Creek Nation.

....

STATEMENT AND ORDER.

The record in this case shows that on April 13, 1905, application was made, in affidavit form, for the enrollment of Randolph Huckaby, deceased, as a citizen by blood of the Creek Nation, under the provisions of the Act of Congress approved March 3, 1905.

It appears from the affidavit filed in this matter that said Randolph Huckaby, deceased, was born December 7, 1904, and died December 8, 1904.

The Act of Congress approved March 3, 1905, (33 Stats., 1048), provided[sic]:

Applications for Enrollment of Creek Newborn
Act of 1905 Volume XI

"That the Commission to the Five Civilized Tribes is authorized for sixty days after the date of the approval of this act to receive and consider applications for enrollment, of children, <u>born subsequent to May twenty-fifth, nineteen hundred and one, and prior to March fourth, nineteen hundred and five, and living on said latter date</u>, to citizens of the Creek tribe of Indians whose enrollment has been approved by the Secretary of the Interior prior to the approval of this act; and to enroll and make allotments to such children."

It is, therefore, ordered that the application for the enrollment of said Randolph Huckaby, deceased, as a citizen by blood of the Creek Nation be, and the same is, hereby dismissed.

Tams Bixby Commissioner.

Muskogee, Indian Territory.
JAN 4 – 1907

BIRTH AFFIDAVIT.

DEPARTMENT OF THE INTERIOR.
COMMISSION TO THE FIVE CIVILIZED TRIBES.

IN RE APPLICATION FOR ENROLLMENT, as a citizen of the Creek Nation, of Ora Huckaby, born on the *(blank)* day of *(blank)*, 1*(blank)*

Name of Father: R.W. Huckaby	a citizen of the U. S.	Nation.
Name of Mother: Elsie Huckaby	a citizen of the Creek	Nation.

Postoffice   Okmulgee, I. T.

AFFIDAVIT OF MOTHER.

UNITED STATES OF AMERICA, Indian Territory,
    Western   DISTRICT.

I, Elsie Huckaby, on oath state that I am 33 years of age and a citizen by blood, of the Creek Nation; that I am the lawful wife of R. W. Huckaby, who is a citizen, by *(blank)* of the United States Nation; that a female child was born to me on 29th day of March, 1903, that said child has been named Ora Huckaby, and was living March 4, 1905.

Elsie Huckaby

Witnesses To Mark:

Applications for Enrollment of Creek Newborn
Act of 1905   Volume XI

Subscribed and sworn to before me this 14th day of November , 1905.

Fred H Smith
Notary Public.
My Commission expires Mch 12" 1907.

BIRTH AFFIDAVIT.
DEPARTMENT OF THE INTERIOR.
COMMISSION TO THE FIVE CIVILIZED TRIBES.

IN RE APPLICATION FOR ENROLLMENT, as a citizen of the Creek Nation, of Ora May Huckaby, born on the 29th day of March , 1903

Name of Father: R.W. Huckaby   non a citizen of the   Creek   Nation.
Name of Mother: Elcy Huckaby   a citizen of the   Creek   Nation.

Postoffice   Okmulgee, Ind. Ter.

AFFIDAVIT OF MOTHER.

UNITED STATES OF AMERICA, Indian Territory, }
       Western   DISTRICT.

I, Elcy Huckaby , on oath state that I am 32 years of age and a citizen by birth, of the Creek   Nation; that I am the lawful wife of R. W. Huckaby , who is not a citizen, by *(blank)* of the Creek   Nation; that a Female   child was born to me on 29th day of March , 1903 , that said child has been named Ora May Huckaby , and was living March 4, 1905.

Elcy Huckaby
Witnesses To Mark:
{

Subscribed and sworn to before me this 23rd day of October , 1905.

Fred H Smith
Notary Public.
My Commission expires March 12th 1907.

Applications for Enrollment of Creek Newborn
Act of 1905 Volume XI

BIRTH AFFIDAVIT.
DEPARTMENT OF THE INTERIOR.
COMMISSION TO THE FIVE CIVILIZED TRIBES.

IN RE APPLICATION FOR ENROLLMENT, as a citizen of the Creek Nation, of Ora Huckaby, born on the 26[sic] day of March , 1903

Name of Father: R.W. Huckaby   a citizen of the United States ~~Nation~~.
Name of Mother: Elcy Huckaby (nee Lynch)   a citizen of the   Creek   Nation.
Arbaka Deep Fork Town
          Postoffice   Okmulgee, Ind. Ter.

AFFIDAVIT OF MOTHER.

UNITED STATES OF AMERICA, Indian Territory,
  Western   DISTRICT.   Child is present

   I, Elcy Huckaby , on oath state that I am 33 years of age and a citizen by blood, of the Creek Nation; that I am the lawful wife of R. W. Huckaby , who is a citizen, ~~by~~ *(blank)* of the United States Nation; that a female child was born to me on 26 day of March , 1903 , that said child has been named Ora Huckaby , and was living March 4, 1905.

               Elcy Huckaby
Witnesses To Mark:
{

   Subscribed and sworn to before me this 10 day of April , 1905.

              Drennan C Skaggs
              Notary Public.

AFFIDAVIT OF ATTENDING PHYSICIAN OR MID-WIFE.

UNITED STATES OF AMERICA, Indian Territory,
  Western   DISTRICT.

                     my wife
   I, R. W. Huckaby , ~~a (blank)~~ , on oath state that I attended on ^ Mrs. Elcy Huckaby , ~~wife of~~ *(blank)* on the 26 day of March , 1903 ; that there was born to her on said date a female child; that said child was living March 4, 1905, and ~~is said to have been~~ has named Ora Huckaby
              R W Huckaby
Witnesses To Mark:
{

Applications for Enrollment of Creek Newborn
Act of 1905   Volume XI

Subscribed and sworn to before me this 10 day of April, 1905.

                                      Drennan C Skaggs
                                      Notary Public.

NC 894

                              Muskogee, Indian Territory, October 19, 1905.

Elcy Huckaby,
    Care R.W. Huckaby,
        Okmulgee, Indian Territory.

Dear Madam:

    In the matter of the application for the enrollment of your minor child, Ora Huckaby, born March 26, 1903, as a citizen by blood of the Creek Nation, this office desires affidavit of the midwife or physician in attendance at the birth of said child and a blank for that purpose is enclosed herewith.

    In the event that there was no physician or midwife in attendance when said child was born, it will be necessary for you to furnish this office with the affidavits of two disinterested witnesses relative to her birth. Said affidavits must set forth the name of said child, the date of her birth, the names of her parents, and whether or not she was living on March 4, 1905.

                    Respectfully,

BC   Commissioner.
Env.

N.C. 894

                              Muskogee, Indian Territory, October 30, 1905.

Elsie Huckaby,
    Care R.W. Huckaby,
        Okmulgee, Indian Territory.

Dear Madam:

    In the matter of the application for the enrollment of your minor child, Ora Huckaby, as a citizen by blood of the Creek Nation; you state in your affidavit executed April 10, 1905, that said child was born March 26, 1903; your name is signed to both of said affidavits Elcy Huckaby and you are identified on the final roll of citizens by blood of the Creek Nation as Elsie Huckaby.

    In order that these discrepancies may be corrected, there is herewith enclosed form of birth affidavit which has been partially filled out; you are requested to execute

Applications for Enrollment of Creek Newborn
Act of 1905   Volume XI

same, giving the correct date of the birth of said Ora Huckaby and sign your name to said affidavit as the same appears in the body thereof.

This matter should receive your prompt attention.

NC 894
Respectfully,
Commissioner.

NC-894

OKMULGEE, I. T. November 14th, 1905.

Hon. Tams Bixby,
   Commissioner to the Five Civilized Tribes,
      Muskogee, I. T.

Dear Sir: N. C. 894

In the matter of the enrollment of my minor child, Ora Huckaby, I herewith return affidavit enclosed in yours of Oct. 30th duly sworn to.

Regarding the discrepancy in the date of the child's birth, I beg to say that the correct date if March 29th 1903, and I so intended to give it in my affidavit of April 10th 1905, and if it is given therein as of March 26th it is an error.

Respectfully,
(signed)   ELSIE HUCKAR[sic].

BIRTH AFFIDAVIT.

DEPARTMENT OF THE INTERIOR.
COMMISSION TO THE FIVE CIVILIZED TRIBES.

IN RE APPLICATION FOR ENROLLMENT, as a citizen of the Creek Nation, of Mary Morrison , born on the 24 day of September, 1903

Name of Father: Watie Morrison   a citizen of the   Creek   Nation.
Coweta Town
Name of Mother: Eliza Morrison   a citizen of the   Creek   Nation.
Coweta Town

Applications for Enrollment of Creek Newborn
Act of 1905   Volume XI

Postoffice   Lenna, I.T.

AFFIDAVIT OF MOTHER.

UNITED STATES OF AMERICA, Indian Territory,
Western   DISTRICT.

I, Eliza Morrison , on oath state that I am about 24 years of age and a citizen by blood , of the Creek Nation; that I am the lawful wife of Watie Morrison , who is a citizen, by blood of the Creek Nation; that a female child was born to me on 24 day of September , 1903 , that said child has been named Mary Morrison , and was living March 4, 1905.

Eliza Morrison

Witnesses To Mark:

Subscribed and sworn to before me this 4 day of April , 1905.

Drennan C Skaggs
Notary Public.

AFFIDAVIT OF ATTENDING PHYSICIAN OR MID-WIFE.

UNITED STATES OF AMERICA, Indian Territory,
Western   DISTRICT.

I, Peggie Turk , a midwife , on oath state that I attended on Mrs. Eliza Morrison , wife of Watie Morrison on the 24 day of September , 1903 ; that there was born to her on said date a *(blank)* child; that said child was living March 4, 1905, and is said to have been named Mary Morrison

her
Peggie Turk x
Witnesses To Mark: mark
 Roley McIntosh
 Thomas McIntosh

Subscribed and sworn to before me 27 day of April, 1905.
My commission
May 19th 1908   Preston Janway

Notary Public.

Applications for Enrollment of Creek Newborn
Act of 1905   Volume XI

Central District Indian Territory
U S - America
Before me a duly authorized Notary Public in and for above named District --- Personally appeared Lizzy Richard and upon Her oath stated that Enos Vay Mikey was in truthe[sic] and *(illegible)* the son of Josiah Mikey and His wife Lizzy Mikey born to them in Her presence *(illegible)* July the 10- 1901

Lizzie Richard

S C *(Illegible)*
Notary Public

NC. 896.

Muskogee, Indian Territory, July 15, 1905.

Chief Clerk,
    Chickasaw Enrollment Division,
        Muskogee, Indian Territory.

Dear Sir:

    April 29, 1905, application was made to the Commission to the Five Civilized Tribes for the enrollment of Enos Vey Mikey, born July 10, 1901, as a citizen by blood of the Creek Nation. It is stated in said application that the father of said child is Josiah Mikey, a citizen of the Chickasaw Nation, and that the mother is Lizzie Mikey, a citizen of the Creek Nation.

    You are requested to inform the Creek Enrollment Division as to whether application has been made for the enrollment of said Enos Vey Mikey, as a citizen of the Chickasaw Nation, and if so, what disposition has been made of the same.

Respectfully,
Commissioner.

Applications for Enrollment of Creek Newborn
Act of 1905   Volume XI

A B

REFER IN REPLY TO THE FOLLOWING:
19-152
NC 152

DEPARTMENT OF THE INTERIOR,
COMMISSIONER TO THE FIVE CIVILIZED TRIBES.

Muskogee, Indian Territory, July 26, 1905.

Clerk in Charge,
    Creek Enrollment Division.

Dear Sir:

    Receipt is hereby acknowledged of your letter of July 15, 1905, requesting to be informed if application has been made for the enrollment as a citizen of the Chickasaw Nation of Enos Vey Mikey, child of Josiah Mikey, a citizen of the Chickasaw Nation and Lizzie Mikey, a citizen of the Creek Nation and if so what disposition has been made of the same.

    In reply to your letter you are advised that it appears from the records of this office that Josiah Mikey is a Chickasaw freedman and it does not that application was ever made to the Commission to the Five Civilized Tribes for the enrollment of Enos Vey Mikey as a Chickasaw freedman.

                      Respectfully,
                             Tams Bixby   Commissioner.

NC 896

Muskogee, Indian Territory, November 13, 1906.

Chief Clerk,
    Choctaw-Chickasaw Enrollment Division,
        General Office.

Dear Sir:

    You are hereby advised that the name of Enos Vey Mikey, born July 10, 1901 to Josiah Mikey, an alleged citizen of the Chickasaw Nation and Lizzie Mikey, a citizen by blood of the Creek Nation, is contained in schedule of minor citizens by blood of the Creek Nation, approved by the Secretary of the Interior, November 27, 1905 opposite Roll number 840.

                      Respectfully,
                                    Commissioner.

Applications for Enrollment of Creek Newborn
Act of 1905   Volume XI

BIRTH AFFIDAVIT.

DEPARTMENT OF THE INTERIOR,
COMMISSION TO THE FIVE CIVILIZED TRIBES.

In Re- Application for Enrollment, as a citizen of the Creek Nation, of Enos Vey Mikey, born on the 10 day of July , 1901

Name of Father: Josiah Mikey (Chickasaw Freedman) Nation.
Name of Mother: Lizzie Mikey a citizen of the Creek Nation.

Post-office   Bristow Ind Tey

AFFIDAVIT OF MOTHER.

UNITED STATES OF AMERICA,
   INDIAN TERRITORY,
Western   District.

I, Lizzie Mikey , on oath state that I am 29 years of age and a citizen by Birth , of the Creek Nation; that I am the lawful wife of Josiah Mikey , who is a citizen, by Chickasaw Freedman Nation; that a male child was born to me on 10 day of July , 1901 , that said child has been named Enos Vey Mikey , and is now living.

                                   Lizzie Mikey

Witnesses To Mark:
  W. J. Ladd

Subscribed and sworn to before me this 27 day of Mch, 1905.

                                   E.W. Sims
                                        Notary Public.

AFFIDAVIT OF ATTENDING PHYSICIAN OR MID-WIFE.

UNITED STATES OF AMERICA,
   INDIAN TERRITORY,
Western   District.

I, Lizzie Richard , a Midwife , on oath state that I attended on Mrs. Lizzie Mikey , wife of Josiah Mikey on the 10 day of July , 1901; that there was born to her on said date a male child; that said child is now living and is said to have been named Enos Vey Mikey

                                   Lizzie Richard

Applications for Enrollment of Creek Newborn
Act of 1905   Volume XI

Witnesses To Mark:
{ Charley Williams
{ Chas Abrams

Subscribed and sworn to before me this 22 day of April, 1905.

E. J. Ball
Notary Public.

BIRTH AFFIDAVIT.

DEPARTMENT OF THE INTERIOR.
COMMISSION TO THE FIVE CIVILIZED TRIBES.

IN RE APPLICATION FOR ENROLLMENT, as a citizen of the Creek Nation, of Susannah Tiger, born on the 21 day of Dec, 1903

Name of Father: John Tiger   a citizen of the   Creek   Nation.
Euchee
Name of Mother: Millie Tiger   a citizen of the   Creek   Nation.
(Euchee)

Postoffice   Bixby

AFFIDAVIT OF MOTHER.

Child Present

UNITED STATES OF AMERICA, Indian Territory,
    Western   DISTRICT.

I, Millie Tiger, on oath state that I am 24 years of age and a citizen by blood, of the Creek Nation; that I am the lawful wife of John Tiger, who is a citizen, by blood of the Creek Nation; that a female child was born to me on 21 day of Dec, 1903, that said child has been named Susannah Tiger, and was living March 4, 1905.

Her
Millie x Tiger
mark

Witnesses To Mark:
{ David Shelby
{ Jesse McDermott

Applications for Enrollment of Creek Newborn
Act of 1905   Volume XI

Subscribed and sworn to before me this 24 day of April, 1905.

>Edw C Griesel
>Notary Public.

AFFIDAVIT OF ATTENDING ~~PHYSICIAN~~ OR MID-WIFE.

UNITED STATES OF AMERICA, Indian Territory, }
    Western   DISTRICT.

I, Rachel Bigpond , a Mid wife , on oath state that I attended on Mrs. Millie Tiger , wife of John Tiger on the 21 day of December , 1903 ; that there was born to her on said date a female child; that said child was living March 4, 1905, and is said to have been named Susannah Tiger

>Mrs. Rachel Bigpond

Witnesses To Mark:
{

Subscribed and sworn to before me 26 day of April, 1905.

(Seal)
>Edw C Griesel
>Notary Public.

BIRTH AFFIDAVIT.

DEPARTMENT OF THE INTERIOR,
COMMISSION TO THE FIVE CIVILIZED TRIBES.

In Re Application for Enrollment, as a citizen of the Muskogee Nation, of Marcellus Holleyman , born on the 13th day of January , 1903

Name of Father: T.E. Holleyman   a citizen of the United States Nation.
Name of Mother: Maggie Holleyman   a citizen of the Muskogee   Nation.

                  Post-office   Okmulgee, Ind. Terry

Applications for Enrollment of Creek Newborn
Act of 1905   Volume XI

AFFIDAVIT OF MOTHER.

UNITED STATES OF AMERICA,
INDIAN TERRITORY,
Western   District.

I, Maggie G Holleyman , on oath state that I am 33 years of age and a citizen by Blood , of the Muskogee Nation; that I am the lawful wife of T.E. Holleyman , who is a citizen, of the U. S. of ~~the~~ A. Nation; that a male child was born to me on the 13th day of January , 1903 , that said child has been named Marcellus Holleyman, and is now living.

Maggie G. Holleyman

WITNESSES TO MARK:
{ T.E. Holleyman
{ Mary Hodge

Subscribed and sworn to before me this 4th day of April , 1903.

Perry K Morton
NOTARY PUBLIC.

AFFIDAVIT OF ATTENDING PHYSICIAN OR MID-WIFE.

UNITED STATES OF AMERICA,
INDIAN TERRITORY,
Western   District.

I, Rebecca L. Mashburn , a mid-wife , on oath state that I attended on Mrs. Maggie Holleyman, wife of T.E. Holleyman on the 13th day of January , 1903 ; that there was born to her on said date a male child; that said child is now living and is said to have been named Marcellus Holleyman

Rebecca L. Mashburn

WITNESSES TO MARK:
{ T.E. Holleyman
{ Mary Hodge

Subscribed and sworn to before me this 4th day of April , 1903.

Perry K Morton
NOTARY PUBLIC.

Applications for Enrollment of Creek Newborn
Act of 1905 Volume XI

BIRTH AFFIDAVIT.
DEPARTMENT OF THE INTERIOR.
COMMISSION TO THE FIVE CIVILIZED TRIBES.

IN RE APPLICATION FOR ENROLLMENT, as a citizen of the Creek Nation, of Marcellus Holleyman, born on the 13 day of January, 1903

Name of Father: T.E. Holleyman   a citizen of the United States Nation.
Name of Mother: Maggie G. Holleym an   a citizen of the Creek Nation.
Eufaula Deep Fork Town
                    Postoffice   Okmulgee, Ind. Ter.

AFFIDAVIT OF MOTHER.

UNITED STATES OF AMERICA, Indian Territory,   Child is not present
Western   DISTRICT.

     I, T.E. Holleyman, on oath state that I am 54 years of age and a citizen by (blank), of the United States Nation; that I am the lawful wife husband of Maggie G. Holleyman, who is a citizen, by blood of the Creek Nation; that a male child was born to me her on 13 day of January, 1903, that said child has been named Marcellus Holleyman, and was living March 4, 1905. That I assisted the mid-wife at the birth of the child; that I was unable to have the midwife to appear in person to make application for the child on account of illness

                                        T. E. Holleyman
Witnesses To Mark:

     Subscribed and sworn to before me this 10 day of April, 1905.

                                        Drennan C Skaggs
                                        Notary Public.

BIRTH AFFIDAVIT.
DEPARTMENT OF THE INTERIOR,
COMMISSION TO THE FIVE CIVILIZED TRIBES.

     In Re Application for Enrollment, as a citizen of the Muskogee Nation, of Marcella Holleyman, born on the 13th day of January, 1903

Name of Father: T.E. Holleyman   a citizen of the United States Nation.
Name of Mother: Maggie Holleyman   a citizen of the Muskogee Nation.

                    Post-office   Okmulgee, Ind. Terry

Applications for Enrollment of Creek Newborn
Act of 1905   Volume XI

AFFIDAVIT OF MOTHER.

UNITED STATES OF AMERICA,
   INDIAN TERRITORY,
Western   District.

I, Maggie G Holleyman , on oath state that I am 33 years of age and a citizen by Blood , of the Muskogee Nation; that I am the lawful wife of T.E. Holleyman , who is a citizen, of the U. S. of ~~the~~ A. Nation; that a female child was born to me on the 13$^{\underline{th}}$ day of January , 1903 , that said child has been named Marcella Holleyman, and is now living.

                                             Maggie G. Holleyman

WITNESSES TO MARK:
- T.E. Holleyman
- Mary Hodge

Subscribed and sworn to before me this 4th day of April , 1903.

                                             Perry K Morton
                                                  NOTARY PUBLIC.

AFFIDAVIT OF ATTENDING PHYSICIAN OR MID-WIFE.

UNITED STATES OF AMERICA,
   INDIAN TERRITORY,
Western   District.

I, Rebecca L. Mashburn , a mid-wife , on oath state that I attended on Mrs. Maggie G. Holleyman, wife of T.E. Holleyman on the 13$^{\underline{th}}$ day of January , 1903 ; that there was born to her on said date a female child; that said child is now living and is said to have been named Marcella Holleyman

                                               her
                                      Rebecca x L. Mashburn

WITNESSES TO MARK: mark
- T.E. Holleyman
- Mary Hodge

Subscribed and sworn to before me this 4th day of April , 1903.

                                             Perry K Morton
                                                  NOTARY PUBLIC.

Applications for Enrollment of Creek Newborn
Act of 1905   Volume XI

BIRTH AFFIDAVIT.
DEPARTMENT OF THE INTERIOR.
COMMISSION TO THE FIVE CIVILIZED TRIBES.

IN RE APPLICATION FOR ENROLLMENT, as a citizen of the Muskogee (or Creek) Nation, of Marcellus Holleyman, born on the 13$\underline{th}$ day of January, 1903

Name of Father: T.E. Holleyman   a citizen of the   U.S.   Nation.
Name of Mother: Maggie G Holleyman   a citizen of the Muskogee (or Creek)Nation.

Postoffice   Okmulgee, Ind. Terry.

AFFIDAVIT OF MOTHER.

UNITED STATES OF AMERICA, Indian Territory, ⎫
　　Western　　　　　　DISTRICT.　　　　　⎭

I, Maggie G. Holleyman, on oath state that I am 35 years of age and a citizen by blood, of the Muskogee (or Creek) Nation; that I am the lawful wife of T.E. Holleyman, who is a citizen, ~~by~~ *(blank)* of the United States Nation; that a male child was born to me on the 13$\underline{th}$ day of January, 1903, that said child has been named Marcellus Holleyman, and was living March 4, 1905.

　　　　　　　　　　　　　　　　Maggie G. Holleyman
Witnesses To Mark:
⎰ T.E. Holleyman
⎱ Mary Hodge
　　her
　Mary x Bowman
　　mark

Subscribed and sworn to before me this 27th day of April, 1905.

My commission expires Feb 2nd 1907.   L.E. Sherwood
　　　　　　　　　　　　　　　　　　　　　　　　　　Notary Public.

Applications for Enrollment of Creek Newborn
Act of 1905   Volume XI

BIRTH AFFIDAVIT.
DEPARTMENT OF THE INTERIOR.
COMMISSION TO THE FIVE CIVILIZED TRIBES.

IN RE APPLICATION FOR ENROLLMENT, as a citizen of the Creek Nation, of Marcella Holleyman, born on the 13 day of January, 1903

Name of Father: T.E. Holleyman   a citizen of the United States Nation.
Name of Mother: Maggie G. Holleym an   a citizen of the   Creek   Nation.
Eufaula Deep Fork Town
                            Postoffice   Okmulgee, Ind. Ter.

AFFIDAVIT OF MOTHER.

UNITED STATES OF AMERICA, Indian Territory, ⎱   Child is not present
     Western   DISTRICT.   ⎰

I, T.E. Holleyman, on oath state that I am 54 years of age and a citizen by (blank), of the United States Nation; that I am the lawful wife husband of Maggie G. Holleyman, who is a citizen, by blood of the Creek Nation; that a female child was born to me her on 13 day of January, 1903, that said child has been named Marcella Holleyman, and was living March 4, 1905. That I assisted the mid-wife with birth of the child; that I was unable to have the midwife appear in person; that application for the child on account of illness

                                T. E. Holleyman
Witnesses To Mark:
⎰
⎱
       Subscribed and sworn to before me this 10 day of April, 1905.

                                Drennan C Skaggs
                                    Notary Public.

BIRTH AFFIDAVIT.
DEPARTMENT OF THE INTERIOR.
COMMISSION TO THE FIVE CIVILIZED TRIBES.

IN RE APPLICATION FOR ENROLLMENT, as a citizen of the Muskogee (or Creek) Nation, of Marcella Holleyman, born on the 13$\underline{th}$ day of January, 1903

Name of Father: T.E. Holleyman   a citizen of the   U.S.   Nation.
Name of Mother: Maggie G Holleyman   a citizen of the Muskogee (or Creek) Nation.

Applications for Enrollment of Creek Newborn
Act of 1905 Volume XI

Postoffice   Okmulgee, Ind. Terry.

AFFIDAVIT OF MOTHER.

UNITED STATES OF AMERICA, Indian Territory, ⎱
Western   DISTRICT.   ⎰

I, Maggie G. Holleyman , on oath state that I am 35 years of age and a citizen by blood , of the Muskogee (or Creek) Nation; that I am the lawful wife of T.E. Holleyman , who is a citizen, ~~by~~ *(blank)* of the United States Nation; that a female child was born to me on the 13$\underline{th}$ day of January , 1903 , that said child has been named Marcella Holleyman , and was living March 4, 1905.

                                             Maggie G. Holleyman

Witnesses To Mark:
⎰ T.E. Holleyman
⎱ Mary Hodge
      her
    Mary x Bowman
          mark

Subscribed and sworn to before me this 27th day of April , 1905.

My commission expires Feb 2nd 1907.   L.E. Sherwood
                                                    Notary Public.

NC 898

Marcellus Holleyman
Marcella   "
Lula Laura   "

applicants for enrollment as citizen by blood of Creek Nation
Father T.E. Holleyman alleged Cherokee Desire status of all as Cherokees
                                                        ABO

No application ~~being~~ made for
Marcellus Holleyman
Marcella   "
Lula Laura   "   as citizens of the Cherokee Nation
                             (Name Illegible)

Applications for Enrollment of Creek Newborn
Act of 1905   Volume XI

Schulter, I.T. Oct. 31st 05.

To the Hon. Tams Bixby,
Commissioner to the five civilized tribes[sic]

This is to certify that we, W.H. Russell and *(blank space)* do hereby certify and testify that Marcellus and Marcella Holleyman were born unto Mrs. Maggie and T.E. Holleyman on the 13th day of January, 1903. Also said twin children are Creek Indians by blood as their mother, Maggie G. Holleyman is a Creek citizen by blood. Said children were living on the 4th day of March 1905 and both of them are living now with their parents about 2 miles north west of Schulter, I.T.

W.H. Russell
T.P. Moseley

Subscribed and sworn to before me this 31st day of October 1905

My commission expires Feb 2nd 1907

L.E. Sherwood
Notary Public

NC. 898.

Muskogee, Indian Territory, July 15, 1905.

Chief Clerk,
Cherokee Enrollment Division,
Muskogee, Indian Territory.

Dear Sir:

April 13, 1905, application was made to the Commission to the Five Civilized Tribes for the enrollment of Marcellus, and Marcella Holleyman, both born January 13, 1903, as citizens by blood of the Creek Nation. It is stated in said application that the father of said children is T.E. Holleyman, a citizen of the Cherokee Nation, and that the mother is Maggie Holleyman, identified as Maggie G. Hodge, a citizen of the Creek Nation.

You are requested to inform the Creek Enrollment Division as to whether application has been made for the enrollment of said children as citizens of the Cherokee Nation, and if so, what disposition has been made of the same.

Respectfully,
Commissioner.

Applications for Enrollment of Creek Newborn
Act of 1905 Volume XI

REFER IN REPLY TO THE FOLLOWING:

DEPARTMENT OF THE INTERIOR,
COMMISSIONER TO THE FIVE CIVILIZED TRIBES.

Muskogee, Indian Territory, July 18, 1905.

Chief Clerk,
    Creek Enrollment Division,
        Muskogee, Indian Territory.

Dear Sir:

    Replying to your letter of July 15, 1905, (NC. 898) asking to be advised whether or not any application has ever been made for the enrollment, as citizens of the Cherokee Nation, of Marcellus and Marcella Holleyman, children of T. E. Holleyman, a citizen of the Cherokee Nation, and Maggie Holleyman, a citizen of the Creek Nation, you are advised that from an examination of the records of the Cherokee Enrollment Division it does not appear that any application has ever been made for the enrollment of said children, as citizens of that nation.

                             Respectfully,
GHL   Tams Bixby   Commissioner.

                             Okmulgee, Ind. Terry Sept. 25th 1905

Hon Mr Tams Bixby

        Dear Sir:

    Will you kindly inform me when I am to file for my twins Marcellus and Marcella Holleyman I want to look their land up so as to be in readiness I am informed that some of the people are filing already. Please let me know what to do at once.

                             Maggie G. Holleyman
                             Okmulgee Ind Ter

Applications for Enrollment of Creek Newborn
Act of 1905   Volume XI

N.C. 898

Muskogee, Indian Territory, September 30, 1905.

Maggie G. Holleyman,
    Okmulgee, Indian Territory.

Dear Madam:

    Receipt is acknowledged of your communication in which you ask as to the status of the application for enrollment of your minor children, Marcellus and Marcella Holleyman, as citizens by blood of the Creek Nation.

    In reply you are advised that the matter of said application is pending before this office and when final action is had therein, you will be duly notified.

                Respectfully,
                            Commissioner.

NC 898

Muskogee, Indian Territory, October 19, 1905.

Maggie G. Holleyman,
    Care T.E. Holleyman,
        Okmulgee, Indian Territory.

Dear Madam:

    In the matter of the application for the enrollment of your minor children, Marcellus and Marcella Holleyman, both born January 13, 1903, as citizens by blood of the Creek Nation, this office desires the affidavits to two disinterested witnesses relative to their birth. Said affidavits must set forth the names of said children, the date of their birth, the names of their parents, and whether or not they were living on March 4, 1905.

                Respectfully,
                            Commissioner.

NC 898

Muskogee, Indian Territory, November 13, 1906

Chief Clerk,
    Cherokee Enrollment Division,
        General Office.

Dear Sir:

Applications for Enrollment of Creek Newborn
Act of 1905 Volume XI

You are hereby advised that the names of Marcellus and Marcella Holleyman, twin children born January 13, 1903 to T. E. Holleyman, an alleged citizen of the Cherokee Nation and Maggie G. Holleyman a citizen by blood of the Creek Nation, are contained in schedule of minor citizens by blood of the Creek Nation, approved by the Secretary of the Interior January 4, 1906, opposite Roll numbers 993 and 994.

Respectfully,
Commissioner.

THE WESTERN UNION TELEGRAPH COMPANY.
----------INCORPORATED----------
24,000 OFFICES IN AMERICA.   CABLE SERVICE TO ALL THE WORLD.
ROBERT C. CLOWRY, President and General Manager.

Receiver's No. 53	Time filed	Check
		Of. B. Govt. Rate. *44 paid Gen.*

SEND the following message subject to the terms on back hereof, which are hereby agreed to.

February 16, 1907.

T. E. Holleyman,
    Schulter, I. T.

In the matter of the application for the enrollment of your minor child Lula Laura Holleyman, you are requested to furnish this office immediately proof as to whether said child was living March Fourth, nineteen hundred and six.

BIXBY, Commissioner.

☞ READ THE NOTICE AND AGREEMENT ON BACK

NC 898.

Muskogee, Indian Territory, February 16, 1907.

T. E. Holleyman,
    Schulter, Indian Territory.

Dear Sir:

    In the matter of the application for the enrollment of your minor child, Lula Laura Holleyman, you are advised that this office requires proof as to whether said child was living March 4, 1906, and a blank form is enclosed herewith for the purpose which you are requested to have executed and returned to this office at once.

Applications for Enrollment of Creek Newborn
Act of 1905   Volume XI

The Act of Congress approved April 26, 1906, (Public No. 129), provides as follows:

"That the rolls of the tribes affected by this Act shall be fully completed on or before the fourth day of March, nineteen hundred and seven, and the Secretary of the Interior shall have no jurisdiction to approved the enrollment of any person after said date."

You are requested to furnish said proof immediately.

Respectfully,
Commissioner.

BIRTH AFFIDAVIT.
DEPARTMENT OF THE INTERIOR.
COMMISSION TO THE FIVE CIVILIZED TRIBES.

IN RE APPLICATION FOR ENROLLMENT, as a citizen of the Creek Nation, of Lulu Laura Holleyman, born on the 30 day of Mar , 1905

(Cherokee?)
Name of Father: T.E. Holleyman   a citizen of the   U.S.   Nation.
Name of Mother: Maggie G. Holleym an a citizen of the   Creek   Nation.
Eufaula D.F.
                                Postoffice   Okmulgee

AFFIDAVIT OF ~~MOTHER~~. Father

UNITED STATES OF AMERICA, Indian Territory,
   Western   DISTRICT.

I, T.E. Holleyman , on oath state that I am 54 years of age and a citizen by *(blank)* , of the   U.S. Nation; that I am the lawful ~~wife~~ Husband of   Maggie G. Holleyman , who is a citizen, by blood of the Creek Nation; that a female child was born to me on 30 day of March , 1905 , that said child has been named   Lulu Laura Holleyman , and was living March 4, 1905.

T. E. Holleyman
Witnesses To Mark:
{   (Seal)

Subscribed and sworn to before me this 11 day of April , 1905.

Edw C Griesel
Notary Public.

Applications for Enrollment of Creek Newborn
Act of 1905   Volume XI

NC 898.

DEPARTMENT OF THE INTERIOR,
COMMISSIONER TO THE FIVE CIVILIZED TRIBES.
NEAR SCHULTER, I. T., FEBRUARY 23, 1907.

In the matter of the application for the enrollment of Lula Laura Holleyman as a citizen by blood of the Creek Nation.

MAGGIE G. HOLLEYMAN, being first duly sworn by Alex Posey, a Notary Public, and examined on behalf of the Commissioner, testified as follows:

BY THE COMMISSIONER:

Q What is your name? A Maggie G. Holleyman.
Q How old are you? A 36.
Q What is your postoffice address? A Schulter.
Q Are you a citizen of the Creek Nation? A I am.
Q To what Creek town do you belong? A Eufaula Deepfork.
Q Who are your parents? A Johnson Hodge.
Q Who is your mother? A Margaret.
Q Under what name are you enrolled? A Maggie G. Holleyman.
Q Have you a child named Lula Laura Holleyman? A I have.
Q Is that child living? A No, dead.
Q Who is the father of the child? A T. E. Holleyman.
Q Is he a Creek citizen? A No sir, non-citizen.
Q When did your minor child, ~~Lau~~ Lula Laura Holleyman, die? A September 1, 1905.
Q You are positive that that is the correct date of the child's death? A Yes sir.
Q When was she born? A March 30, 1905.
Q Who attended on you at the birth of this child? A Mary Bowman.

- - - - - - - - - -

J. B. Myers, being first duly sworn, states, that as stenographer to the Commissioner to the Five Civilized Tribes, he recorded the testimony in the foregoing proceedings, and that the above is a true, and correct transcript of his stenographic notes thereof.

JB Myers

Subscribed and sworn to before me
this, the 25th day of February, 1907.

Alex Posey
Notary Public.

JBM

Applications for Enrollment of Creek Newborn
Act of 1905 Volume XI

REFER IN REPLY TO THE FOLLOWING:

NC 898.

DEPARTMENT OF THE INTERIOR,
COMMISSIONER TO THE FIVE CIVILIZED TRIBES.

Henryetta, Indian Territory, February 25, 1907.

Commissioner to the Five Civilized Tribes,
    Muskogee, Indian Territory.

Sir:

    There is herewith inclosed the testimony of Maggie G. Holleyman, taken by the Creek Field Party February 23, 1907, in the matter of the application for the enrollment of Lulu Laura Holleyman, deceased, as a citizen by blood of the Creek Nation.

              Respectfully,
                        Alex Posey
                        In Charge,
                        Creek Field Party.

JBM

NC 898.

                Muskogee, Indian Territory, February 27, 1907.

Maggie G. Holleyman,
    c/o T.E. Holleyman,
        Schulter, Indian Territory.

Dear Madam:

    There is herewith enclosed one copy of the statement and order of the Commissioner to the Five Civilized Tribes, dated February 27, 1907, dismissing the application made by you for the enrollment of your minor child, Lula Laura Holleyman, as a citizen by blood of the Creek Nation.

               Respectfully,
                              Commissioner.

Register.
LM-20.2.

Applications for Enrollment of Creek Newborn
Act of 1905   Volume XI

NC 898.   SAM
                                                                                                                 EK
DEPARTMENT OF THE INTERIOR
COMMISSIONER TO THE FIVE CIVILIZED TRIBES.

In the matter of the application for the enrollment of Lulu Laura Holleyman, deceased, as a citizen by blood of the Creek Nation.

STATEMENT AND ORDER.

The record in this case shows that on April 13, 1905, application was made, in affidavit form, for the enrollment of Lulu Laura Holleyman as a citizen by blood of the Creek Nation. Further proceedings were had February 23, 1907.

It appears from the evidence and the records in the possession of this office that said applicant was the minor child of T. E. Holleyman, a non citizen, and Maggie G. Holleyman, whose name appears on a partial schedule of citizens by blood of the Creek Nation approved by the Secretary of the Interior March 13, 1902, opposite number 2847.

The evidence in this case shows that said applicant was born on March 30, 1905 and died September 1, 1905.

In view of the foregoing, I am of the opinion that there is no authority of law for the enrollment of Lulu Laura Holleyman, deceased, as a citizen by blood of the Creek Nation blood of the Creek Nation and the application for her enrollment as such is accordingly dismissed.

                                                                    Tams Bixby COMMISSIONER.
Muskogee, Indian Territory.
     FEB 27 – 1907

Muskogee, Indian Territory, October 19, 1905.

Sam R. Keys,
         Care J.B. Morrow,
                  Checotah, Indian Territory.

Dear Sir:

In the matter of the application for the enrollment of your minor child, James Keys, born August 15, 1901, as a citizen by blood of the Creek Nation, this office desires the affidavits of two disinterested witnesses relative to his birth. Said affidavits must set forth said child's name, the date of his birth, the names of his parents and whether or not he was living on March 4, 1905.

217

Applications for Enrollment of Creek Newborn
Act of 1905 Volume XI

You are further advised that this office desires proof of the marriage of yourself and Martha Keys, deceased, said proof may consist of either the original or a certified copy of your marriage license and certificate.

         Respectfully,
             Commissioner.

         CHECOTAH, I. T., November 16th 1905

Indian Territory }
Western District }

  Samuel R. Keys being duly sworn, states on his oath that he was married to Martha Miller now deceased, under the laws of the Creek Nation Indian Territory, by Judge Wm I. McIntosh now deceased in the presence of John T. Miller and T.F. McIntosh whose affidavits are hereto attached and that at the time of his marriage, the date of which he has forgotten, no License was required and no certificates of marriage were issued.

          Samuel R. Keys

Subscribed and sworn to before me this 16th day of November 1905.

         J.B. Morrow
           Notary Public

My Commission Expires July 1, 1906.

J. B. MORROW, MAYOR. D. W. FRY, RECORDER. CHAS. R. FREEMAN, CITY ATTY. G. W. ODOM, MARSHAL.	**INCORPORATED** **TOWN OF CHECOTAH** **MAYOR'S OFFICE.**	COUNCIL A. H. LIVINGSTON. R. H. RUSSELL. J. F. ADAMS. J. E. ADAIR. J. W. CRAWFORD.

         CHECOTAH, I. T., Apr. 26, 1905 190

The Commission To The Five Civilized Tribes
   Muskogee Ind. Ter.

Dear Sirs.

  In presenting the enclosed applications for enrollment, of James Keys and Emmett Dyer, I beg to state that they have been executed in accordance with instructions by telephone this day, at my request, from the Chief Clerk of the Creek Enrolling Division of your Office.

As the time is short, for enrolling the parents of these children respectfully request you to advise me at Checotah in case any further evidence is required in either or both cases, as they live in the country.

Applications for Enrollment of Creek Newborn
Act of 1905 Volume XI

I have known Fred S. Dyer & wife and Sam R. Keys for 15 years, "intimately", and do hereby certify that their integrity is unquestionable, and that they are entitled to credit for truthfulness.

Also that Martha Keys, mother of James Keys is dead.

Very Respectfully

J.B. Morrow
My Commission Expires July 1, 1906. **Notary Public**

BIRTH AFFIDAVIT.
DEPARTMENT OF THE INTERIOR.
COMMISSION TO THE FIVE CIVILIZED TRIBES.

IN RE APPLICATION FOR ENROLLMENT, as a citizen of the Creek Nation, of James Keys, born on the 15$\underline{th}$ day of August, 1901

Name of Father: Samuel R. Keys   a citizen of the Creek Nation.
Name of Mother: Martha Keys (now decd.)   a citizen of the United StatesNation.

Postoffice   Checotah Ind Ter

Acquaintance.
AFFIDAVIT OF ~~MOTHER~~.

UNITED STATES OF AMERICA, Indian Territory,
Western   DISTRICT.

I, John T. Miller, on oath state that I am 38 years of age of *(Illegible)* Ind. Ter. I was present and witnesses the marriage of Samuel R. Keys and my sister, Martha Miller, now deceased. I know James Keys their child who was born on the 15th day of August 1901, that said child has been named James Keys, and is now living.

John T. Miller

Witnesses To Mark:

Subscribed and sworn to before me this 15th day of November, 1905.

J. B. Morrow
Notary Public.

My Commission Expires July 1, 1906.

Applications for Enrollment of Creek Newborn
Act of 1905 Volume XI

AFFIDAVIT OF ATTENDING PHYSICIAN OR MID-WIFE.

UNITED STATES OF AMERICA, Indian Territory, ⎫
    Western   DISTRICT.   ⎬

I, T. F. McIntosh , a *(blank)* , on oath state that I am 38 years of age, and a citizen of the Creek Nation Ind. Ter. I was present at, and witnessed the marriage of Samuel R. Keys and Martha Miller now deceased. I know James Keys their child who was born on the 15th day of August 1901 and that said child is now living and is said to have been named James Keys.

                                    T.F. McIntosh

Witnesses To Mark:
{

Subscribed and sworn to before me this 16th day of November , 1905.

                                    J. B. Morrow
                                    Notary Public.

My Commission Expires July 1, 1906.

BIRTH AFFIDAVIT.

DEPARTMENT OF THE INTERIOR.
COMMISSION TO THE FIVE CIVILIZED TRIBES.

IN RE APPLICATION FOR ENROLLMENT, as a citizen of the Creek Nation, of James Keys , born on the 15th day of August , 1901

Name of Father: Sam R. Keys   a citizen of the   Creek   Nation.
Name of Mother: Martha Keys, deceased   a citizen of the United StatesNation.

                          Postoffice   Checotah Ind Ter

                                Father
                       AFFIDAVIT OF ~~MOTHER~~.

UNITED STATES OF AMERICA, Indian Territory, ⎫
    Western   DISTRICT.   ⎬

I, Sam R. Keys , on oath state that I am 35 years of age and a citizen by Blood, of the Creek   Nation; that I ~~am~~ was the lawful ~~wife~~ husband of Martha Keys, deceased, who ~~is~~ was a citizen, by *(blank)* of the United States   Nation; ~~that~~ I was present when a male   child was born to ~~me~~ the said Martha Keys on   15$^{\underline{th}}$ day of August , 1901 , that said child has been named James Keys , and was living March 4, 1905.

                                  Sam R. Keys

Applications for Enrollment of Creek Newborn
Act of 1905   Volume XI

Witnesses To Mark:

{

Subscribed and sworn to before me this 26th day of April , 1905.

J. B. Morrow
Notary Public.

My Commission Expires July 1, 1906.

AFFIDAVIT OF ATTENDING PHYSICIAN OR MID-WIFE.

UNITED STATES OF AMERICA, Indian Territory,
Western   DISTRICT.

I, Eliza Dyer , a Midwife , on oath state that I attended on Mrs. Martha Keys, deceased , wife of Sam R. Keys on the 15th day of August , 1901 ; that there was born to her on said date a male child; that said child was living March 4, 1905, and is said to have been named   James Keys

Eliza Dyer

Witnesses To Mark:

{

Subscribed and sworn to before me this 26th day of April , 1905.

J. B. Morrow
Notary Public.

My Commission Expires July 1, 1906.

N.C. 900

Muskogee, Indian Territory, October 19, 1905.

Eliza Dyer,
    Care Fred S. Dyer,
        Checotah, Indian Territory.

Dear Madam:

In the matter of the application for the enrollment of your minor child, Emmett Dyer, born May 20, 1902, as a citizen by blood of the Creek Nation, this office desires the affidavits of two disinterested witnesses relative to the birth of said child. Said

221

Applications for Enrollment of Creek Newborn
Act of 1905   Volume XI

affidavits must set forth said child's name, the date of his birth, the names of his parents and whether or not he was living on March 4, 1905.

          Respectfully,
               Commissioner.

BIRTH AFFIDAVIT.
DEPARTMENT OF THE INTERIOR.
COMMISSION TO THE FIVE CIVILIZED TRIBES.

  IN RE APPLICATION FOR ENROLLMENT, as a citizen of the Creek Nation, of Emmett Dyer, born on the 20th day of May, 1902

Name of Father: Fred S. Dyer   a citizen of the United States Nation.
Name of Mother: Eliza Dyer   a citizen of the   Creek   Nation.

        Postoffice   Checotah Ind. Ter

          Acquaintance
     AFFIDAVIT OF ~~MOTHER~~.

UNITED STATES OF AMERICA, Indian Territory,
  Western   **DISTRICT.**

  I, Jessie Acker , on oath state that I am 24 years of age I know Emmett Dyer son of Fred S Dyer and Eliza Dyer; who is said to have been born May 20th 1902 which I believe to be true, as I live and have lived for the past 5 years within a half mile of his house, and was at his home a few days after his birth, and that said child has been named Emmett Dyer , and was living March 4, 1905.

            Jessie Acker
Witnesses To Mark:

  Subscribed and sworn to before me this 24th day of April , 1905.

            J. B. Morrow
             Notary Public.
My Commission Expires July 1, 1906.

Applications for Enrollment of Creek Newborn
Act of 1905 Volume XI

Acquaintance
AFFIDAVIT OF ~~ATTENDING PHYSICIAN OR MID-WIFE~~.

UNITED STATES OF AMERICA, Indian Territory,
Western DISTRICT.

I, Samuel R. Keys , a *(blank)* , on oath state that I am 35 years of age. My Post Office is Checotah Ind. Ter. I know Emmett Dyer, son of Fred S. Dyer and Eliza Dyer, who was born on the 20th day of May, 1902; that said child was living March 4, 1905, and is said to have been named Emmett Dyer

Samuel R. Keys

Witnesses To Mark:
{

Subscribed and sworn to before me this 15th day of November , 1905.

J. B. Morrow
Notary Public.

My Commission Expires July 1, 1906.

BIRTH AFFIDAVIT.

DEPARTMENT OF THE INTERIOR.
COMMISSION TO THE FIVE CIVILIZED TRIBES.

IN RE APPLICATION FOR ENROLLMENT, as a citizen of the Creek Nation, of Emmett Dyer, born on the 20th day of May, 1902

Name of Father: Fred S. Dyer   a citizen of the United States Nation.
Name of Mother: Eliza Dyer   a citizen of the Creek Nation.

Postoffice Checotah Ind. Ter.

AFFIDAVIT OF MOTHER.

UNITED STATES OF AMERICA, Indian Territory,
Western DISTRICT.

I, Eliza Dyer , on oath state that I am 34 years of age and a citizen by Blood , of the Creek Nation; that I am the lawful wife of Fred S. Dyer , who is a citizen, by *(blank)* of the United States Nation; that a male child was born to me on 20th day of May , 1902, that said child has been named Emmett Dyer, and was living March 4, 1905.

Eliza Dyer

Witnesses To Mark:
{

Applications for Enrollment of Creek Newborn
Act of 1905   Volume XI

Subscribed and sworn to before me this 26th day of April , 1905.

                                            J. B. Morrow
                                            Notary Public.

My Commission Expires July 1, 1906.

AFFIDAVIT OF ATTENDING PHYSICIAN OR MID-WIFE.

UNITED STATES OF AMERICA, Indian Territory,
    Western   DISTRICT.

I, Fred S Dyer , Father of Emmett Dyer , on oath state that I attended on Mrs. Eliza Dyer , my wife ~~of~~ *(blank)* on the 20th day of May , 1902 ; that there was born to her on said date a   male   child; that said child was living March 4, 1905, and ~~is said to have~~ has been named Emmett Dyer, and that the whereabouts of the midwife in this case is unknown to me.

                                            Fred S Dyer

Witnesses To Mark:

Subscribed and sworn to before me this 26th day of April , 1905.

                                            J. B. Morrow
                                            Notary Public.

My Commission Expires July 1, 1906.

BIRTH AFFIDAVIT.

DEPARTMENT OF THE INTERIOR.
COMMISSION TO THE FIVE CIVILIZED TRIBES.

IN RE APPLICATION FOR ENROLLMENT, as a citizen of the Creek Nation, of Leotta Dyer, born on the 8th day of February , 1904

Name of Father: Fred S. Dyer   a citizen of the United States   Nation.
Name of Mother: Eliza Dyer   a citizen of the   Creek   Nation.

                        Postoffice   Checotah Ind. Ter.

Applications for Enrollment of Creek Newborn
Act of 1905   Volume XI

AFFIDAVIT OF MOTHER.

UNITED STATES OF AMERICA, Indian Territory,
Western   DISTRICT.

  I, Eliza Dyer, on oath state that I am 34 years of age and a citizen by Blood, of the Creek Nation; that I am the lawful wife of Fred S. Dyer, who is a citizen, by *(blank)* of the United States Nation; that a Female child was born to me on 8th day of February, 1904, that said child has been named Leotta Dyer, and was living March 4, 1905.

Eliza Dyer

Witnesses To Mark:

  Subscribed and sworn to before me this 26th day of April, 1905.

J. B. Morrow
Notary Public.

My Commission Expires July 1, 1906.

AFFIDAVIT OF ATTENDING PHYSICIAN OR MID-WIFE.

UNITED STATES OF AMERICA, Indian Territory,
Western   DISTRICT.

  I, J.B. West, a Physician, on oath state that I attended on Mrs. Eliza Dyer, wife of Fred S. Dyer on the 8th day of February, 1904 ; that there was born to her on said date a Female child; that said child was living March 4, 1905, and is said to have been named Leotta Dyer

J.B. West

Witnesses To Mark:

  Subscribed and sworn to before me this 29th day of April, 1905.

J. B. Morrow
Notary Public.

My Commission Expires July 1, 1906.

Applications for Enrollment of Creek Newborn
Act of 1905 Volume XI

DEPARTMENT OF THE INTERIOR.
COMMISSION TO THE FIVE CIVILIZED TRIBES.

In the matter of the death of Amandy Johnson a citizen of the Creek Nation, who formerly resided at or near Okmulgee , Ind. Ter., and died on the 10th day of July , 1906

AFFIDAVIT OF RELATIVE.

UNITED STATES OF AMERICA, Indian Territory, }
Western DISTRICT. }

I, Enah[sic] Johnson or Daniel , on oath state that I am 34 years of age and a citizen by blood , of the Creek Nation; that my postoffice address is Okmulgee , Ind. Ter.; that I am Uncle of Amandy Johnson who was a citizen, by blood , of the Creek Nation and that said Amandy Johnson died on the 10th day of July , 1906

Unah Johnson or Daniel

Witnesses To Mark:
{

Subscribed and sworn to before me this 16th day of November, 1906.

Edward Merrick
Notary Public.

BIRTH AFFIDAVIT.
DEPARTMENT OF THE INTERIOR.
COMMISSION TO THE FIVE CIVILIZED TRIBES.

IN RE APPLICATION FOR ENROLLMENT, as a citizen of the Creek Nation, of Amandy Johnson , born on the 17 day of August, 1903

Name of Father: Wiley Johnson a citizen of the Creek Nation.
Tuledega Arbeka Town
Name of Mother: Kizzie Johnson (nee Scott) a citizen of the Creek Nation.
Cussehta Town

Postoffice Okmulgee, Ind. Ter.

Applications for Enrollment of Creek Newborn
Act of 1905   Volume XI

Child present.
AFFIDAVIT OF MOTHER.

UNITED STATES OF AMERICA, Indian Territory, ⎫
   Western   DISTRICT. ⎬

I, Kizzie Johnson , on oath state that I am 20 years of age and a citizen by blood , of the Creek Nation; that I am the lawful wife of Wiley Johnson , who is a citizen, by blood of the Creek Nation; that a female child was born to me on 17 day of August , 1903 , that said child has been named Amandy Johnson , and was living March 4, 1905.

                                  Kizzie Johnson

Witnesses To Mark:
{

Subscribed and sworn to before me this 10 day of April , 1905.

                                    Drennan C Skaggs
                                    Notary Public.

AFFIDAVIT OF ATTENDING PHYSICIAN OR MID-WIFE.

UNITED STATES OF AMERICA, Indian Territory, ⎫
   Western   DISTRICT. ⎬

I, Mulley Scott , a mid-wife , on oath state that I attended on Mrs. Kizzie Johnson , wife of Wiley Johnson on or about the 17 day of August , 1903 ; that there was born to her on said date a female child; that said child was living March 4, 1905, and is said to have been named Amandy Johnson

                                        her
                                Mulley x Scott

Witnesses To Mark: mark
{ DC Skaggs
  Alex Posey

Subscribed and sworn to before me 10 day of April, 1905.

                                    Drennan C Skaggs
                                    Notary Public.

Applications for Enrollment of Creek Newborn
Act of 1905 Volume XI

BIRTH AFFIDAVIT.

DEPARTMENT OF THE INTERIOR.
COMMISSION TO THE FIVE CIVILIZED TRIBES.

IN RE APPLICATION FOR ENROLLMENT, as a citizen of the Creek Nation, of Eloise Posey, born on the 28 day of June, 1904

Name of Father: Frank Posey	a citizen of the Creek	Nation.
Name of Mother: Carrie Posey	a citizen of the Creek	Nation.

Postoffice   Coweta, I.T.

AFFIDAVIT OF MOTHER.

UNITED STATES OF AMERICA, Indian Territory,
   Western   DISTRICT.

I, Carrie Posey, on oath state that I am 20 years of age and a citizen by blood, of the Creek Nation; that I am the lawful wife of Frank Posey, who is a citizen, by blood of the Creek Nation; that a female child was born to me on 28 day of June, 1904, that said child has been named Eloise Posey, and was living March 4, 1905.

                                        Carrie Posey

Witnesses To Mark:
   Hattie Adkins Deere
   Annie Lovett

Subscribed and sworn to before me this 26th day of April, 1905.

                                        R C Allen
                                           Notary Public.
My Com. Ex. Mch. 15, 1908.

AFFIDAVIT OF ATTENDING PHYSICIAN OR MID-WIFE.

UNITED STATES OF AMERICA, Indian Territory,
   Western   DISTRICT.

I, Kizzie Lovett, a midwife, on oath state that I attended on Mrs. Carrie Posey, wife of Frank Posey on the 28th day of June, 1904; that there was born to her on said date a female child; that said child was living March 4, 1905, and is said to have been named Eloise Posey   her
                              Kizzie x Lovett
                                    mark

Applications for Enrollment of Creek Newborn
Act of 1905   Volume XI

Witnesses To Mark:
{ Hattie Adkins
{ Annie Lovett

Subscribed and sworn to before me 5th day of April, 1905.

Bert J. Beavers
Notary Public.

My commission expires Dec 19-1908

NC 903.

DEPARTMENT OF THE INTERIOR,
COMMISSIONER TO THE FIVE CIVILIZED TRIBES.
MUSKOGEE, INDIAN TERRITORY.
November 8, 1906.

In the matter of the application for the enrollment of William Arpoika as a citizen by blood of the Creek Nation.

Lena Simmer, being duly sworn by H.G. Hains, a Notary Public, testified as follows, through Official Interpreter Lona Merrick.

Examination by Commissioner.
Q What is your name? A Lena Simmer.
Q What is your age? A 36.
Q What is your post office address? A Weleetka.
Q Do you know Sissie Arpoika? A Yes sir, she was my sister.
Q Sissie's father's name was what? A Muska.
Q What is the name of your mother? A Mateloka.
Q Your sister Sissie is dead is she not? A Yes sir.
Q Did Sissie have a child named William Arpoika? A Yes sir.
Q What was the name of the father of this child? A George Arpoika.
Q Is he living? A No sir.
Q When did he die? A About four months ago.
Q July--last July? A Yes sir.
Q This office wrote several letters more than a year ago to George Arpoika telling him what was necessary in order to enroll his child, William Arpoika and he never paid any attention to these letters? A He was sick at the time he got those letters and couldn't answer them.

Applications for Enrollment of Creek Newborn
Act of 1905 Volume XI

Q Is William Arpoika living? A Yes sir.
Q With whom does he live? A With me.
Q When was he born? A He was born in July.
Q How many years ago? A He is three years old now.
Q Isn't he over four years? A No sir. He is over three years old.
Q We have the affidavit of David Knight and Levi Mitchell and they swore he was over four years old? A They were mistaken, this child is not over four years old but is early four years old now.
Q There are on file in this office the affidavit of David Knight and Levi Mitchell in which they state that they were acquainted with William Arpoika a citizen by blood of the Creek Nation; that said William Arpoika was born on the 2nd day of July, 1902 and was living on the 4th day of March, 1904, is that a mistake a mistake in the year? A Yes sir, they were mistaken.
Q Well you are advised that in the place of the affidavits of the parents of this child this office requires the affidavits of two disinterested witnesses, that means two people that are not kin to either of the parents or this child, and that said affidavit must state the name of the child, the names of its parents, the date of its birth and whether it was living March 4, 1905; that affidavit must be properly executed and filed in this case.
Q When these two witnesses made affidavit that the child was living March 4, 1904, was it the fact that the child was living March 4, 1905 and is now living? A Yes sir.
Q You are sure then that this child is three years old going on four instead of four years going on five? A Yes sir, he is three years old going on four.
Q Were you present when he was born, the names of his parents and whether or not he was living on March 4, 1905? A No sir.

----------------oOo------------

Lona Merrick, being duly sworn, states that the above and foregoing is a true and correct transcript of her stenographic notes as taken in said cause on said date.

Lona Merrick

Subscribed and sworn to before me this 10th day of November, 1906.

Edward Merrick
Notary Public.

AFFIDAVIT OF DISINTERESTED WITNESSES.

UNITED STATES OF AMERICA,
INDIAN TERRITORY, SS
Western DISTRICT.

We, the undersigned, on oath state that we are personally acquainted with Sissie Arpoika Dec'd wife of George Arpoika Dec'd ; that there was born to her a male child on or about the month ~~day~~ of July going on 4 years; that the

Applications for Enrollment of Creek Newborn
Act of 1905   Volume XI

said child has been named   William Arpoika   , and was living March 4, 1906. & is now living.   his
                                                                    John x *(Illegible)*
                                                                         mark
WITNESSES: her
                                                                 Sofarche x Deere
Lona Merrick   mark
HGHains

Subscribed and sworn to before me this 18 day of October, 1906.

                                        HG Hains
                                            Notary Public.

———————

_____ District
Indian Territory   SS

     We, the undersigned, on oath state that we are personally acquainted with Sissie Arpoika   wife of   George Arpoika   and that on or about the 12 day of July , 1902 , a male   child was born to them and has been named   William Arpoika; and that said child was living March 4, 1905.

     We further state that we have no interest in the above case.

                                        S.W. Scott

                                        (Name Illegible)

Witness to mark:

_____
_____
_____
_____

Subscribed and sworn to before
me this 28 day of Feb 1906
                                        Benjamin F. Hannan
                                            Notary Public.

My Commission Expires July 29-1909

———————

Applications for Enrollment of Creek Newborn
Act of 1905   Volume XI

Birth Affidavit.

Department of the Interior,
Commission to the Five Civilized Tribes.

IN RE APPLICATION FOR ENROLLMENT, as a citizen of the Creek Nation, of William Arpoika, born on the 12th day of July, 1902.

Name of Father, George Arpoika, a citizen of the Creek Nation.
Name of Mother, Sissie Arpoika, a citizen of the Creek Nation.

Post Office, Tuskegee, Ind. Terr.

Affidavit of an acquaintance.

United State of America, Indian Territory,
Western District.

I, David Knight, on oath, state that i[sic] am 34 years of age, and a citizen of the Creek Nation, by blood, that I am an acquaintance of William Arpoika, who is a citizen of the Creek Nation, by blood: that said William Arpoika was born on the 12th day of July, 1902; that said child has been named William Arpoika, and was living on the 4th day of March, 1904.

David Knight

Witnesses to mark.
C.H. Greenwood
J.W. Bowman

Subscribed and sworn to before me this 22nd day of November, 1905.

T.W. Flynn
Notary Public.

Birth Affidavit.

Department of the Interior,
Commission to the Five Civilized Tribes.

IN RE APPLICATION FOR ENROLLMENT, as a citizen of the Creek Nation, of William Arpoika, born on the 12th day of July, 1902.

Name of Father, George Arpoika, a citizen of the Creek Nation.
Name of Mother, Sissie Arpoika, a citizen of the Creek Nation.

Post Office, Tuskegee, Ind. Terr.

Applications for Enrollment of Creek Newborn
Act of 1905   Volume XI

Affidavit of an acquaintance.

United State of America, Indian Territory,
Western District.

I, Levi Mitchell, on oath, state that I am 54 years of age, and a citizen of the Creek Nation by blood, that I am an acquaintance of William Arpoika, who is a citizen of the Creek Nation: that said William Arpoika, was born on the 12th, day of July, 1902; that the said child has been named William Arpoika, and was living March 4th, 1904.

                                                his
                                       Levi Mitchell x
Witnesses to mark.   mark
C.H. Greenwood
J.W. Bowman

Subscribed and sworn to before me this 22nd day of November, 1905.

                                        T.W. Flynn
                                              Notary Public.

BIRTH AFFIDAVIT.
DEPARTMENT OF THE INTERIOR.
COMMISSION TO THE FIVE CIVILIZED TRIBES.

IN RE APPLICATION FOR ENROLLMENT, as a citizen of the Creek Nation, of   William Arpoika , born on the 12th   day of July , 1902

Name of Father: George Arpoika   a citizen of the   Creek   Nation.
Name of Mother: Sissie Arpoika, - Deceased   a citizen of the   Creek   Nation.

                                  Postoffice   Tuskegee, Ind Terr.

                         AFFIDAVIT OF ~~MOTHER~~. Father

UNITED STATES OF AMERICA, Indian Territory, }
    Western   DISTRICT.

I, George Arpoika , on oath state that I am 38 years of age and a citizen by Blood , of the Creek Nation; that I am the Father of William Arpoika , who is a citizen, by blood of the Creek Nation; that a male child was born to me on 12th day of July , 1902 , that said child has been named William Arpoika , and was living March 4, 1905.

                                        George Arpoika

Applications for Enrollment of Creek Newborn
Act of 1905   Volume XI

Witnesses To Mark:
{ J M Longfellow
{ C.O. Crane

Subscribed and sworn to before me this Fifth day of April, 1905.

T.W. Flynn
Notary Public.

AFFIDAVIT OF ATTENDING PHYSICIAN OR MID-WIFE.

UNITED STATES OF AMERICA, Indian Territory, }
Western   DISTRICT.   }

I, Katie Bear , a Mid-wife , on oath state that I attended on Mrs. Sissie Arpoika, wife of George Arpoika on the 12th day of July , 1902 ; that there was born to her on said date a male child; that said child was living March 4, 1905, and is said to have been named William Arpoika   her

Witnesses To Mark: Katie Bear x
{ J M Longfellow   mark
{ C.O. Crane

Subscribed and sworn to before me this 5th day of April, 1905.

T.W. Flynn
Notary Public.

N.C. 903
C.I. 2493

Muskogee, Indian Territory, October 19, 1905.

George Arpoika,
   Tuskegee, Indian Territory.

Dear Sir:

In the matter of the application for the enrollment of your minor child, William Arpoika, born July 12, 1902, a a citizen by blood of the Creek Nation, this office desires the affidavits of two disinterested witnesses relative to his birth. Said affidavits must set forth the name of said child, the date of his birth, the names of his parents and whether or not he was living on March 4, 1905.

You state in your affidavit filed in said case that Sissie Arpoika, the mother of said William Arpoika, is dead.

Applications for Enrollment of Creek Newborn
Act of 1905 Volume XI

There is herewith enclosed a blank form of death affidavit which this office desires filled out and properly executed and returned to the Commissioner to the Five Civilized Tribes, in the enclosed envelope.

Respectfully,

Tams Bixby
DA   Commissioner.
Env.

HGH

REFER IN REPLY TO THE FOLLOWING:
NC-903

DEPARTMENT OF THE INTERIOR,
COMMISSIONER TO THE FIVE CIVILIZED TRIBES.

Muskogee, Indian Territory, December 16, 1905.

George Arpoika,
    Tuskegee, Indian Territory.

Dear Sir:

In the matter of the application for the enrollment of your minor child, William Arpoika, born July 12, 1902, as a citizen by blood of the Creek Nation blood of the Creek Nation; you are advised that the affidavits of Levi Mitchell and David Knight, disinterested witnesses in said case, are defective, inasmuch as the affiants do not state in the bodies of the affidavits the names of the parents of William Arpoika. Said affiants state in their affidavits that said William Arpoika was living March 4, 1904, but do not state whether he was living March 4, 1905.

There is herewith enclosed a blank form of affidavit for disinterested witnesses, which you are requested to have executed and returned in the enclosed envelope.

Respectfully,
                        Tams Bixby   Commissioner.
Dis

Applications for Enrollment of Creek Newborn
Act of 1905   Volume XI

JWH

N C 903

Muskogee, Indian Territory, March 1, 1907.

    Simmer
Lena Quinner[sic],
    Weleetka, Indian Territory.

Dear Madam :--

    You are hereby advised that on February 15, 1907, the Secretary of the Interior approved the enrollment of William Arpoika as a citizen by blood of the Creek Nation, and that the name of said child appears upon the roll of New Born citizens by blood of the Creek Nation, enrolled under the Act of Congress approved March 3, 1905, as number 1175.

    This child is now entitled to allotment and application therefor should be made without delay at the Creek Land Office, Muskogee, Indian Territory.

                      Respectfully,
                              Commissioner.

(The above letter given again.)

N.C. 904.

DEPARTMENT OF THE INTERIOR,
COMMISSIONER TO THE FIVE CIVILIZED TRIBES.
Muskogee, Indian Territory, August 16, 1905

    In the matter of the application for the enrollment of Melissa Canard as a citizen by blood of the Creek Nation.

    Martin Cannard[sic] being duly sworn testified as follows partly through Alex Posey Official Interpreter.

Q What is your name? A Martin Cannard.
Q What is the name of your father? A James Cannard
Q What [sic] the name of your mother? [sic] Pitchee Cannard.

Applications for Enrollment of Creek Newborn
Act of 1905   Volume XI

Witness is identified as Martin Kannard on Creek Indian card 1377 opposite roll No. 4388.

Q How old are you? A I couldn't tell, white men keep their ages, Indians dont[sic], may be 30 or 35 years but I dont[sic] know.
Q What is your post office address? A Okmulgee
Q You are enrolled as Martin Kannard and you spell your name in this affidavit Cannard? A My certificate has on it Kannard but we some times write it Cannard.
Q Have you a child named Melissa? A Yes, sir
Q That child you spell its name Cannard? [sic] We spell it both ways.
Q Is that child living? A Yes, sir

Witness is advised that this office requires in lieu of the affidavit of the midwife the affidavit of two disinterested witnesses as to the birth of this child and the office further requires the affidavit of Mimah[sic] Kannard, the Seminole mother, electing in which nation she desires to have the child enrolled.

Q If it should be found that this child Melissa is entitled to rights in either the Creek or Seminole Nation, in which nation do you elect to have it enrolled and take its share of land.[sic] A In the Creek Nation.

Anna Garrigues

Subscribed and sworn to before me
this 16th day of August 1905.

Edw C Griesel
Notary Public.

United States of America, Indian Territory,
   Western Judicial District.

Be it remembered, that on this, the 21st day of October, 1905, the undersigned Notary Public, within and for the Western District of the Indian Territory, duly commissioned and acting as such, Eli Williams, a citizen by blood of the Creek Nation, residing about five miles West of the town of Okmulgee, Indian Territory, and made oath in du[sic] form of law that he is acquainted with Melissa Kannard; that he has known Martin Kannard, father of said child and Minah Kannard, mother of said child for about ten years; that he now lives within a mile and one half of the home of said Martin Kannard; that he saw said child shortly after its birth, and when it was wrapped in cloth used at the birth of children, and that said child now called Melissa Kannard was born near the middle of the month of November of the year of 1903, and to the best of his recolection[sic] the birth was on the 15th day of said month, and that it was about the middle of November without without[sic] question.

Affiant further states that said minor child is now living and was living on March the 4th, 1905, and that the facts herein stated are from his own personal knowledge.

Applications for Enrollment of Creek Newborn
Act of 1905   Volume XI

Affiant further states that he is about forty eight years old and that he has no interest direct or indirect in the result of the application for enrollment of the child Melissa Kannard.

his
Eli x Williams
mark

Sworn and subscribed to before me this 21st day of October, 1905.

My Commission Expires April 27th, 1908.

George C. Beidleman
Witness: Notary Public.
Geo C. Beidleman
J.H. Winston

United States of America, Western District,
Indian Territory.

Be it remembered, That on this, the 21st day of October, 1905, came before me, the undersigned   W.E. Wood a Notary Public   within and for the Western Judicial District of the Indian Territory aforesaid, duly commissioned and acting on such, Phillip Marshall, a citizen by blood of the Creek Nation, residing about four miles west of Okmulgee, Indian Territory, and made oath in due form of law that he is acquainted with Melissa Kannard, the minor child of Martin Kannard and his wife, Minah Kannard; that he has known Martin Kannard and his wife Minah from their childhood; that he lives only a short distance from the home of said Martin Kannard and was so living, when the child Melissa Kinnard[sic] was born; that he saw the child a few days after its birth and that the said child was born in the middle of November, 1903, about the fifteenth of said month.

Affiant further states that said minor child is now living and was living on March 4th - 1905; that he is well acquainted with the minor child Melissa Kannard and her parents, whose names are Martin Kannard and Minah Kannard; that he lives close to said parties, within a mile distant, and that the facts herein stated are of his own personal knowledge.

Affiant further states that he is about sixty seven years old and has no interest direct or indirect in the result of the application for enrollment of the child Melissa Kannard.

Sworn to and subscribed before me this the 21st day of October, 1905.

his
Philip x Marshall
mark

Witness
J.H. Winston   W.E. Wood
My commission expires Nov. 14th, 1907.   Notary Public.

Applications for Enrollment of Creek Newborn
Act of 1905 Volume XI

BIRTH AFFIDAVIT.
DEPARTMENT OF THE INTERIOR.
COMMISSION TO THE FIVE CIVILIZED TRIBES.

IN RE APPLICATION FOR ENROLLMENT, as a citizen of the Creek Nation, of Melissa Cannard, born on the 15th day of November, 1903

Name of Father: Martin Cannard   a citizen of the Creek Nation.
Name of Mother: Minah Cannard   a citizen of the Seminole Nation.

Postoffice   Okmulgee, Indian Territory

AFFIDAVIT OF MOTHER.

UNITED STATES OF AMERICA, Indian Territory,
Western Judicial   DISTRICT.

    I, Mineh[sic] Cannard, on oath state that I am 32 years of age and a citizen by Blood, of the Seminole Nation; that I am the lawful wife of Martin Cannard, who is a citizen, by Blood of the Creek Nation; that a Female child was born to me on 15th day of November, 1905[sic], that said child has been named Melissa Cannard, and was living March 4, 1905.

                                     her
                                Minah x Cannard
Witnesses To Mark: mark
  { George C. Beidleman
     J.H. Winston

    Subscribed and sworn to before me this 22nd day of April, 1905.

                                 George C. Beidleman
                                 Notary Public.
Commission Expires April 27th, 1908

AFFIDAVIT OF ATTENDING PHYSICIAN OR MID-WIFE.

UNITED STATES OF AMERICA, Indian Territory,
Western Judicial   DISTRICT.

    I, Martin Cannard Husband of Minah Cannard, on oath state that I attended on Mrs. Minah Cannard, my wife, ~~wife of~~ *(blank)* on the 15th day of November, 1903; that there was born to her on said date a Female child; that said child was living March 4, 1905, and is said to have been named Melissa Cannard

Applications for Enrollment of Creek Newborn
Act of 1905 Volume XI

Martin Cannard

Witnesses To Mark:
{ George C. Beidleman
{ J.H. Winston

Subscribed and sworn to before me this 22nd day of April, 1905.

George C. Beidleman
Notary Public.

Commission Expires April 27th, 1908

BIRTH AFFIDAVIT.

DEPARTMENT OF THE INTERIOR.
COMMISSION TO THE FIVE CIVILIZED TRIBES.

IN RE APPLICATION FOR ENROLLMENT, as a citizen of the Creek Nation, of Melissa Cannard, born on the 15 day of November, 1 *(blank)*

Name of Father: Martin Cannard   a citizen of the   Creek   Nation.
Name of Mother: Minah Cannard   a citizen of the   Seminole   Nation.

Postoffice   Okmulgee

AFFIDAVIT OF MOTHER.

UNITED STATES OF AMERICA, Indian Territory,
   Western   DISTRICT.

     I, Minah Cannard, on oath state that I am 32 years of age and a citizen by blood, of the Seminole Nation; that I am the lawful wife of Martin Cannard, who is a citizen, by blood of the Creek Nation; that a female child was born to me on 15 day of November, 1903, that said child has been named Melissa Cannard, and was living March 4, 1905.

                                       her
                            Minah x Cannard
Witnesses To Mark: mark
{ George C. Beidleman
{ John H. Winston

Subscribed and sworn to before me this 1st day of November, 1905.

George C. Beidleman
Notary Public.

Com Exp Apr 27th 1908.

Applications for Enrollment of Creek Newborn
Act of 1905   Volume XI

GEO. C. BEIDLEMAN   JOHN H. WINSTON
BEIDLEMAN & WINSTON
LAWYERS
OKMULGEE, IND. TER.

#213.

Okmulgee, I. T. August 19th, 1905.

Commissioner to the Five Civilized Tribes,
Muskogee, I. T.

Dear Sir:----

Replying to your letter relative to the selection of an allotment for my minor child, Melissa Kanard, have to say that I desire to take for her an allotment in the Creek Nation, and make this as my application for such allotment.

You will remember that I am a citizen of the Seminole Nation and the child's father is a Creek Citizen.

Very truly,
                    her
Mineh[sic] x Kanard

Witness to Signiture[sic] & Mark
George C. Beidleman
Jack W. Stephens

NC 904

Muskogee, Indian Territory, October 19, 1905.

Minah Kannard,
   Care Martin Kannard,
      Okmulgee, Indian Territory.

Dear Madam:
   In the matter of the application for the enrollment of your minor child, Melissa Kannard, born November 15, 1903, as a citizen by blood of the Creek Nation blood of the Creek Nation, it will be necessary for you to furnish this office with the affidavits of two disinterested witnesses relative to her birth. Said affidavits must set forth said child's name, the date of her birth, the names of her parents and whether or not she was living on March 4, 1905.

   This matter should receive your prompt attention.

Respectfully,
                    Commissioner.

Applications for Enrollment of Creek Newborn
Act of 1905 Volume XI

N.C. 904.
Muskogee, Indian Territory, October 30, 1905.

Minah Kannard,
    Care Beidleman & Winston,
        Okmulgee, Indian Territory.

Dear Madam:

    In the matter of the application for the enrollment of Melissa Kannard, as a citizen by blood of the Creek Nation, it is stated in your affidavit executed April 22, 1905, that said Melissa Kannard was born November 15, 1905. This is obviously an error and for the purpose of correcting same, there is herewith enclosed form of birth affidavit which you are requested to execute and return to this office in the enclosed envelop.

    Care should be taken that the notary affix his name and notarial seal and that you sign your name as the same appears in the body of the affidavit.

                Respectfully,
                              Commissioner.
NC 904

N.C. 904.
Muskogee, Indian Territory, October 30, 1905.

Chief Clerk,
    Seminole Enrollment Division.

Dear Sir:

    In the matter of the application for the enrollment of Melissa Kannard, daughter of Martin Kannard, a citizen of the Creek Nation, and Minah Kannard a citizen of the Seminole Nation; you are requested to advise the Creek Enrollment Division whether any application has been made for the enrollment of said Melissa Kannard as a citizen of the Seminole Nation.

                Respectfully,
                              Commissioner.

Applications for Enrollment of Creek Newborn
Act of 1905 Volume XI

REFER IN REPLY TO THE FOLLOWING:

DEPARTMENT OF THE INTERIOR,
COMMISSIONER TO THE FIVE CIVILIZED TRIBES.

Muskogee, Indian Territory, November 2, 1905.

Chief Clerk,
    Creek Enrollment Division.

Dear Sir

    Your letter N. C. 904. You are advised that it does not appear from the records of the Seminole Enrollment Division that any application has been made for the enrollment of Malissa Kannard, as a citizen by blood of the Seminole Nation.

                          Respectfully,
                                    Tams Bixby   Commissioner.

NC 904

                      Muskogee, Indian Territory, November 13, 1906

Chief Clerk,
    Seminole Enrollment Division,
        General Office.

Dear Sir:

    You are hereby advised that the name of Mellisa[sic] Cannard, born November 15, 1903 to Martin Cannard, a citizen by blood of the Creek Nation and Minah Cannard, an alleged citizen of the Seminole Nation, is contained in schedule of minor citizens by blood of the Creek Nation, approved by the Secretary of the Interior, January 4, 1906, opposite Roll number 996.

                          Respectfully,
                                          Commissioner.

Applications for Enrollment of Creek Newborn
Act of 1905   Volume XI

DEPARTMENT OF THE INTERIOR,
COMMISSIONER TO THE FIVE CIVILIZED TRIBES.
Okmulgee, I. T., April 10, 1905.

In the matter of the application for the enrollment of Addie Lindsey as a citizen by blood of the Creek Nation.

HETTIE LINDSEY, being duly sworn, testified as follows:

Through Alex Posey Official Interpreter:

BY COMMISSION:
Q What is your name? A Hettie Lindsey.
Q How old are you? A Twenty-eight.
Q What is your post office address? A Wewoka.
Q Are you a citizen of the Creek Nation? A No, sir, I am a Seminole.
Q Do you make application for the enrollment of your minor child, Addie Lindsey, as a citizen by blood of the Creek Nation? A Yes, sir.
Q What is the name of the child's father? A Walter Lindsey.
Q Is he a citizen of the Creek Nation? A Yes, sir.
Q To what town does he belong? A Tuckabatche.
Q Is Walter Lindsey your lawful husband? A Yes, sir.
Q If it should be found that your minor child, Addie Lindsey, is entitled to enrollment in either the Creek or Seminole Nations in which nation do you desire to have him enrolled? A In the Creek Nation.

---oooOOOooo---

I, D. C. Skaggs, on oath state that the above and foregoing is a full and true transcript of my stenographic notes as taken in said cause on said date.

D. C. Skaggs

Subscribed and sworn to before me this 22 day of July, 1905.

J. McDermott
Notary Public.

Applications for Enrollment of Creek Newborn
Act of 1905   Volume XI

NC. 905.

Muskogee, Indian Territory, July 15, 1905.

Chief Clerk,
    Seminole Enrollment Division,
    Muskogee, Indian Territory.

Dear Sir:

    April 13, 1905, application was made to the Commission to the Five Civilized Tribes for the enrollment of Addie Lindsey, born January 5, 1903, as a citizen by blood of the Creek Nation. It is stated in said application that the father of said child is Walter Lindsey, a citizen of the Creek Nation; and that the mother is Hettie Lindsey, a citizen of the Seminole Nation.

    You are requested to inform the Creek Enrollment Division as to whether application has been made for the enrollment of said Addie Lindsey as a citizen of the Seminole Nation, and if so, what disposition has been made of the same.

Respectfully,
Commissioner.

N.F.
DEPARTMENT OF THE INTERIOR.
COMMISSION TO THE FIVE CIVILIZED TRIBES.

Muskogee, Indian Territory, July 19, 1905.

Chief Clerk,
    Creek Enrollment Division.

Dear Sir:

    Receipt is acknowledged of your letter of July 15, 1905, (NC-905) stating that application was made to the Commission to the Five Civilized Tribes for the enrollment of Addie Lindsey, born January 5, 1903, child of Walter Lindsey, a citizen of the Creek Nation, and Hettie Lindsey, a citizen of the Seminole Nation, as a citizen by blood of the Creek Nation and requesting to be informed as to whether application was made for the enrollment of said child as a citizen of the Seminole Nation.

    In reply to your letter you are advised that it does not appear from an examination of the records of this office that any application was made for the enrollment of said Addie Lindsey as a citizen of the Seminole Nation.

Respectfully,
Tams Bixby   Commissioner.

Applications for Enrollment of Creek Newborn
Act of 1905   Volume XI

NC 905

Muskogee, Indian Territory, October 19, 1905.

Hettie Lindsey,
    Wewoka, Indian Territory.

Dear Madam:

    In the matter of the application for the enrollment of your minor child, Addie Lindsey, born January 5, 1903, as a citizen by blood of the Creek Nation, this office desires affidavit of the midwife or physician in attendance at the birth of said child and a blank for that purpose is enclosed herewith.

    In the event that there was no physician or midwife in attendance when said child was born, it will be necessary for you to furnish this office with the affidavits of two disinterested witnesses relative to her birth. Said affidavits must set forth said child's name, the date of her birth, the names of her parents and whether or not she was living on March 4, 1905.

    This matter should receive your prompt attention.

        Respectfully,
                Commissioner.

NC-905

Muskogee, Indian Territory, November 10, 1905.

B. F. Davis,
    Wewoka, Indian Territory.

Dear Sir:

    Receipt is acknowledged of your letter of November 6, 1905, in which you state that Walter Linsley[sic] has requested you, as his attorney, to obtain the status of the application for the enrollment of his minor child, Addie Linsley, as a citizen of the Creek Nation.

    You are advised that this Office requires proof of marriage between Walter Lindsay[sic] and Hettie Lindsay, parent of said Addie Lindsay; said proof may consist of either the original or a certified copy of your marriage license and certificate.

        Respectfully,
                Commissioner.

Applications for Enrollment of Creek Newborn
Act of 1905 Volume XI

NC-905

Muskogee, Indian Territory, November 10, 1905.

Hettie Lindsay,
    Care of Walter Lindsay,
        Wewoka, Indian Territory.

Dear Madam:

    In the matter of the application for the enrollment of your minor child, Addie Lindsay, as a citizen by blood of the Creek Nation, this Office requires proof of your marriage to Walter Lindsay, the father of said child; said proof may consist of either the original or a certified copy of your marriage license and certificate.

                Respectfully,
                          Commissioner.

NC 905

Muskogee, Indian Territory, November 13, 1905

Chief Clerk,
    Seminole Enrollment Division,
        General Office.

Dear Sir:

    You are hereby advised that the name of Addie Lindsey born January 5, 1903 to Walter Lindsey, a citizen by blood of the Creek Nation and Hettie Lindsey an alleged citizen of the Seminole Nation, is contained in schedule of minor citizens by blood of the Creek Nation, approved by the Secretary of the Interior, January 4, 1905, opposite Roll number 997.

                Respectfully,
                          Commissioner.

Applications for Enrollment of Creek Newborn
Act of 1905 Volume XI

BIRTH AFFIDAVIT.
DEPARTMENT OF THE INTERIOR.
COMMISSION TO THE FIVE CIVILIZED TRIBES.

IN RE APPLICATION FOR ENROLLMENT, as a citizen of the Creek Nation, of Addie Lindsey , born on the 5 day of January , 1903

Name of Father: Walter Lindsey a citizen of the   Creek   Nation.
Tuckabatche Town
Name of Mother: Hettie Lindsey (nee Bruner)   a citizen of the Seminole   Nation.

Postoffice   Wewoka, Ind. Ter.

AFFIDAVIT OF MOTHER.

UNITED STATES OF AMERICA, Indian Territory, ⎫   Child is present
   Western   DISTRICT.   ⎭

I, Hettie Lindsey , on oath state that I am 28 years of age and a citizen by blood , of the Seminole Nation; that I am the lawful wife of Walter Lindsey , who is a citizen, by blood of the Creek Nation; that a female child was born to me on 5 day of January , 1903 , that said child has been named Addie Lindsey , and was living March 4, 1905.

Hattie[sic] Lindsey
Witnesses To Mark:
{

Subscribed and sworn to before me this 10 day of April , 1905.

Drennan C Skaggs
Notary Public.

AFFIDAVIT OF ATTENDING PHYSICIAN OR MID-WIFE.

UNITED STATES OF AMERICA, Indian Territory, ⎫
   Western   DISTRICT.   ⎭

I, Mattie Marks , a midwife , on oath state that I attended on Mrs. Hettie Lindsey , wife of Walter Lindsey on the 5 day of January , 1903 ; that there was born to her on said date a female child; that said child was living March 4, 1905, and is said to have been named Addie Lindsey

her
Mattie x Marks
mark
Witnesses To Mark:
{ Alex Posey
  DC Skaggs

Applications for Enrollment of Creek Newborn
Act of 1905 Volume XI

Subscribed and sworn to before me 10 day of April, 1905.

Drennan C Skaggs
Notary Public.

DEPARTMENT OF THE INTERIOR,
COMMISSIONER TO THE FIVE CIVILIZED TRIBES.

In the matter of the Enrollment of Addie Lindsey, born January 5, 1903, as a citizen by blood of the Creek Nation.
Father, Walter Lindsey; citizen of the Creek Nation, P. O. Wewoka, Indian Territory
Mother, Hattie Lindsey, Seminole citizen, P. O. Wewoka, I.T.

AFFIDAVIT OF MID-WIFE.

United States of America, Indian Territory,
Western Judicial District.

I, Mattie Marks, being of lawful age, and first duly sworn, on my oath depose and say that on the 5th day of January, 1903, I was present at the home of Walter Lindsey and Hattie Lindsey, husband and wife, the former a citizen by blood of the Creek Nation, the latter a citizen by blood of the Seminole Nation, when a xxmale[sic] child was born to said Walter and Hattie Lindsey; that at that time I attended on said Hattie Lindsey in the capacity of mid-wife; that said child has been named Addie Lindsey, is well known to me, was alive on the 4th day of March, 1905, and is still alive.

Witness
Jno W. Willmott
Hattie Lindsey

her
Mattie Marks x
mark

Subscribed and sworn to before me, at Wewoka, I.T., on this the 15th day of November, A.D., 1905.

John W. Willmott
Notary Public.

My com. expires Oct. 5-1906

Applications for Enrollment of Creek Newborn
Act of 1905 Volume XI

DEPARTMENT OF THE INTERIOR,
COMMISSIONER TO THE FIVE CIVILIZED TRIBES.

In the Matter of the Application for the Enrollment of Addie Lindsay, as a citizen by blood of the Creek Nation.

Father, ~~Hettie~~ Walter Lindsay, Wewoka, I.T., citizen of the Creek Nation.
Mother, Hettie Lindsay, Wewoka, I.T., citizen of the Seminole Nation.

United States of America, Indian Territory,
    Western Judicial District.

I, Walter Lindsay, being first duly sworn, on his oath states that he was married to Hettie Bruner, at Wewoka, I.T., about nine years ago, by a minister named Duncan; that said marriage was according to the customs of the Seminole nation; that he has since ~~hr~~ resided at Wewoka, where he has continuously lived with his wife, Hettie Lindsey; that three children have been born of said marriage, all of whom are now alive. That there is no certificate or license showing said marriage.   his
    Attest: Walter Lindsay x
    Jno. W. Willmott   mark

Subscribed and sworn to before me, this 25th day of November, 1905.

                                    John W. Willmott
My com. expires Oct. 5, 1906.   Notary Public.

United States of America, Indian Territory,
    Western Judicial District.

Chissie Harjo and Caesar Bowlegs, being first duly sworn, on their oaths depose and say, each for himself, that he is above the age of sixty years, a citizen of the Seminole Nation, that he has long been personally well acquainted with Walter Lindsay and his wife, Hettie Lindsay, who was formerly Hettie Bruner; that said Walter Lindsay and Hettie Lindsay have been living together as man and wife near Wewoka for something over eight years; that they were married according to the Indian laws and customs, have held themselves out as husband and wife, and are generally so regarded by the people of the community where they live. That they have reared three children, all of whom are now alive.   his
                                            Chissie Harjo x
                                                  mark
                                                   his
                                       Caesar Bowlegs x
                                                   mark

Applications for Enrollment of Creek Newborn
Act of 1905 Volume XI

Subscribed and sworn to before me, this 25th day of November, 1905; and I hereby certify that I am personally well acquainted with said Chissie Harjo and Caesar Bowlegs, and that they are respectable citizens and entitled to credit.

My com. expires Oct. 5, 1906.

John W. Willmott
Notary Public.

(The above Affidavit given again.)

MISCELLANEOUS. R E C E I V E D JUN 24 1919 ENCL. TO No. 50539 SUPT. FIVE CIVILIZED TRIBES

STATE OF OKLAHOMA, |
                           | ss.   AFFIDAVIT.
HUGHES COUNTY. |

John Cordell, of lawful age, being duly sworn, deposeth and saieth: That he is a citizen of Hughes County, Oklahoma, and he legally appointed and acting guardian of Addie Lindsey, New Born Creek Roll Number 992, now about 16 years of age; that he is personally acquainted with the said Addie Lindsey and has known him for the past nine (9) years and that the said Addie Lidsey is a male person and not a female person as his name would indicate.

Further affiant saieth not.

John Cordell

SUBSCRIBED and sworn to before me this 20th day of June, 1919.

My commission expires: Nov 30-1922

J S Meyers

. . . .

STATE OF OKLAHOMA,
HUGHES COUNTY. . . . . .SS.

We, the undersigned, adult citizens of Hughes County, Oklahoma, being duly sworn on oath state: That we are acquainted with John Cordell of Holdenville, Indian Territory Oklahoma, and Addie Lindsey, #997, and know that the above and foregoing affidavit of John Cordell, as to the age and sex of the said Addie Lindsey is true. Further affiants saieth not.

(Illegible) Leader
Alfred F. Goat

Applications for Enrollment of Creek Newborn
Act of 1905   Volume XI

SUBSCRIBED and sworn to before me this 20th day of June, 1919.

My commission expires:
Nov 30 1922

J S Meyers
Notary Public - Hughes County.
Oklahoma.

Department of the Interior
United States Indian Service
Local Field Representative

LEASE #39330
Lease on land of
Addie Lindsey, minor.

MISCELLANEOUS.
R E C E I V E D
JUN 24 1919
ENCL. TO
No.   50539
SUPT. FIVE CIVILIZED TRIBES

Wewoka, Okla.,
Dec. 15, 1919.

Testimony of Hettie Lindsey, mother of Addie Lindsey, minor, New Born Creek #997.

Q. What is your name.
A. Hettie Lindsey.
Q. Where do you live.
A. About three miles north of Lima, Okla., this county.
Q. Are you married.
A. Yes.
Q. Have you been married before.
A. Yes.
Q. What was your first husband's name.
A. Walter Lindsey, a Creek Indian.
Q. How many Children have you.
A. Three.
Q. What are their names.
A. Addie, Noah and Willie.
Q. Is Addie a boy or girl.
A. Addie is a boy, but he is enrolled as a girl, he is living with me at home.

Hetty Lindsey

Applications for Enrollment of Creek Newborn
Act of 1905 Volume XI

L A N D
WHA:LFS
1-17-20
In re: correction of record
of sex of ADDIE LINDSEY, New
Born Creek, Roll No. 997.
E?CLS-4-

The Honorable,   January 17, 1920.
The Commissioner of Indian Affairs.

Dear Mr. Commissioner:

                      On partial schedule of the New Born Creek citizens by blood approved by the Secretary of the Interior on January 4, 1906, there appears the following:

No.	Name	Age	Sex	Blood	Card No.
997	Lindsey, Addie	2	F	1/2	905.

                      From papers filed in this office in connection with oil and gas lease executed by the guardian of said enrollee, it appears that this person is a male instead of a female. The matter was thereupon investigated and evidence was obtained consisting of the testimony of Hettie Lindsey, the mother of said Addie Lindsey, and affidavit of John Cordell, the guardian, showing that Addie Lindsey is a male instead of a female. It also appears from testimony of said Hettie Lindsey, taken on April 10, 1905, and affidavit of Mattie Marks, the mid-wife who attended at the birth of this child made November 15, 1905, that said Addie Linsey is a male instead of a female. Copies of said testimony and affidavits are herewith enclosed.

                      It appearing clearly from the evidence obtained that said Addie Lindsey is a male instead of a female, it is respectfully recommended that the letter "M" be substituted in place of "F" in the sex column opposite the name of said Addie Lindsey at No. 997 upon the approved roll of the New Born Creek Indian Roll in the possession of the Indian Office, and that this office be authorized to make like notation upon the approved New Born Creek Indian roll in its possession.

                                         Sincerely yours,
No reply
Dec 4, 1923   Superintendent for the
                                                       Five Civilized Tribes.

Applications for Enrollment of Creek Newborn
Act of 1905 Volume XI

Land 12/5/23 PLo-TKK
Correction of record as to
sex of Addie Lindsey, New
Born Creek 997. *(Illegible)*   December 5, 1923.

The Honorable
    The Commissioner of Indian Affairs.

Sir:

    On the partial schedule of New Born Creek citizens by blood approved by the Secretary of the Interior on January 4, 1906, appears the following:

No.	Name.	Age.	Sex.	Blood.	Card No.
997	Lindesy[sic], Addie	2	F.	1/2	905

    This Office having been informed that an error was made in the designation of the sex of the above named allottee, which is shown on Census Card No. 905 as female instead of male, the matter was investigated and evidence obtained consisting of the testimony of Hetty Lindsey, the mother of said Addie Lindsey, and affidavit of John Cordell, the guardian, showing that Addie Lindsey is a male instead of a female. Copies of said testimony, affidavit, and census card are enclosed.

    It appearing clearly from the evidence that the said Addie Lindsey is a male instead of a female, it is respectfully recommended that the letter be substituted in the place of "F" in the sex column opposite the name of said Addie Lindsey at No. 997 upon the approved roll of New Born Creek Indians in the possession of the Indian Office and that this Office be authorized to make a like notation upon the approved New Born Creek Indian Roll in its possession.

                                                Respectfully,
                                                               Superintendent.

                                     56663
Land-F.T.

94587-23
O G P

DEPARTMENT
R E C E I V E D
DEC 26 1923
No.   7672
Supt. Five Civilized Tribes

DEC 20 1923

The Honorable
    The Secretary of the Interior.

Sir:

    There is transmitted herewith a report dated December 5, 1923, from the Superintendent for the Five Civilized Tribes, with inclosures, relative to an error appearing in the final approved roll of New Born Creek citizens by blood, in reference to

Applications for Enrollment of Creek Newborn
Act of 1905 Volume XI

the designation of the sex of Addie Lindsey, whose name appears opposite No. 997 on the roll. It appears that Addie Lindsey was designated on the roll as a female, and should have been designated as a male.

This Office therefore recommends that the letter "F" appearing in the sex column opposite the name of Addie Lindsey, No. 997 on the final approved roll of New Born Creek citizens by blood, be cancelled, and that the letter "M" be substituted therefor, and that this Office and the Superintendent for the Five Civilized Tribes be authorized to make a similar correction upon the copies of the rolls in their possession.

Respectfully,

(Signed) E.B. Meritt

12-LW-18   Assistant Commissioner.
DEC 20 1923
Approved.   Census Card No. 905
                                                Creek New Born Roll
(Sgd.) F. M. GOODWIN.
Assistant Secretary,

BIRTH AFFIDAVIT.
DEPARTMENT OF THE INTERIOR.
COMMISSION TO THE FIVE CIVILIZED TRIBES.

IN RE APPLICATION FOR ENROLLMENT, as a citizen of the Creek Nation, of Sarah Miller, born on the 18th day of November, 1904

Name of Father: Seborn Miller   a citizen of the   Creek   Nation.
Name of Mother: Effa Miller   a citizen of the   Creek   Nation.

                       Postoffice   Okmulgee, Ind. Ter.

AFFIDAVIT OF MOTHER.

UNITED STATES OF AMERICA, Indian Territory, ⎫
         Western   DISTRICT.   ⎭

I, Effa Miller , on oath state that I am 23 years of age and a citizen by Blood , of the Creek Nation; that I am the lawful wife of Seborn Miller , who is a citizen, by

Applications for Enrollment of Creek Newborn
Act of 1905 Volume XI

Blood of the Creek Nation; that a female child was born to me on 18th day of November, 1904, that said child has been named Sarah Miller, and is now living.

                                                          Her
                                    Effa Miller x
Witnesses To Mark: mark
{ E H Moore
  Seborn Miller

Subscribed and sworn to before me this 26th day of October, 1905.

My Com Ex Sept 12, 1906   E H Moore

                                                        Notary Public.

AFFIDAVIT OF ATTENDING PHYSICIAN OR MID-WIFE.

UNITED STATES OF AMERICA, Indian Territory, }
    Western   DISTRICT.

    I, Sarah Chamblen, a midwife, on oath state that I attended on Mrs. Effa Miller, wife of Seborn Miller on the 18th day of November, 1904 ; that there was born to her on said date a female child; that said child is now living and is said to have been named Sarah Miller

                                        Sarah Chamblen
Witnesses To Mark:
{ E H Moore
  Seborn Miller

Subscribed and sworn to before me this 26th day of October, 1905.

My Com Ex Sept 12, 1906   E H Moore

                                                        Notary Public.

NC 907

                                 Muskogee, Indian Territory, October 19, 1905.

Effa Miller,
    Care Seborn Miller,
        Okmulgee, Indian Territory.

Dear Madam:

    In the matter of the application for the enrollment of your minor child, Sarah Miller, born November 18, 1904, as a citizen by blood of the Creek Nation, this office

Applications for Enrollment of Creek Newborn
Act of 1905   Volume XI

desires affidavit of the midwife or physician in attendance at the birth of said child and a blank for that purpose is inclosed herewith.

In the event that there was no physician or midwife in attendance when said child was born, it will be necessary for you to furnish this office with the affidavits of two disinterested witnesses relative to her birth. Said affidavits must set forth said child's name, the date of her birth, the names of her parents and whether or not she was living on March 4, 1905.

Respectfully,

Commissioner.

BA
Env.

BIRTH AFFIDAVIT.

DEPARTMENT OF THE INTERIOR.
COMMISSION TO THE FIVE CIVILIZED TRIBES.

IN RE APPLICATION FOR ENROLLMENT, as a citizen of the Creek Nation, of Sarah Miller, born on the 18 day of Nov, 1904

Name of Father: Seborn Miller   a citizen of the   Creek   Nation.
Tulsa Canadian Town
Name of Mother: Effie Miller   a citizen of the   Creek   Nation.
Con charte Town
                                       Postoffice   Okmulgee, Ind. Ter.

AFFIDAVIT OF MOTHER.

UNITED STATES OF AMERICA, Indian Territory,
   Western   DISTRICT.   Child is present

I, Effie Miller, on oath state that I am about 23 years of age and a citizen by blood, of the Creek Nation; that I am the lawful wife of Seborn Miller, who is a citizen, by blood of the Creek Nation; that a female child was born to me on 18 day of November, 1904, that said child has been named Sarah Miller, and was living March 4, 1905.

                                            her
                                        Effie x Miller

Witnesses To Mark: mark
   { Alex Posey
     DC Skaggs

Applications for Enrollment of Creek Newborn
Act of 1905   Volume XI

Subscribed and sworn to before me this 10 day of April, 1905.

Drennan C Skaggs
Notary Public.

AFFIDAVIT OF ATTENDING PHYSICIAN OR MID-WIFE.

UNITED STATES OF AMERICA, Indian Territory,
Western   DISTRICT.

my wife
I, Seborn Miller, a ~~(blank)~~ , on oath state that I attended on ^ Mrs. Effie Miller, ~~wife of~~ *(blank)* on the 18 day of Nov, 1904; that there was born to her on said date a female child; that said child was living March 4, 1905, and ~~is said to have been~~ has been named Sarah Miller

Seborn Miller
Witnesses To Mark:

Subscribed and sworn to before me this 10 day of April, 1905.

Drennan C Skaggs
Notary Public.

N.C. 908

DEPARTMENT OF THE INTERIOR,
COMMISSIONER TO THE FIVE CIVILIZED TRIBES.
Muskogee, Indian Territory, March 17, 1906.

In the matter of the application for the enrollment of Bessie Wildcat as a citizen by blood of the Creek Nation.

MATILDA WESLEY, being duly sworn, testified as follows through Jesse McDermott official interpreter.

Q What is your name? A My present name is Matilda Wesley; I am enrolled as Matilda Benson.
Q What is the name of your father? A Jim Benson.
Q Is he living? A No
Q What is the name of your mother? A Mary Benson.

Applications for Enrollment of Creek Newborn
Act of 1905   Volume XI

Q Is she living? A No.
Q Have you a sister enrolled with you if so what is her name? A Kokey
Q How old are you? A About thirty.
Q What is your post office address? A Dustin.

Witness is identified as Matilda Benson on Creek Indian care 2845 opposite roll No. 8029.

Q What is the name of this child here? A Bessie
Q Bessie what? A I suppose her name is Bessie Wildcat.
Q What is the name of the father of the child? A Willie Wildcat.
Q What is the name of Willie's father? A Sandy.
Q What [sic] the name of his mother? A Sechalagee.

Said Willie is identified on Creek Indian card 1487 opposite roll No. 1487.

Q Were you ever known by the name of Matilda Sunday? A Yes, sir.
Q Did you make application for this child under the name of Bessie Sunday? A Yes
Q Bessie Wildcat and Bessie Sunday is the same child? A Yes
Q How old is this child? A The child will be four years old next fall
Q Then the affidavit you made out for it under the name of Bessie Sunday on March 16, 1905 saying it was born in 1903 would be incorrect would it? A Yes, 1902 is correct.
Q Who was the midwife when the child was born? A Martha Hains.
Q Do you know the exact day and month that the child will be four years old? A I do not remember the exact day; the father of the child says September 13th.
Q We have affidavits here in which it is stated the child was born the 6th, 15 and blank day of September which is correct, do you now think the 13th is correct? A The 13th is the correct date.
Q Were you married to Willie Wildcat when this child was born? A No
Q Are you married to him now? A No
Q Are you married to this man Wesley whose name you have now? A Yes
Q Was Willie ever known by the name of Willie Sunday? A He is generally known among the Indians as Willie Sunday. That is the reason why the affidavit made out for the child was Bessie Sunday and he probably got that name from his father's name of Sandy Wildcat--from the first name Sandy.
Q You haven't two child named Bessie have you? [sic] No I have only one.

I, Anna Garrigues, on oath state that the above and foregoing is a true and correct transcript of my stenographic notes as taken in said cause on said date.

                                        Anna Garrigues
Subscribed and sworn to before
me this 17 day of March 1906.
                                        J McDermott
                                           Notary Public.

Applications for Enrollment of Creek Newborn
Act of 1905   Volume XI

BIRTH AFFIDAVIT.

DEPARTMENT OF THE INTERIOR,
COMMISSION TO THE FIVE CIVILIZED TRIBES.

In Re Application for Enrollment, as a citizen of the Creek Nation, of Bessie Wildcat, born on the 15th day of September, 1902

Name of Father: Willie Wildcat	a citizen of the Creek	Nation.
Name of Mother: Matilda Wildcat	a citizen of the Creek	Nation.

Post-office   Spokogee

AFFIDAVIT OF MOTHER.

UNITED STATES OF AMERICA,
   INDIAN TERRITORY,
   Western   District.

    I, Matilda Wildcat, on oath state that I am 25 years of age and a citizen by birth, of the Creek Nation; that I am the lawful wife of Willie Wildcat (deceased), who ~~is~~ was a citizen, by birth of the Creek Nation; that a female child was born to me on 15th day of September, 1902, that said child has been named Bessie Wildcat, and is now living.

                                        Her
                            Matilda x Wildcat
WITNESSES TO MARK: mark
    W.E. McQueen
    Geo Kanard

    Subscribed and sworn to before me this 22^{d} day of April, 1903.

                                   J.P. *(Illegible)*
My Com Expires Aug 16th 1906.   NOTARY PUBLIC.

AFFIDAVIT OF ATTENDING PHYSICIAN OR MID-WIFE.

UNITED STATES OF AMERICA,
   INDIAN TERRITORY,
   Western   District.

    I, Martha Haynes, a Midwife, on oath state that I attended on Mrs. Matilda Wildcat, wife of Willie Wildcat on the 15th day of September, 1902; that there was born to her on said date a female child; that said child is now living and is said to have been named Bessie Wildcat

Applications for Enrollment of Creek Newborn
Act of 1905 Volume XI

WITNESSES TO MARK:
{ W.E. McQueen
{ Geo Kanard

Her
Martha x Haynes
mark

Subscribed and sworn to before me this 22^d day of April , 1903.

My Com Expires Aug 16th 1906.

J.P. *(Illegible)*
NOTARY PUBLIC.

BIRTH AFFIDAVIT.
DEPARTMENT OF THE INTERIOR.
COMMISSION TO THE FIVE CIVILIZED TRIBES.

IN RE APPLICATION FOR ENROLLMENT, as a citizen of the CREEK Nation, of Bessie Sunday, born on the 15 day of Sept. , 1903

Name of Father: Willie Sunday   a citizen of the Creek   Nation.
Name of Mother: Matilda "   a citizen of the "   Nation.

Postoffice   Dustin

Child Present - Gr

AFFIDAVIT OF MOTHER.

UNITED STATES OF AMERICA, Indian Territory, }
    WESTERN   DISTRICT. }

    I, Matilda Sunday , on oath state that I am 26 years of age and a citizen by blood , of the Creek Nation; that I am the lawful wife of Willie Sunday , who is a citizen, by blood of the Creek Nation; that a female child was born to me on 15 day of Sept. , 1903 , that said child has been named Bessie Sunday , and is now living.

Witnesses To Mark:
{ J McDermott
{ EC Griesel

Her
Matilda x Sunday
mark

Subscribed and sworn to before me this 16 day of March , 1905.

Edw C Griesel
Notary Public.

261

Applications for Enrollment of Creek Newborn
Act of 1905 Volume XI

BIRTH AFFIDAVIT.
DEPARTMENT OF THE INTERIOR.
COMMISSION TO THE FIVE CIVILIZED TRIBES.

IN RE APPLICATION FOR ENROLLMENT, as a citizen of the Creek Nation, of Bessie Sunday, born on or about the 6 day of September, 1902

Name of Father: Willie Sunday   a citizen of the   Creek   Nation.
Name of Mother: Tilda Sunday   a citizen of the   Creek   Nation.

Postoffice   Dustin, Ind. Ter.

AFFIDAVIT OF MOTHER.

UNITED STATES OF AMERICA, Indian Territory,
Western DISTRICT.

     I, Tilda Sunday, on oath state that I am about 26 years of age and a citizen by blood, of the Creek Nation; that I am the lawful wife of Willie Sunday, who is a citizen, by blood of the Creek Nation; that a female child was born to me on or about 6 day of September, 1902, that said child has been named Bessie Sunday, and was living March 4, 1905.

                                         her
                                Tilda x Sunday
Witnesses To Mark: mark
   { Alex Posey
   { DC Skaggs

     Subscribed and sworn to before me this 23 day of March, 1905.

                                Drennan C Skaggs
                                   Notary Public.

AFFIDAVIT OF ATTENDING PHYSICIAN OR MID-WIFE.

UNITED STATES OF AMERICA, Indian Territory,
Western DISTRICT.

     I, Annie Canard, a (blank), on oath state that I attended on Mrs. Tilda Sunday, wife of Willie Sunday on or about the 6 day of September, 1902; that there was born to her on said date a female child; that said child was living March 4, 1905, and is said to have been named Bessie Sunday

                                         her
                                Annie x Canard
Witnesses To Mark: mark
   { Alex Posey
   { DC Skaggs

Applications for Enrollment of Creek Newborn
Act of 1905   Volume XI

Subscribed and sworn to before me this 23 day of March , 1905.

Drennan C Skaggs
Notary Public.

___

SUPPLEMENTAL PROOF.

DEPARTMENT OF THE INTERIOR,
COMMISSION TO THE FIVE CIVILIZED TRIBES.

___

IN RE Application for Enrollment, as a citizen of the Creek (or Muskogee) Nation, of Bessie Wildcat , born on the 13 day of Sept , 1902

Name of Father: Willie Wildcat　　　a citizen of the　Creek　Nation.
Name of Mother: Matilda Wesley　　　a citizen of the　Creek　Nation.

Postoffice　　Dustin IT

___

AFFIDAVIT OF PARENT.
(To be made if child is now living)

UNITED STATES OF AMERICA,
Indian Territory,
Western　　　DISTRICT.

I,　Matilda Wesley , on oath state that I am about 30 years of age and a citizen by blood , of the Creek (or Muskogee) Nation; that I am the mother   of Bessie Wildcat a   female   child who was born on the   13"   day of Sept , 1902, that said child is now living.　　　　　　　　　　　　　　　　　　　　his[sic]
　　　　　　　　　　　　　　　　　　　Matilda x Wesley
Witnesses To Mark:　　　　　　　　　　　mark
{ *(Name Illegible)*
{ Jesse McDermott

Subscribed and sworn to before me this 17th *day of March, 1906.*

My Commission　　　　　　　J McDermott
Expires July 25" 1907　　　　　　　　*Notary Public.*

___

263

Applications for Enrollment of Creek Newborn
Act of 1905   Volume XI

BIRTH AFFIDAVIT.

DEPARTMENT OF THE INTERIOR.
COMMISSION TO THE FIVE CIVILIZED TRIBES.

IN RE APPLICATION FOR ENROLLMENT, as a citizen of the Creek Nation, of Bessie Wildcat, born on the *(blank)* day of Sept, 1902

Name of Father: Willie Wildcat	a citizen of the Creek	Nation.
Name of Mother: Matilda Wildcat	a citizen of the Creek	Nation.

Postoffice   Dustin Ind Ter

AFFIDAVIT OF MOTHER.

UNITED STATES OF AMERICA, Indian Territory, ⎫
   Western   DISTRICT.   ⎬

I, Matilda Wildcat, on oath state that I am 27 years of age and a citizen by Birth, of the Creek Nation; that I am the lawful wife of Willie Wildcat, who is a citizen, by Birth of the Creek Nation; that a Female child was born to me on *(blank)* day of September, 1902, that said child has been named Bessie Wildcat, and was living March 4, 1905.

                            her
                      Matilda x Wildcat
Witnesses To Mark: mark
  { W.E. McQueen
    Geo Canard

Subscribed and sworn to before me this 9 day of Feb, 1906.

                        Dan Upton
                        Notary Public.

AFFIDAVIT OF ATTENDING PHYSICIAN OR MID-WIFE.

UNITED STATES OF AMERICA, Indian Territory, ⎫
   Western   DISTRICT.   ⎬

I, Martha Haynes, a Midwife, on oath state that I attended on Mrs. Matilda Wildcat, wife of Willie Wildcat on the *(blank)* day of September, 1902 ; that there was born to her on said date a Female child; that said child was living March 4, 1905, and is said to have been named Bessie Wildcat.

                        her
                    Martha x Haynes
Witnesses To Mark: mark
  { W.E. McQueen
    Geo Canard

Applications for Enrollment of Creek Newborn
Act of 1905   Volume XI

Subscribed and sworn to before me this 9 day of Feb , 1906.

                          Dan Upton
                          Notary Public.

HGH

COMMISSIONERS:
TAMS BIXBY,
THOMAS B. NEEDLES,
C.R. BRECKINBRIDGE.

DEPARTMENT OF THE INTERIOR,
COMMISSIONER TO THE FIVE CIVILIZED TRIBES.

REFER IN REPLY TO THE FOLLOWING:

NC-441.

WM. O. BEALL
Secretary

ADDRESS ONLY THE
COMMISSION TO THE FIVE CIVILIZED TRIBES.

Muskogee, Indian Territory, May 31, 1905.

Matilda Sunday,
    Dustin, Indian Territory.

Dear Madam:

    In the matter of the application for the enrollment of your minor child, Bessie Sunday, as a citizen of the Creek Nation, you are advised that the Commission requires the affidavit of the midwife or physician at the birth of said child.

    There is herewith enclosed blank form of birth affidavit. In executing same, care should be taken to see that all blanks are properly filled, all names written in full and in the event that the person signing the affidavit is unable to write, signature by mark must be attested by two witnesses.

                      Respectfully,

                            Tams Bixby
                            Chairman.

1 B A

NC-262.

                        Muskogee, Indian Territory, July 26, 1905.

Willie Sunday,
    Dustin, Indian Territory.

Dear Sir:

    On March 16, 1905 your wife Matilda Sunday appeared before the Commission to the Five Civilized Tribes and made application for the enrollment of your daughter Bessie Sunday as a citizen by blood of the Creek Nation and at that time submitted her affidavit as to the birth of said child, from which it appears that she was born September 5, 1903. Subsequently your wife and Annie Canard appeared before one of the field

Applications for Enrollment of Creek Newborn
Act of 1905   Volume XI

parties of said Commission and made affidavit that said child was born on or about the 6th day of September 1902.

For the purpose of correcting this discrepancy there is inclosed herewith a blank for proof of bityh[sic] partially filled out which you are requested to have wholly filled out, properly executed and return to this office in the inclosed envelope.

Be careful to see that the notary public before whom the affidavits are sworn to attaches his name and seal to each affidavit. In case any signature is by mark it must be attested by two disinterested witnesses.

It is stated in the affidavits as to the birth of your said daughter that you are a citizen by blood of the Creek Nation. This office is unable to identify you upon the approved roll of citizens by blood of the Creek Nation.

You are, therefore, requested to state the name under which you are finally enrolled, your final roll number as it appears from your deed or allotment certificate and the names of your parents and other members of your family.

Please give this matter your prompt attention.

Respectfully,

Commissioner.

CTD.4
Env.

BA-NE.-95.

Muskogee, Indian Territory, January 24, 1906.

Matilda Wildcat,
    Dustin, Indian Territory.

Dear Madam:

In the matter of the application for the enrollment of your minor child, Bessie Wildcat, born September 15, 1902, you are advised that this office requires proof of death of said child.

There is inclosed herewith a blank form of death affidavit and you are requested to execute before an officer authorized to administer oaths and return it to this office in the inclosed envelope.

In the event said child is not dead your affidavit and the affidavit of the mid-wife in attendance at its birth will be required; said affidavits should state the name of the child, the names of its parents, the date of its birth and whether or not it was living March 4, 1905.

Applications for Enrollment of Creek Newborn
Act of 1905 Volume XI

This matter should receive your immediate attention.

Respectfully,

Acting Commissioner.

1-DA.

N.C. 908.

Muskogee, Indian Territory, February 7, 1906.

Matilda Wildcat,
    Dustin, Indian Territory.

Dear Madam:

In the matter of the application for the enrollment of your minor child, Bessie Wildcat, you are advised that this office is unable to identify you or the father of said child on its rolls of citizens of the Creek Nation.

You are requested to write this office at an early date giving the names of your respective parents, the Creek Indian Towns to which each of you belong and your names and roll numbers as same appear upon your allotment certificates or deeds to lands in the Creek Nation.

Your affidavit and the affidavit of the mid-wife, Martha Haynes, are required, setting forth the name of the child, the names of the parents, the date of its birth and whether or not it was living on March 4, 1905, a blank for which purpose is herewith inclosed.

Respectfully,

Acting Commissioner.

1 B.A.

Applications for Enrollment of Creek Newborn
Act of 1905   Volume XI

(The letter below typed as given.)

COPY N.C. 908

THE DUSTIN MERCANTILE COMPANY.
(Incorporated)

DUSTIN? I.T.   2/9   1906

Commissioners for Five Cilized Tribes
Muskogee, I.T.

Gentlemen:

My Fathers Name was James Benson
I Belong to Thlewahle Town
My P O address is Dustin I.T.

Respc Yours

SIGNED MATILDA WILDCAT

(The letter below typed as given.)

NC 908

THE DUSTIN MERCANTILE COMPANY,
Dustin, I. T. 3/5/1906

Com to Five Cvilized Tribes,
Muskogee, I. T.

Dear Sir, Refering to your letter of 19 inst to Mattie Wilcat who hase a minor child and who is a citizen of the Creek Nation.

Is there any way for her to have this child enrolled without coming before the Com. She is a widow woman and has no money to pay R R Farr and Hotel bills and I see no chance for her to get it. Please advise if this can be done, if not how much time yet has she to come before the Com and present the child for enrollment.

Thanking you for an inmmediate reply,

Respectfully,
J.H. Swafford

for Matilda Wilcat

Applications for Enrollment of Creek Newborn
Act of 1905 Volume XI

N C 908

Muskogee, Indian Territory, March 1, 1907.

Matilda Wesley,
% Willie Wildcat,
Dustin, Indian Territory.

Dear Madam :--

You are hereby advised that on February 15, 1907, the Secretary of the Interior approved the enrollment of your minor child, Bessie Wildcat, as a citizen by blood of the Creek Nation, and that the name of said child appears upon the roll of New Born citizens by blood of the Creek Nation, enrolled under the Act of Congress approved March 3, 1905, as number 1176.

This child is now entitled to allotment and application therefor should be made without delay at the Creek Land Office, Muskogee, Indian Territory.

Respectfully,
Commissioner.

BIRTH AFFIDAVIT.
DEPARTMENT OF THE INTERIOR.
COMMISSION TO THE FIVE CIVILIZED TRIBES.

IN RE APPLICATION FOR ENROLLMENT, as a citizen of the Creek Nation, of Linda Barnett, born on the 21st day of Oct, 1902

Name of Father: Daniel Barnett   a citizen of the   Creek   Nation.
Name of Mother: Samara Barnett   a citizen of the   Creek   Nation.

Postoffice   Stonebluff I.T.

Applications for Enrollment of Creek Newborn
Act of 1905   Volume XI

AFFIDAVIT OF MOTHER.

UNITED STATES OF AMERICA, Indian Territory,
  Western   DISTRICT.

I, Samara Barnett , on oath state that I am 25 years of age and a citizen by Blood , of the Creek Nation; that I am the lawful wife of Daniel Barnett , who is a citizen, by Blood of the Creek   Nation; that a Female   child was born to me on 21st day of Oct , 1902 , that said child has been named Linda Barnett , and is now living.

Samara Barnett

Witnesses To Mark:

Subscribed and sworn to before me this 23rd day of March , 1905.

Ralph Dresback
Notary Public.

AFFIDAVIT OF ATTENDING PHYSICIAN OR MID-WIFE.

UNITED STATES OF AMERICA, Indian Territory,
  Western   DISTRICT.

I, Louvina Colbert , a Midwife , on oath state that I attended on Mrs. Samara Barnett , wife of Daniel Barnett on the 21st day of Oct , 1902 ; that there was born to her on said date a female child; that said child is now living and is said to have been named Linda Barnett

her
Louvina x Colbert
mark

Witnesses To Mark:
  { Louis Isaac
  { Nellie Dresback

Subscribed and sworn to before me this 23rd day of March , 1905.

Ralph Dresback
Notary Public.

Applications for Enrollment of Creek Newborn
Act of 1905 Volume XI

NC 911

Muskogee, Indian Territory, October 19, 1905.

Molleanna Snakeya,
  Care David Snakeya,
    Okmulgee, Indian Territory.

Dear Madam:

In the matter of the application for the enrollment of your minor child, Heness Snakeya, as a citizen by blood of the Creek Nation, there is on file with this office your affidavit relative to the birth of said child. The name of said child is given in said affidavit as Heness Nekeeyah and your name is signed thereto, Mullie Nekeeyah.

You are identified on the final roll of citizens by blood of the Creek Nation as Molleanna Snakeya and David Nekeeyah is identified on said roll as David Snakeya.

There is herewith enclosed form of birth affidavit, properly filled out, and if it correctly states thr[sic] facts, you are requested to have same executed before a notary public, being careful to sign your name as it appears in the body of the affidavit. Signature by mark must be attested by two witnesses must be attested by two witnesses.

This office further desires affidavit of the midwife or physician in attendance at the birth of said child and a blank for that purpose is enclosed herewith.

In the event that there was no physician or midwife in attendance when said child was born, it will be necessary for you to furnish this office with the affidavits of two disinterested witnesses relative to her birth. Said affidavits must set forth said child's name, the date of her birth, the names of her parents and whether or not she was living on March 4, 1905.

Respectfully,

Commissioner.

G-1

BIRTH AFFIDAVIT.

DEPARTMENT OF THE INTERIOR.
COMMISSION TO THE FIVE CIVILIZED TRIBES.

IN RE APPLICATION FOR ENROLLMENT, as a citizen of the Creek Nation, of Heness Nekeeyah, born on the 20 day of March, 1904

Name of Father: Davis Nekeeyah	a citizen of the	Creek	Nation.
Cussehta Town			
Name of Mother: Mullie Nekeeyah	a citizen of the	Creek	Nation.
Tulwa Thlocco Town			

Applications for Enrollment of Creek Newborn
Act of 1905   Volume XI

Postoffice   Okmulgee, Ind. Ter.

AFFIDAVIT OF MOTHER.

UNITED STATES OF AMERICA, Indian Territory, ⎫
   Western   DISTRICT. ⎬   Child is present

I, Mullie Nekeeyah , on oath state that I am about 25 years of age and a citizen by blood , of the Creek Nation; that I am the lawful wife of Davis Nekeeyah , who is a citizen, by blood of the Creek Nation; that a female child was born to me on 20 day of March , 1904 , that said child has been named Heness Nekeeyah , and was living March 4, 1905.

                                                       her
Witnesses To Mark: Mullie x Nekeeyah
  { Alex Posey   mark
  { DC Skaggs

Subscribed and sworn to before me this 10 day of April , 1905.

                                 Drennan C Skaggs
                                 Notary Public.

AFFIDAVIT OF ATTENDING PHYSICIAN OR MID-WIFE.

UNITED STATES OF AMERICA, Indian Territory, ⎫
   Western   DISTRICT. ⎬

                                                             my wife
I, Davis Nekeeyah , ~~a (blank)~~ , on oath state that I attended on ^ Mrs. Mullie Nekeeyah , ~~wife of~~ *(blank)* on the 20 day of March , 1904 ; that there was born to her on said date a female child; that said child was living March 4, 1905, and ~~is said to have~~ has been named Heness Nekeeyah

                                                  his
Witnesses To Mark: Davis x Nekeeyah
  { Alex Posey   mark
  { DC Skaggs

Subscribed and sworn to before me this 10 day of April, 1905.

                                 Drennan C Skaggs
                                 Notary Public.

Applications for Enrollment of Creek Newborn
Act of 1905 Volume XI

BIRTH AFFIDAVIT.
DEPARTMENT OF THE INTERIOR.
COMMISSION TO THE FIVE CIVILIZED TRIBES.

IN RE APPLICATION FOR ENROLLMENT, as a citizen of the Creek Nation, of Heness Snakeya, born on the 20 day of March, 1904

Name of Father: David Snakeya   a citizen of the Creek Nation.
Name of Mother: Molleanna Snakeya   a citizen of the Creek Nation.

Postoffice   Okmulgee, I.T.

AFFIDAVIT OF MOTHER.

UNITED STATES OF AMERICA, Indian Territory,
Western DISTRICT.

I, Molleanna Snakeya, on oath state that I am about 25 years of age and a citizen by blood, of the Creek Nation; that I am the lawful wife of David Snakeya, who is a citizen, by blood of the Creek Nation; that a female child was born to me on 20 day of March, 1904, that said child has been named Heness Snakeya, and was living March 4, 1905.

                                                 her
                           Molleanna x Snakeya
Witnesses To Mark: mark
   Noty Tiger
   J.A. Roper

Subscribed and sworn to before me this 15 day of Nov., 1905.

My Com Ex Nov. 18-1908   E. P. Blakemore
                                                Notary Public.

AFFIDAVIT OF ATTENDING PHYSICIAN OR MID-WIFE.

UNITED STATES OF AMERICA, Indian Territory,
Western DISTRICT.

I, Wm Cott, a Physician, on oath state that I attended on Mrs. Molleanna Snakeya, wife of David Snakeya on the 20 day of March, 1904; that there was born to her on said date a female child; that said child was living March 4, 1905, and is said to have been named Heness Snakeya

                                    Wm Cott MD

Witnesses To Mark:

Applications for Enrollment of Creek Newborn
Act of 1905 Volume XI

Subscribed and sworn to before me 18 day of Nov., 1905.

My Commission Expires Nov. 18, 1908

E. P. Blakemore
Notary Public.

N.C. 912

DEPARTMENT OF THE INTERIOR,
COMMISSIONER TO THE FIVE CIVILIZED TRIBES.
Muskogee, Indian Ter. July 12, 1905

In the matter of the application for the enrollment of Clarence B. Davis and Harvie L. Davis as citizens of the Creek Nation.

Susanna Davis being duly sworn testified as follows:

By Commission.

Q What is your name? [sic] Susanna Davis.
Q How old are you? A Thirty two.
Q What is your post office? A Red Bird
Q Are you a citizen of the Creek Nation? A No, sir.
Q What are the names of your two young children? A Clarance B/[sic] Davis and Harvie L. Davis
Q What is the name of the father of those children? A Lewis Davis
Q Is he a citizen of the Creek Nation? A Yes, sir.
Q Is he living? A Yes, sir, here he is.
Q When was Clarance born? A November 21st
Q Is he living? A Yes, sir.
Q How old will he be next November? A Three this coming November
Q A boy is it? A Yes, sir
Q When was Harvie L. born? [sic] January 21, 1905
Q Is he living? A No, sir.
Q How long did he live? A Until May 7th.
Q How many months did he live? A A little over two months, was born in January.
Q Wither you have the wrong date for his birth or you are poor in arithmetic, how old was he when he died? A He was over three months old. I know he was born in January and died in May.
Q How do you know the day he was born? A I have it down

Applications for Enrollment of Creek Newborn
Act of 1905   Volume XI

Q What have you it down in? A In the bible where I keep all my childrens[sic] births like that.
Q You didn't bring that bible with you? A No, sir, we always set them all down
Q Do you remember going before a notary public you and the midwife and making out affidavit about Harvie L. Davis? A Yes, sir.
Q What was his name? A Barber.
Q Up at Red Bird? A Yes, sir
Q Was this child living at the time you went before him? A Yes, sir
Q Did you have it with you? A No, sir.
Q The child was living then? A Yes, sir
Q Did you have a doctor when he died? A Yes, sir.
Q What was his name? A C.W. Payne of Red Bird
Q Do you know the date of his death, is it on the tombstone or headboard over his grave? A We have none
Q Did you write in your bible about the birth and death of the child? A He wrote it
Q He said in his affidavit that he didn't know when it died? A I told him.
Q Do you know what he wrote it with, pen or pencil? A I don't know for sure, generally writes with a pen

    Lewis Davis, being duly sworn, testified as follows:

Q What is your name? A Lewis Davis.
Q How old are you? [sic] About twenty nine
Q Are you a citizen of the Creek Nation? A Yes, sir.
Q What is the name of your father? A Sam Davis
Q What is the name of your mother? A Mahala Burk or Watson
Q Are you the father of Clarance B. and Harvie L. Davis? A Yes, sir
Q You made out an affidavit here in which you state Harvie was born in 1905-no month and no day and died in that year and you do not know the month? A Yes, sir.
Q Do you know the month and day now,[sic]? A No, only what I heard her say.
Q Don't you live at home? A Yes, sir
Q You ought to know about how long that youngest child lived? A I got so much business to attend to, I don't think about it, I just write it down in a book and that ends it. I never thought to get the correct day but it is all right, it is just like she says it was if it is not I can bring the book down

---

I, Anna Garrigues, on oath state that the above and foregoing is a true and correct transcript of my stenographic notes as taken in said case on said date.

                           Anna Garrigues

Subscribed and sworn to before me this 12th day of July 1905

                           J McDermott
                           Notary public[sic].

Applications for Enrollment of Creek Newborn
Act of 1905   Volume XI

BIRTH AFFIDAVIT.

DEPARTMENT OF THE INTERIOR.
COMMISSION TO THE FIVE CIVILIZED TRIBES.

    IN RE APPLICATION FOR ENROLLMENT, as a citizen of the Creek Nation, of Harvie L. Davis, born on the ~~(blank) day of (blank)~~ , 1905

Name of Father:	Lewis H. Davis	a citizen of the	Creek	Nation.
Name of Mother:	Susanna Davis	a citizen of the	U. S.	Nation.

                   Postoffice   Redbird, I.T.

AFFIDAVIT OF ~~MOTHER~~.
                   father

UNITED STATES OF AMERICA, Indian Territory,
    Western   DISTRICT.

    I, Lewis H. Davis , on oath state that I am 29 years of age and a citizen by blood , of the Creek Nation; that I am the lawful ~~wife~~ husband of   Susanna Davis , who is a citizen, by ~~(blank)~~ of the U. S. Nation; that a male child was born to me on ~~(blank)~~ day of ~~(blank)~~ , 1905 , that said child has been named Harvie L. Davis , and ~~was living March 4, 1905~~. died in 1905; dont[sic] know month

                                    Lewis H. Davis

Witnesses To Mark:

    Subscribed and sworn to before me this 3" day of July, 1905.

                                    Henry G. Hains
                                       Notary Public.

BIRTH AFFIDAVIT.

DEPARTMENT OF THE INTERIOR.
COMMISSION TO THE FIVE CIVILIZED TRIBES.

    IN RE APPLICATION FOR ENROLLMENT, as a citizen of the Creek or Muskogee Nation, of Harvie L. Davis, born on the 21 day of January, 1905

Name of Father: Lewis H. Davis	a citizen of the Creek	Nation.
Name of Mother: Susanna Davis	a citizen of the United States	Nation.

                   Postoffice   Red Bird Ind. Terr.

Applications for Enrollment of Creek Newborn
Act of 1905   Volume XI

AFFIDAVIT OF MOTHER.

UNITED STATES OF AMERICA, Indian Territory,
Western Judical[sic]   DISTRICT.

I, Susanna Davis , on oath state that I am 23   years of age and a citizen by ……………….., of the …………………… Nation; that I am the lawful wife of Lewis H. Davis , who is a citizen, by blood of the Creek or Muskogee Nation; that a boy child was born to me on 21   day of January , 1905 , that said child has been named Harvie L. Davis , and was living March 4, 1905.

Susanna Davis

Witnesses To Mark:

Subscribed and sworn to before me this 28 day of April , 1905.

E. L. Barber
Notary Public.

My Com Exp 13 Jun 1908

AFFIDAVIT OF ATTENDING PHYSICIAN OR MID-WIFE.

UNITED STATES OF AMERICA, Indian Territory,
Western Judical[sic]   DISTRICT.

I, Bettie TURner[sic] , a Mid Wife , on oath state that I attended on Mrs. Susanna Davis , wife of Lewis H. Davis on the 21   day of January , 1905 ; that there was born to her on said date a boy child; that said child was living March 4, 1905, and is said to have been named Harvie L. Davis

her
Bettie x Turner
mark

Witnesses To Mark:
  C.W. Paine
  C. Knight

Subscribed and sworn to before me this 28 day of April , 1905.

E. L. Barber
Notary Public.

My Com Exp 13 Jun 1908

Applications for Enrollment of Creek Newborn
Act of 1905 Volume XI

BIRTH AFFIDAVIT.

DEPARTMENT OF THE INTERIOR.
COMMISSION TO THE FIVE CIVILIZED TRIBES.

IN RE APPLICATION FOR ENROLLMENT, as a citizen of the Creek Nation, of Clarance B. Davis, born on the 21" day of Nov., 1902

Name of Father: Lewis H. Davis   a citizen of the   Creek   Nation.
Name of Mother: Susanna Davis   a citizen of the   U. S.   Nation.

Postoffice   Red Bird, I.T.

AFFIDAVIT OF ~~MOTHER~~.
father

UNITED STATES OF AMERICA, Indian Territory,
Western   DISTRICT.

I, Lewis H. Davis, on oath state that I am 29 years of age and a citizen by blood, of the Creek Nation; that I am the lawful ~~wife~~ husband of Susanna Davis, who is a citizen, by ~~(blank)~~ of the U. S. Nation; that a male child was born to ~~me~~ her ~~on (blank)~~ in winter day of ~~(blank)~~, 1902, that said child has been named Clarance B. Davis, and was living March 4, 1905.

Lewis H. Davis

Witnesses To Mark:
{

Subscribed and sworn to before me this 3" day of July, 1905.

Henry G. Hains
Notary Public.

BIRTH AFFIDAVIT.

DEPARTMENT OF THE INTERIOR.
COMMISSION TO THE FIVE CIVILIZED TRIBES.

IN RE APPLICATION FOR ENROLLMENT, as a citizen of the Creek or Muskogee Nation, of Clarance B. Davis, born on the 21 day of November, 1902

Name of Father: Lewis Davis   a citizen of the   Creek   Nation.
Name of Mother: Susanna Davis   a citizen of the United States   Nation.

Postoffice   Red Bird Ind. TEr.[sic]

Applications for Enrollment of Creek Newborn
Act of 1905   Volume XI

AFFIDAVIT OF MOTHER.

UNITED STATES OF AMERICA, Indian Territory, }
  Western Judical[sic]   DISTRICT.

I, Susanna Davis , on oath state that I am 23 years of age and a citizen by ...., of the .... Nation; that I am the lawful wife of Lewis H. Davis , who is a citizen, by Blood of the Creek or Muskogee Nation; that a boy child was born to me on 21 day of November , 1902 , that said child has been named Clarance B. Davis , and was living March 4, 1905.

Susanna Davis

Witnesses To Mark:
{

Subscribed and sworn to before me this 28 day of April , 1905.

E. L. Barber
Notary Public.

My Com Exp 13 Jun 1908

AFFIDAVIT OF ATTENDING PHYSICIAN OR MID-WIFE.

UNITED STATES OF AMERICA, Indian Territory, }
  Western Judical[sic]   DISTRICT.

I, Nellie Prence , a Mid Wife , on oath state that I attended on Mrs. Susanna Davis , wife of Lewis H. Davis on the 21 day of November , 1902 ; that there was born to her on said date a boy child; that said child was living March 4, 1905, and is said to have been named Clarance B. Davis

her
Nellie x Prence
mark

Witnesses To Mark:
{ B. *(Illegible)*
  C. W. Paine

Subscribed and sworn to before me this 28 day of April , 1905.

E. L. Barber
Notary Public.

My Com Exp 13 Jun 1908

Applications for Enrollment of Creek Newborn
Act of 1905 Volume XI

BIRTH AFFIDAVIT.

DEPARTMENT OF THE INTERIOR.
COMMISSION TO THE FIVE CIVILIZED TRIBES.

IN RE APPLICATION FOR ENROLLMENT, as a citizen of the CREEK Nation, of Moses Pitman, born on the 8 day of August, 1902

Name of Father: Edward Pitman	a citizen of the Creek	Nation.
Name of Mother: Susie Pitman	a citizen of the Creek	Nation.

Postoffice   Brokenorrow[sic]

AFFIDAVIT OF MOTHER.

UNITED STATES OF AMERICA, Indian Territory, }
    WESTERN   DISTRICT.

marriage
I, Susie Pitman, on oath state that I am 28 years of age and a citizen by ~~Creek~~, of the Creek Nation; that I am the lawful wife of Edward Pitman, who is a citizen, by blood of the Creek Nation; that a male child was born to me on 8 day of August, 1902, that said child has been named Moses Pitman, and is now living.

Susie Pitman

Witnesses To Mark:
{

Subscribed and sworn to before me this 18 day of April, 1905.

J.C. Atkinson asistant[sic]
Notary Public. P.M.

AFFIDAVIT OF ATTENDING PHYSICIAN OR MID-WIFE.

UNITED STATES OF AMERICA, Indian Territory, }
    WESTERN   DISTRICT.

I, Becky Meeks, a mid-wife, on oath state that I attended on Mrs. Susie Pitman, wife of Ed. Pitman on the 8 day of August, 1902; that there was born to her on said date a male child; that said child is now living and is said to have been named Moses Pitman

Becky x Meeks
her mark

Witnesses To Mark:
{ W. H. Grant
  William Meeks

Applications for Enrollment of Creek Newborn
Act of 1905 Volume XI

Subscribed and sworn to before me this 18 day of April, 1905.

                    J.C. Atkinson   assistant
                    Notary Public. P.M.

BIRTH AFFIDAVIT.

DEPARTMENT OF THE INTERIOR.
COMMISSION TO THE FIVE CIVILIZED TRIBES.

IN RE APPLICATION FOR ENROLLMENT, as a citizen of the Creek Nation, of Moses Pitman, born on the 8 day of August, 1902

Name of Father: Edward Pitman   a citizen of the Creek Nation.
Coweta Town
Name of Mother: Susie Pitman   a citizen of the United StatesNation.

                Postoffice   Stidham, Ind. Ter.

AFFIDAVIT OF MOTHER.

UNITED STATES OF AMERICA, Indian Territory,
    Western   **DISTRICT.**   Child is not present

    I, Edward Pitman, on oath state that I am 22 years of age and a citizen by blood, of the Creek Nation; that I ~~am~~ was formerly the lawful ~~wife~~ husband of Susie Pitman, who is a citizen, by *(blank)* of the United States ~~Nation~~; that a male child was born to ~~me~~ her on 8 day of August, 1902, that said child has been named Moses Pitman, and was living March 4, 1905. That the mother of the child and I have separated and she has the custody of the child and has removed from the country

                    Edward Pitman
Witnesses To Mark:

Subscribed and sworn to before me this 7 day of April, 1905.

                    Preston Janway
                    Notary Public.

Applications for Enrollment of Creek Newborn
Act of 1905 Volume XI

AFFIDAVIT OF ATTENDING PHYSICIAN OR MID-WIFE.

UNITED STATES OF AMERICA, Indian Territory, }
    Western   DISTRICT.

    I, Rose Pitman , a midwife , on oath state that I attended on Mrs. Susie Pitman, wife of Edward Pitman on the 8 day of August , 1902 ; that there was born to her on said date a male child; that said child was living March 4, 1905, and is said to have been named Moses Pitman

                                                     Rose Pitman
Witnesses To Mark:
{

    Subscribed and sworn to before me this 7 day of April , 1905.

My commission   Preston Janway
Expires May 19th 1908   Notary Public.

BIRTH AFFIDAVIT.
DEPARTMENT OF THE INTERIOR.
COMMISSION TO THE FIVE CIVILIZED TRIBES.

    IN RE APPLICATION FOR ENROLLMENT, as a citizen of the CREEK Nation, of Moses Pitman, born on the 8 day of August, 1902

Name of Father: Ed Pitman   a citizen of the Creek   Nation.
Name of Mother: Susie Pitman   a citizen of the U. S.   Nation.

                        Postoffice   Broken Arrow, I.T.

AFFIDAVIT OF MOTHER.

UNITED STATES OF AMERICA, Indian Territory, }
    WESTERN   DISTRICT.

    I, Susie Pitman , on oath state that I am 28 years of age and a citizen by ~~U.S.~~ , of the U.S. Nation; that I am the lawful wife of Ed Pitman , who is a citizen, by Blood of the Creek Nation; that a male child was born to me on 8th day of August, 1902 , that said child has been named Moses Pitman , and is now living.

                                                Susie Pitman
Witnesses To Mark:
{

Applications for Enrollment of Creek Newborn
Act of 1905 Volume XI

Subscribed and sworn to before me this 14th day of April, 1905.

My Com expires Apr. 11, 1909

Zera E Parrish
Notary Public.

BIRTH AFFIDAVIT.

DEPARTMENT OF THE INTERIOR.
COMMISSION TO THE FIVE CIVILIZED TRIBES.

IN RE APPLICATION FOR ENROLLMENT, as a citizen of the Creek Nation, of Sammie Shepherd, born on the 28 day of Sep., 1902

Name of Father: George Shepherd who is not   a citizen of the   Creek   Nation.
Name of Mother: Annie Shepherd   a citizen of the   Creek   Nation.

Postoffice   Beggs, I.T.

AFFIDAVIT OF MOTHER.

UNITED STATES OF AMERICA, Indian Territory,
Western   DISTRICT.

I, Annie Shepherd, on oath state that I am 27 years of age and a citizen by blood, of the Creek Nation; that I am the lawful wife of George Shepherd who is not ~~who is~~ a citizen, by *(blank)* of the Creek Nation; that a male child was born to me on 28 day of September, 1902, that said child has been named Sammie Shepherd, and was living March 4, 1905.

Annie Shepherd

Witnesses To Mark:
{

Subscribed and sworn to before me this 28 day of April, 1905.

My Commission Expires July 14, 1906.   N. N. Barker
Notary Public.

Applications for Enrollment of Creek Newborn
Act of 1905 Volume XI

AFFIDAVIT OF ATTENDING PHYSICIAN OR MID-WIFE.

UNITED STATES OF AMERICA, Indian Territory, }
Western DISTRICT.

I, Maggie Washington , a mid-wife , on oath state that I attended on Mrs. Annie Shepherd , wife of George Shepherd on the 28 day of September , 1902 ; that there was born to her on said date a male child; that said child was living March 4, 1905, and is said to have been named Sammie Shepherd

Maggie Washington

Witnesses To Mark:
{

Subscribed and sworn to before me this 28 day of April , 1905.

My Commission Expires July 14, 1906. N. N. Barker
Notary Public.

N.C. 915.

DEPARTMENT OF THE INTERIOR,
COMMISSIONER TO THE FIVE CIVILIZED TRIBES.
Muskogee, I. T., February 6, 1906.

In the matter of the application for the enrollment of Robert Daniel as a citizen by blood of the Creek Nation.

UNAH DANIEL, being duly sworn, testified as follows:

BY THE COMMISSIONER:
Q What is your name? A Unah Daniel. I am sometimes called in my neighborhood, Unah Johnson or Unah Daniel Johnson. The way they got it mixed up my father's name is Daniel Johnson. I am enrolled Unah Daniel. I have received my deed with the name Unah Daniel on it and I have a new born child by Mary Daniel, the woman from whom I am now divorced, and so I have no desire to have my name changed f[sic] from Daniel, which is on my deed and on the rolls of the Commission, to Johnson, by which I am sometimes called and desire that this child be enrolled as Robert Daniel instead of Robert Johnson.
Q What is the name of your mother? A Nicey Scott.

Applications for Enrollment of Creek Newborn
Act of 1905 Volume XI

The witness is identified as Unah Daniel, Creek Indian Card 95, opposite Roll No. 353. A notation on said card shows that he appears on the 1890 Roll as Unah Daniel Johnson.

Q Who is the mother of your child, Unah Daniel, Jr.? A Mary Daniel
Q Is she living? A Yes, sir.
Q Is Unah living? A Yes, sir.
Q When were you divorced from Mary Daniel? A About three years ago.
Q Were you divorced before or after Unah was born? A After he was born.
Q How long after? A It was along about in the same year.
Q Is your child, Robert Daniel, living? A Yes, sir.
Q How old is he? A He will be one year old this month.
Q What day? A The 25th.
Q What is the name of Robert's mother? A Miley Alexander.
Q What is the name of Miley's father? A Arty Alexander.
Q What was the name of her mother? A Nancy Alexander.

Miley Alexander is identified on Creek Indian Care 95, opposite Roll No. 359.

Q Are you married to her? A Yes, sir.
Q When were you married to her? A I think it was about in the Fall of 1902, I guess.
Q How long had you been married to her before you had a child by her? A The child died.
Q How long after you were married to her before the child was born? A About a year and a little over, I guess.
Q What was that child's name? A Joseph.
Q Is Joseph living? A No, sir.
Q When did he die? A He died in 1903, I think it was. On March the 11th.---------------
It was 1904, March 11.
Q Are you sure that your child, Robert, was born in February? A Yes, sir.
Q Where is that child? A There he is. (indicating a child in arms)
Q What month was last month? A Last month was January.
Q What will next month be? A March.
Q How do you remember that this child was born February 25, 1903? A I have the date of his birth.
Q You have it written down? A Yes, sir.
Q You have it written down? A Yes, sir.[sic]
Q What is it written in? A The Bible.
Q Have you that Bible with you? A We haven't got it with us.
Q You what[sic] this child enrolled, if it should be enrolled, as Robert Daniel, do you? A Yes, sir.
Q Was there any mid-wife present when Robert was born? A No, sir.
Q You are offering here the affidavits of two disinterested witnesses instead of the affidavit of the mid-wife are you? A Yes, sir.
Q What is your post office address? A Okmulgee.
Q Have you a child named John? A Yes, sir.
Q Is he living? A Yes, sir.

Applications for Enrollment of Creek Newborn
Act of 1905   Volume XI

Q Who is he living with? A With his mother.
Q Who is Unah Daniel, Jr., living with? A With his mother.
Q You are not living in the same house with her, are you? A No, sir.
Q You are living with Miley? A Yes, sir.
Q To what town do you belong? A Cussehta.

---oooOOOooo---

I, D. C. Skaggs, on oath state that the above and foregoing is a full and true transcript of my stenographic notes as taken in said cause on said date.

D. C. Skaggs
23   July
Subscribed and sworn to before me this 6" day of Mch 1906.

HG Hains
Notary Public.

Western District
Indian Territory SS

We, the undersigned, on oath state that we are personally acquainted with Miley Alexander   wife of   Unah Daniel (Johnson)   ; and that on or about the 25th day of   February , 1905, a male child was born to them and has been named Robert Daniel (Johnson)   ; that said child was living March 4, 1905.

We further state that we have no interest in the above case.

his
Henry x Mico
mark
his
Artie x Alexander
Witness to mark.   mark
Wm C. Newman (to both)
O.K. Dickerson   (to both)

Subscribed and sworn to before me
this 27th day of Jan. 1906.   W C McAdoo
Notary Public.
My commission Expires Apr. 23ed[sic]. 1907.

286

Applications for Enrollment of Creek Newborn
Act of 1905   Volume XI

BIRTH AFFIDAVIT.
DEPARTMENT OF THE INTERIOR.
COMMISSION TO THE FIVE CIVILIZED TRIBES.

IN RE APPLICATION FOR ENROLLMENT, as a citizen of the Creek Nation, of Robert Daniel, born on the 25" day of Feby , 1905

Name of Father: Unah Daniel   a citizen of the   Creek   Nation.
Name of Mother: Miley Daniel (nee Alexander) a citizen of the   Creek   Nation.

Postoffice   Okmulgee, I.T.

AFFIDAVIT OF MOTHER.

UNITED STATES OF AMERICA, Indian Territory,
   Western   DISTRICT.

I, Miley Daniel , on oath state that I am 29 years of age and a citizen by blood , of the Creek Nation; that I am the lawful wife of Unah Daniel , who is a citizen, by blood of the Creek Nation; that a male child was born to me on 25" day of Feby , 1905 , that said child has been named Robert Daniel , and is now living.

                                        her
                                Miley x Daniel
Witnesses To Mark: mark
 { H.G. Hains
   DC Skaggs

Subscribed and sworn to before me this 6" day of Feby , 1906.

                        (No name given.)
                        Notary Public.

BIRTH AFFIDAVIT.
DEPARTMENT OF THE INTERIOR.
COMMISSION TO THE FIVE CIVILIZED TRIBES.

IN RE APPLICATION FOR ENROLLMENT, as a citizen of the Creek Nation, of Robert Johnson , born on the 25th day of February, 1905

Name of Father: Unah Johnson   a citizen of the   Creek   Nation.
Name of Mother: Miley Alexander Johnson   a citizen of the   Creek   Nation.

Postoffice   Okmulgee, Indian Territory.

Applications for Enrollment of Creek Newborn
Act of 1905 Volume XI

AFFIDAVIT OF MOTHER.

UNITED STATES OF AMERICA, Indian Territory, }
Western DISTRICT.

I, Miley Alexander Johnson , on oath state that I am 29 years of age and a citizen by Birth , of the Creek Nation; that I am the lawful wife of Unah Johnson , who is a citizen, by Birth of the Creek Nation; that a male child was born to me on 25th day of February , 1 5[sic] , that said child has been named Robert Johnson , and was living March 4, 1905.

                                                                             her
Witnesses To Mark: Miley Alexander x Johnson
{ Wm C. Newman   mark
  Wright Thornburgh

Subscribed and sworn to before me this 28th day of April , 1905.

                                                  Harwood Keaton
                                                  Notary Public.

AFFIDAVIT OF ATTENDING PHYSICIAN OR MID-WIFE.

UNITED STATES OF AMERICA, Indian Territory, }
Western DISTRICT.

I, Unah Johnson, a Father , on oath state that I attended on Mrs. Miley Alexander Johnson , wife of myself, no physician or mid-wife being present when said Robert Johnson was born on the 25th day of February , 1905 ; that there was born to her on said date a male child; that said child was living March 4, 1905, and is said to have been named Robert Johnson

                                                        Unah Johnson
Witnesses To Mark:
{ Wm C. Newman
  Wright Thornburgh

Subscribed and sworn to before me this 28th day of April , 1905.

                                                  Harwood Keaton
                                                  Notary Public.

Applications for Enrollment of Creek Newborn
Act of 1905 Volume XI

BIRTH AFFIDAVIT.
DEPARTMENT OF THE INTERIOR.
COMMISSION TO THE FIVE CIVILIZED TRIBES.

IN RE APPLICATION FOR ENROLLMENT, as a citizen of the Creek Nation, of Joseph Johnson, born on the 10th day of March, 1903

Name of Father: Unah Johnson   a citizen of the Creek   Nation.
Name of Mother: Miley Alexander Johnson   a citizen of the Creek   Nation.

Postoffice   Okmulgee, Indian Territory

AFFIDAVIT OF MOTHER.

UNITED STATES OF AMERICA, Indian Territory,
Western   DISTRICT.

I, Miley Alexander Johnson, on oath state that I am 29 years of age and a citizen by Birth, of the Creek Nation; that I am the lawful wife of Unah Johnson, who is a citizen, by Birth of the Creek Nation; that a male child was born to me on 10th day of March, 1903, that said child has been named Joseph Johnson, ~~and was living March 4, 1905~~. that said Joseph Johnson died on the 11th day of March, 1904

                                                                    her
                              Miley Alexander x Johnson
Witnesses To Mark: mark
{ *(Illegible)* Stanford
{ Wright Thornburgh

Subscribed and sworn to before me this 28th day of April, 1905.

                              Harwood Keaton
                              Notary Public.

AFFIDAVIT OF ATTENDING PHYSICIAN OR MID-WIFE.

UNITED STATES OF AMERICA, Indian Territory,
Western   DISTRICT.

I, Unah Johnson, a Father, on oath state that I attended on Mrs. Miley Alexander Johnson, wife of Myself when said Joseph Johnson was born (no mie-wife being present nor physician) on the 10th day of March, 1903 ; that there was born to her on said date a male child; that said child was living March 4, 1905, and is said to have been named Joseph Johnson

                              Unah Johnson

Applications for Enrollment of Creek Newborn
Act of 1905 Volume XI

Witnesses To Mark:
{ *(Illegible)* Stanford
{ Wright Thornburgh

Subscribed and sworn to before me this 28th day of April, 1905.

Harwood Keaton
Notary Public.

N.C. 915. F.H.W.

DEPARTMENT OF THE INTERIOR,
COMMISSIONER TO THE FIVE CIVILIZED TRIBES.

In the matter of the application for the enrollment of Joseph Daniel, deceased, as a citizen by blood of the Creek Nation.

STATEMENT AND ORDER.

The record in this case shows that on May 2, 1905, an application was filed, in affidavit form, for the enrollment of Joseph Johnson as a citizen by blood of the Creek Nation but inasmuch as the father of the applicant is enrolled under the surname of Daniel, the said application is herein considered as the application of Joseph Daniel. A copy of the transcript of testimony taken on February 6, 1905 in the matter of the application for the enrollment of Robert Daniel as a citizen by blood of the Creek Nation is attached to and made a part of the record herein.

It appears that Joseph Daniel was the child of Unah and Miley Daniel.

It further appears from the records of this office and the evidence that the father is some times known as Johnson but is identified by the name of Unah Daniel on a partial schedule of citizens by blood of the Creek Nation approved by the Secretary of the Interior March 13, 1902, opposite roll No. 353.

The evidence further shows that said Joseph Daniel was born March 10, 1903 and died March 11, 1904.

There is no authority of law for the enrollment of the said applicant as a citizen by blood of the Creek Nation.

It is, therefore, ordered that the application for the enrollment of said Joseph Daniel, deceased, as a citizen by blood of the Creek Nation, be, and the same is, hereby dismissed.

Tams Bixby Commissioner.

Muskogee, Indian Territory.
JAN 24 1907

Applications for Enrollment of Creek Newborn
Act of 1905   Volume XI

N.C. 915

Muskogee, Indian Territory, October 5, 1905.

Unah Johnson,
Okmulgee, Indian Territory.

Dear Sir:

This office is unable to identify you on its roll of citizens of the Creek Nation.

You are requested to state the names of your parents, the Creek Indian town to which you belong, the numbers which appear on your deeds to land in the Creek Nation and any other information that will help to identify you as a citizen of the Creek Nation.

Respectfully,
Commissioner.

NC 915

Muskogee, Indian Territory, October 19, 1905.

Miley Alexander Johnson,
    Care Unah Johnson,
        Okmulgee, Indian Territory.

Dear Madam:

In the matter of the application for the enrollment of your minor child, Robert Johnson, born February 25, 1905, this office desires the affidavits of two disinterested witnesses relative to his birth. Said affidavits must set forth said child's name, the date of his birth, the names of his parents and whether or not he was living on March 4, 1905.

This office is unable to identify Unah Johnson on its roll of approved citizens of the Creek Nation and you are requested to state the names of his parents, the Creek Indian town to which he belongs, the numbers which appear on his deeds to land in the Creek Nation and if he has any children enrolled as citizens of the Creek Nation, state their names.

Respectfully,
Commissioner.

Applications for Enrollment of Creek Newborn
Act of 1905   Volume XI

NC-915

Muskogee, Indian Territory, January 16, 1906.

Millie Johnson,
 Care of Unah Johnson,
  Okmulgee, Indian Territory.

Dear Madam:

Receipt is acknowledged of your letter of January 9, 1906, in which you ask if your children, Robert and Joseph, are enrolled, and if you can file for them now.

In reply you are advised that in the matter of the application for the enrollment of your said children, you will be allowed fifteen days from date hereof within which to appear at this Office with Unah Johnson for the purpose of being examined under oath.

Respectfully,
Commissioner.

NC 915.

Muskogee, Indian Territory, January 24, 1907.

Miley Alexander Johnson,
 c/o Unah Johnson,
  Okmulgee, Indian Territory.

Dear Madam:

There is herewith enclosed one copy of the statement and order of the Commissioner to the Five Civilized Tribes, dated January 14, 1907, dismissing the application made by you for the enrollment of your minor child, Joseph Johnson, as a citizen by blood of the Creek Nation.

Respectfully,
Commissioner.

Register.
LM-91

Applications for Enrollment of Creek Newborn
Act of 1905   Volume XI

See Cr. Field No. 2889.

DEPARTMENT OF THE INTERIOR,
COMMISSION TO THE FIVE CIVILIZED TRIBES.
April 29, 1905, Sapulpa, I.T.

In the matter of the application for the enrollment of Ada Snow, deceased, as a citizen by blood of the Creek Nation.

Pompey Barnett, being duly sworn, by E.C. Griesel, a Notary Public, testified as follows: Through Official interpreter Noah Gregory.

By Commission:
Q What is your name? A Pompey Barnett.
Q How old are you? A 24.
Q What is your post office? A Bristow.
Q Are you a citizen of the Creek Nation? A Yes.
Q Do you know a child by the name of Ada Snow? A Yes sir.
Q Who are the parents of this child? A Ca-pah-ney and Far-lo-con-we-nay.
Q Both of these parents are citizens of the Creek Nation? A Yes.
Q The mother, Far-lo-can-we-nay is sometimes knows as Eliza Hailstone? A She used to be called Eliza Wildcat now Eliza Hailstone.
Q When was this child Ada born? A Last year March 12.
Q Is this child living? [sic] No sir she is dead.
Q When did she die? A March 29, 1905.
Q How do you know it died on March 29, 1905? A She has been sick sometimes and I went to see the child and she died the night I got there.
Q When did you go there? A On the day of the 29th of March, 1905.
Q About how long ago has that been? A About a month I think.
Q Do you know on what day of the week that child died? A I don't know what day of the week it was.
Q[sic]

E.C. Griesel, being duly sworn, on his oath, states that the above and foregoing is a true and correct transcript of his stenographic notes as taken in said cause on said date.

Edw C Griesel

Subscribed and sworn to before me this 5 day of May, 1905.

Zera E Parrish
Notary Public.

Applications for Enrollment of Creek Newborn
Act of 1905   Volume XI

(The note below difficult to read.)

This childs[sic] father selective No 10705
Filed March 28th 1901
Creek Roll Card Filed N2175
allotment on land Ace 3 T 16 K10
W1/2 of S.E.1/4
SW1/4 of ?E1/4 *(illegible)*
?-40 acres of lot 2 of

                    Com Expires 9/8/06
W W Holder

AFFIDAVIT OF DISINTERESTED WITNESSES.

United States of America,
      Indian Territory,
      Western District.

    We, the undersigned, on oath state that we are personally acquainted with   Far lo con we-ney , wife of   Capohney[sic] Snow ; and that there was born to her on or about the 29 day of March , 1904, a Female child; that said child was living March 4, 1905, and is said to have been named   Ada Snow

    We further state that we have no interest in the this case.

                His
                 x   Killie Krinks
               mark
               Her
                 x   Lusanna Krinks
               mark
(2) Witnesses to mark:
W W Holder

T.J. Taggart

Subscribed and sworn to before me this 23 day of December 1905

                              W W Holder
                              Notary Public.

Applications for Enrollment of Creek Newborn
Act of 1905   Volume XI

BIRTH AFFIDAVIT.
DEPARTMENT OF THE INTERIOR.
COMMISSION TO THE FIVE CIVILIZED TRIBES.

IN RE APPLICATION FOR ENROLLMENT, as a citizen of the Creek Nation, of Ada Snow, born on the 12 day of March, 1904

Name of Father: Ka-per-na (or Ca-pah-nay)   a citizen of the   Creek   Nation.
(Euchee)
Name of Mother: Ka-ko-con-ney Wildcat   a citizen of the   "   Nation.
(Euchee)   or (Far-co-con-we-na)
                                                Postoffice   Kellyville

AFFIDAVIT OF MOTHER.

UNITED STATES OF AMERICA, Indian Territory, ⎱
    Western   DISTRICT.   ⎰

I, Ka-ko-con-ney Wildcat or Far-co-con-we-na , on oath state that I am 30 years of age and a citizen by blood , of the Creek Nation; that I am the lawful wife of Ka-per-na , who is a citizen, by blood of the Creek Nation; that a female child was born to me on 12 day of March, 1904, that said child has been named Ada Snow, and was living March 4, 1905. died March 29, 1905
                                                her
                                Ka-ko-con-ney x Wildcat
Witnesses To Mark: or Far-co-con-we-na mark
  ⎰ David Shelby
  ⎱ Jesse McDermott

Subscribed and sworn to before me this 27 day of April, 1905.

(Seal)   Edw C Griesel
                                Notary Public.

AFFIDAVIT OF ATTENDING PHYSICIAN OR MID-WIFE.
                                Father
UNITED STATES OF AMERICA, Indian Territory, ⎱
    Western   DISTRICT.   ⎰

I, Ka-per-na , a *(blank)* , on oath state that I attended on Mrs. Ka-ko-con-ney Wildcat ,my wife of *(blank)* on the 12 day of March, 1904 ; that there was born to her on said date a female child; that said child was living March 4, 1905, and is said to have been named Ada Snow   His
                                Ka-per-na x
                                    father[sic]

Applications for Enrollment of Creek Newborn
Act of 1905 Volume XI

Witnesses To Mark:
{ David Shelby
{ Jesse McDermott

Subscribed and sworn to before me this 27 day of April, 1905.

(Seal) Edw C Griesel
Notary Public.

N.C. 916

Muskogee, Indian Territory, October 20, 1905.

(Name Illegible)
Care Ka per na (or Cap ah ney),
Kellyville, Indian Territory.

Dear Madam:

In the matter of the application for the enrollment of your minor child, Ada Snow, born March 12, 1904, as a citizen by blood of the Creek Nation, this office desires the affidavit of two disinterested witnesses relative to her birth. Said affidavits must set forth said child's name, the date of her birth, the names of her parents and whether or not she was living on March 4, 1905.

From the information at hand this office is unable to identify your husband, Ka per na (or Cap ah ney), on its final roll of citizens by blood of the Creek Nation; you are requested to state the names of his parents, the Creek Indian town to which he belongs and the numbers which appear on his deeds to lands in the Creek Nation.

Respectfully,
Commissioner.

Applications for Enrollment of Creek Newborn
Act of 1905   Volume XI

NC
917

Muskogee, Indian Territory, October 20, 1905.

Panela[sic] Bruner,
    Care John Bruner,
        Bixby, Indian Territory.

Dear Madam:

    In the matter of the application for the enrollment of your minor children, Minnie Bruner, born December 7, 1901, and Archie Bruner, born February 6, 1904, as citizens by blood of the Creek Nation, this office desires the affidavits of two disinterested witnesses relative to their births. Said affidavits must set forth the names of said children, the date of their birth, the names of their parents and whether or not they were living on March 4, 1905.

                    Respectfully,
                                  Commissioner.

AFFIDAVIT OF DISINTERESTED WITNESSES.

United States of America)
Indian Territory   ) SS
Western District   )

    We, the undersigned, on oath state that we are personally acquainted with Permela wife of   John Bruner   ; and that there was born to her on or about the 6th day of Mch 1904, a boy child; that said child was living March 4, 1905, and is said to have been named   Archie Bruner

    We further state that we have no interest in this case.

                                  Daniel Bruner
                                  her
                                Betty x Bruner
(2) Witnesses to mark: mark
    S.M. Jones
    (Name Illegible)

    Subscribed and sworn to before me this 18 day of November 1905.

                                  Carr Peterson
    My Commission Expires Aug 28, 1909   Notary Public.

Applications for Enrollment of Creek Newborn
Act of 1905   Volume XI

Western District
Indian Territory   SS

We, the undersigned, on oath, state that we are personally acquainted with Pamela[sic] Bruner   wife of   John Bruner   and that on or about the 7th day of Dec 1901, a female child was born to them and has been named Minnie Bruner;   that   said child was living March 4, 1905.

We further state that we have no interest in the above case.

                                          John Buck
                                          her
Witness to mark: Rosa x Buck
J.F. Panther   mark

_____
_____

Subscribed and sworn to before
me this 10th day of Jan 1906

                                        J.F. Panther
My com exp July 2-1906   Notary Public.

AFFIDAVIT OF DISINTERESTED WITNESSES.

United States of America   )
Indian Territory   ) SS
Western District   )

We, the undersigned, on oath state that we are personally acquainted with Permela wife of   John Bruner   ; and that there was born to her on or about the 7th   day of Dec. 1901, a girl   child; that said child was living March 4, 1905, and is said to have been named Minnie Bruner

We further state that we have no interest in this case.

                                        Daniel Bruner
                                        her
(2) Witnesses to mark: Betty x Bruner
  S.M. Jones   mark
  Cleo Peterson

Applications for Enrollment of Creek Newborn
Act of 1905 Volume XI

Subscribed and sworn to before me this 18 day of November 1905.

                                          Carr Peterson
My Commission Expires Aug 28, 1909   Notary Public.

BIRTH AFFIDAVIT.
DEPARTMENT OF THE INTERIOR.
COMMISSION TO THE FIVE CIVILIZED TRIBES.

IN RE APPLICATION FOR ENROLLMENT, as a citizen of the Creek Nation, of Minnie Bruner, born on the 7th day of December, 1901

Name of Father: John Bruner   a citizen of the   Creek   Nation.
Name of Mother: Pemala Bruner   a citizen of the   Creek   Nation.

                              Postoffice   Bixby, Indian Territory.

AFFIDAVIT OF MOTHER.

UNITED STATES OF AMERICA, Indian Territory,
    Western   **DISTRICT.**

    I, Pemala Bruner, on oath state that I am 32 years of age and a citizen by Birth, of the Creek Nation; that I am the lawful wife of John Bruner, who is a citizen, by Birth of the Creek Nation; that a Female child was born to me on 7th day of December, 1901, that said child has been named Minnie Bruner, and was living March 4, 1905.
                                                            Her
                                        Pemala Bruner x
Witnesses To Mark: mark
 { EH Moore
  Bluford Miller

Subscribed and sworn to before me this 28th day of April, 1905.

My Com. Ex. Sept. 12, 1906   E H Moore
                                                Notary Public.

Applications for Enrollment of Creek Newborn
Act of 1905   Volume XI

AFFIDAVIT OF ATTENDING PHYSICIAN OR MID-WIFE.

UNITED STATES OF AMERICA, Indian Territory, ⎱
    Western   DISTRICT.   ⎰

I, John Bruner , a *(blank)* , on oath state that I attended on Mrs. Pemala Bruner, wife of John Bruner on the 7th day of December , 1901 ; that there was born to her on said date a Female child; that said child was living March 4, 1905, and is said to have been named Minnie Bruner

                              John Bruner

Witnesses To Mark:

{

Subscribed and sworn to before me this 28th day of April , 1905.

My Com. Ex. Sept. 12, 1906   E H Moore
                                            Notary Public.
                    Moore & Noble, Okmulgee, I.T.

BIRTH AFFIDAVIT.

DEPARTMENT OF THE INTERIOR.
COMMISSION TO THE FIVE CIVILIZED TRIBES.

IN RE APPLICATION FOR ENROLLMENT, as a citizen of the Creek Nation, of Archie Bruner, born on the 6th day of February , 1904

Name of Father: John Bruner	a citizen of the Creek	Nation.
Name of Mother: Pemala Bruner	a citizen of the Creek	Nation.

                    Postoffice   Bixby, Indian Territory.

AFFIDAVIT OF MOTHER.

UNITED STATES OF AMERICA, Indian Territory, ⎱
    Western   DISTRICT.   ⎰

I, Pemala Bruner , on oath state that I am 32 years of age and a citizen by Birth, of the Creek Nation; that I am the lawful wife of John Bruner , who is a citizen, by Birth of the Creek Nation; that a Male child was born to me on 6th day of February , 1904 , that said child has been named Archie Bruner , and was living March 4, 1905.   Her
                                    Pemala Bruner x
Witnesses To Mark: mark
   { EH Moore
     Bluford Miller

Applications for Enrollment of Creek Newborn
Act of 1905 Volume XI

Subscribed and sworn to before me this 28th day of April, 1905.

My Com. Ex. Sept. 12, 1906   E H Moore
                                                 Notary Public.

AFFIDAVIT OF ATTENDING PHYSICIAN OR MID-WIFE.

UNITED STATES OF AMERICA, Indian Territory,
    Western   DISTRICT.

I, John Bruner, a *(blank)*, on oath state that I attended on Mrs. Pemala Bruner, wife of John Bruner on the 6th day of February, 1904; that there was born to her on said date a male child; that said child was living March 4, 1905, and is said to have been named Archie Bruner

                                                 John Bruner
Witnesses To Mark:

Subscribed and sworn to before me this 28th day of April, 1905.

My Com. Ex. Sept. 12, 1906   E H Moore
                                                 Notary Public.
                       Moore & Noble, Okmulgee, I.T.

| REFER IN REPLY TO THE FOLLOWING: NC-918 | **DEPARTMENT OF THE INTERIOR, COMMISSIONER TO THE FIVE CIVILIZED TRIBES.** |

Muskogee, Indian Territory, November 4, 1905.

Clerk in Charge,
    Creek Enrollment Division.

Dear Sir:

Applications for Enrollment of Creek Newborn
Act of 1905 Volume XI

Replying to your verbal inquiry of this date as to whether application for the enrollment as a citizen of the Creek Nation was made for Lula Brown, child of Rosanna Brown, a citizen of the Creek Nation and Jimsey Brown, a citizen of the Seminole Nation, you are advised that no application has been made for the enrollment of said child as a citizen of the Seminole Nation.

Respectfully,

Tams Bixby   Commissioner.

NC-918
DEPARTMENT OF THE INTERIOR,
COMMISSIONER TO THE FIVE CIVILIZED TRIBES.

Muskogee, Indian Territory, July 28, 1905.

In the matter of the application for the enrollment of Lula Brown as a citizen by blood of the Creek Nation.

Jimsey Brown, being duly sworn, testified as follows (through Jesse McDermott, Official Interpreter).

EXAMINATION BY THE COMMISSIONER:
Q What is your name? A Jimsy Brown.
Q How old are you? A About 40.
Q What is your postoffice address? A Henryetta.
Q Have you a child named Lula Brown? A Yes sir.
Q Is she living? A Yes sir; here she is, there.
Q When was she born, do you know? A I don't know.
Q Don't you know about how old she is? A About four years old.
Q What is the name of the mother of that child? A Rosanna.
Q Is she a citizen of the Creek Nation? A Yes sir.
Q You got your land? A Yes sir.
Q If it should be found that this child, Lula, is entitled to enrollment in either the Creek or the Seminole Nation, in which Nation do you elect for her to take her allotment? A In the Creek Nation.
Q You want her enrolled in the Creek Nation? A Yes sir.

Rosanna Brown, being duly sworn, testified as follows (through Jesse McDermott, Official Interpreter):

EXAMINATION BY THE COMMISSIONER:
Q What is your name? A Rosanna Brown.
Q How old are you? A About 32.
Q What is your postoffice address? A Henryetta.
Q Are you a citizen of the Creek Nation? A Yes sir.
Q What is the name of this child, here? A Lula Brown.
Q Your child? A Yes sir.

Applications for Enrollment of Creek Newborn
Act of 1905 Volume XI

Q When was Lula born? A December 17, 1902.
Q How old will she be next December? A She will be four years old.
Q The father of this child is a Seminole, isn't he? A Yes sir.
Q If it should be found that this little girl here is entitled to rights in either the Creek or Seminole Nation, in which Nation do you elect to have her enrolled for her to take her allotment? A In the Creek Nation.

INDIAN TERRITORY, Western District. I, J. Y. Miller, a stenographer to the Commissioner to the Five Civilized Tribes, do hereby certify that the above and foregoing is a true and complete translation of my notes as same appear in my stenographic report of this case.

JY Miller

Subscribed and sworn to before me this the 1st day of August, 1905.

Edw C Griesel Notary Public.

BIRTH AFFIDAVIT.
DEPARTMENT OF THE INTERIOR.
COMMISSION TO THE FIVE CIVILIZED TRIBES.

IN RE APPLICATION FOR ENROLLMENT, as a citizen of the Creek Nation, of Lula Brown , born on the 17 day of December, 1901

Name of Father: Jimsy Brown   a citizen of the   Creek[sic] Nation.
Name of Mother: Rosanna Brown   a citizen of the   Creek   Nation.

Postoffice   Henryetta, Indian Territory

AFFIDAVIT OF MOTHER.

UNITED STATES OF AMERICA, Indian Territory,
Western   DISTRICT.

I, Rosanna Brown , on oath state that I am 32 years of age and a citizen by Blood , of the Creek Nation; that I am the lawful wife of Jimsey Brown , who is a citizen, by Blood of the Creek[sic] Nation; that a female child was born to me on 17 day of December , 1901 , that said child has been named Lula Brown , and was living March 4, 1905.

Rosanna Brown

Witnesses To Mark:

Applications for Enrollment of Creek Newborn
Act of 1905   Volume XI

Subscribed and sworn to before me this 29ᵗʰ day of April, 1905.

                                    J.O. Hamilton
                                    Notary Public.

AFFIDAVIT OF ATTENDING PHYSICIAN OR MID-WIFE.

UNITED STATES OF AMERICA, Indian Territory,
Western   DISTRICT.

    I, Hannah Mitchell, a midwife, on oath state that I attended on Mrs. Rosanna Brown, wife of Jimsy Brown on the 17 day of December, 1901; that there was born to her on said date a female child; that said child was living March 4, 1905, and is said to have been named Lula Brown

                                      her
                            Hannah x Mitchell
Witnesses To Mark: mark
  { John Bastable
    JR Vaughan

    Subscribed and sworn to before me this 29ᵗʰ day of April, 1905.

                                    J.O. Hamilton
                                    Notary Public.
My Commission expires January 18-1908

NC 918

                        Muskogee, Indian Territory, November 13, 1905

Chief Clerk,
       Seminole Enrollment Division,
                General Office.

Dear Sir:

    You are hereby advised that the name of Lula Brown, born December 17, 1901 to Jimsy Brown, an alleged Seminole citizen and Rosanna Brown a citizen by blood of the Creek Nation, is contained in schedule of minor citizens by blood of the Creek Nation, approved by the Secretary of the Interior November 27, 1905, opposite Roll number 850.

                          Respectfully,
                                    Commissioner.

Applications for Enrollment of Creek Newborn
Act of 1905 Volume XI

DEPARTMENT OF THE INTERIOR,
COMMISSIONER TO THE FIVE CIVILIZED TRIBES.,
NEAR SENORA, I.T. April 21, 1905.

In the matter of the application for the enrollment of certain new born children of "Snake" parents:

Asaf Jones, being duly sworn, testified as follows, through Alex Posey, Official Interpreter: Also by Maria Kelley, and Sam Kelley.

Examination by the Commission:
Q What is your name? A Asaf Jones.
Q What is your age? A About 23.
Q What is your post office address? A Weeletka[sic]. I am a citizen of the Creek Nation.

[sic] What is your name? A Maria Kelley.
Q What is your age? A About 35.
Q What is your post office address? A Senora.
Q Are you a citizen of the Creek Nation? A No sir, Seminole Nation.

Q What is your name? A Sam Kelley.
Q What is your age? A I am over 30.
Q What is your post office address? A Senora.
Q Are you a citizen of the Creek Nation? A Yes sir.

Statement: Hillis Harjo of Alabama Town, and Mary Harjo of Hickory Ground have a child about three years old between two and three years--it is a girl-- we saw it-- don't know it's[sic] name.

Sam Emarthla and Leechie, whose maiden name was Taylor, have two children--both boys and living-both under three years old--don't know their names, both parents are of Hickory Ground town.

Roley Taylor and Arcichky of Hickory Ground has one child not a year old. It is a girl and living--don't know it's[sic] bane, (The child appears later one but parents are unwilling to testify)
Q (To Maria) Have you some children you want to make application for? A Yes sir two.
Q What is the name of the oldest one? A Sallie. She is here.
Q How old is she? A Three years old.
Q What is the name of the next one? A David, this baby here.
Q When was David born? A The 25th of February, this year.
Q Do you know when the other was born? A March 10, 1902.
Q What is the name of the father of the child? A Sam Kelley.
Q Is he a citizen of the Creek Nation? A Yes sir.

Applications for Enrollment of Creek Newborn
Act of 1905   Volume XI

Q If it should be found that these children have rights in both the Creek and Seminole Nations, in which Nation do you now elect for them to take their allotment? A In the Creek Nation.

Q (To Sam) What Creek Indian Town do you belong to Sam? A Arbeka North Fork.
Q If it should be found that these children have rights in both the Creek and Seminole Nations, in which Nation do you now elect for them to take their allotment? A In the Creek Nation.

    Statement by Asaf: Some of these children, the parents have not looked after them--I don't know how they stand now, but a while back they were opposed to it--I am a member of Weogufky Town.

    Statement by Louisa Riley, about 40 or over, Dustin, Indian Territory, being duly sworn, through Official Interpreter Alex Posey, states: Turner Scott of Artussee Town and Polly Scott a Seminole, have two children both boys, the oldest if about two years and the other is not quite a year old. Both are living, the post office of the parents is Dustin. I am the grandmother the oldest is named Lumber and Luffus the youngest; the parents want to file for the children in the Creek Nation if they can. I know that, thats[sic] what they told me just the other day.

    Statement by Louisa Riley: Sahala Lewis, Indian name Slow Harjo of Hutchechuppa and Annie Lewis, nee Fields, of Kialigee Town, they have two children, the oldest is named Albert, he is about two years old; I don't know the name of the youngest one and don't know it's[sic] age, but the child is not very old. The parents have been wanting to make application but have not been able to go before the Commission--it was born before New Years I think, I am unable to fix the date, both are living, the post office is Dustin.

    Statement by Asaf Jones: George Thompson of Tookpafka Town and Emma Canard, of Tulwarthlocco, have a child named Isreal Thompson, the child is about three years old, the child is living. Senora is the post office. Also Dick Marshall of Kialigee Town and Liza Marshall, of Arbeka North Fork have a child a girl named Emma about three years old, living, post office Senora.

    Statement by Sam Kelley: Peter and Mully King both of Arbeka North Fork, have a child named Luila, a girl, about two years old and living, also a girl about a year old named Sallie. Their post office is Senora.

    Testimony by Bunny Hicks, who being duly sworn, through Interpreter states:

Q What is your name? A Bunny Hicks.
Q What is your age? A I am about 20.
Q What is your post office? A Senora. Henry Hicks of Quassarte[sic] No 1.(?) and Louisa Hicks of Arbeka, have a child named Joseph over three years old, maybe four years old, don't know the month he was born in, it is living. Joe is my brother. I also have a sister named Kogee Hicks of Quassarte[sic] and she and Hagar Thompson of

Applications for Enrollment of Creek Newborn
Act of 1905 Volume XI

Tookpafka Town, have a child named Newman Thompson, which will be four years old the 24th of this month.

Henry G. Hains, being duly sworn, on his oath, states that the above and foregoing is a true and correct transcript of his stenographic notes as taken in said cause on said date.

Henry G. Hains

Subscribed and sworn to before me this 11th day of May, 1905.

Drennan C Skaggs
Notary Public.

N. C. 919

DEPARTMENT OF THE INTERIOR,
COMMISSIONER TO THE FIVE CIVILIZED TRIBES.
Near Senora, Indian Territory, November 27, 1906.

In the matter of the application for the enrollment of Isreal[sic] Thompson, deceased, as a citizen by blood of the Creek Nation.

CHOTKEY KINHA, being duly sworn, testified as follows (through Jesse McDermott official interpreter):

BY COMMISSIONER:

Q What is your name? A Chotkey Kinha.
Q What is your age? A About 21.
Q What is your postoffice address? A Dustin, c/o Henry Hope.
Q Are you a Creek citizen? A Yes.
Q To which Creek Indian town do you belong? A Tulsa Canadian.

The witness is identified as Chotkey Kinha opposite Creek Roll No. 7728.

Q Have you a child named Isreal Thompson? A Yes.
Q When was he born? A April 8, 1903.
Q Is he living? A No, dead.
Q When did he die do you know? A It is just a little over a year ago since he died.
Q In what month do you know? A No, I do not but the date of his death is written on the headboard at the grave.
Q Who is the father of Isreal? A George Thompson.
Q Were you and George Thompson lawfully married when this child was born? A No.
Q Had you ever lived together as a man and wife prior to the birth of Isreal? A No.
Q Who attended on you when Isreal was born? A Melinda Hope but she is now dead.

Applications for Enrollment of Creek Newborn
Act of 1905   Volume XI

There are on file at the office of the Commissioner to the Five Civilized Tribes two affidavits signed by you, in one you sign your name as Emma Canard and in the other, you sign it as Emma Thompson.

Q Which is your correct name Emma Canard or Emma Thompson? A Neither one is correct. Alex Posey drew up the papers and asked me to sign them Emma Canard and I did so. That is the name that I went by when I attended school at Okmulgee.

On examination of the headboard at the grave of the said Isreal Thompson the following is carved thereon: " ISREAL THOMSON - B - APR. 03 D- SEPT. 05 "

I, Jesse McDermott, on oath state that the above and foregoing is a full and true transcript of my notes as taken in said cause on said date.

Jesse McDermott

Subscribed and sworn to before me this 27th day of November, 1905.

J H Swafford
My Com. Exp. 2/21/1910   Notary Public.

AFFIDAVIT OF DISINTERESTED WITNESS.

UNITED STATES OF AMERICA,
INDIAN TERRITORY,
Western DISTRICT.   SS

We, the undersigned, on oath state that we are personally acquainted with Chotkey Stinha not, the wife of   George Thompson   ; and that there was born to her a male child on or about the 8 day of April 1903, that the said child has been named Isreal Thompson , and was living March 5, 1905, and died the following Sept.

We further state that we have no interest in this case.

	his
Witnesses: J McDermott	Henry x Hope
	mark
Jim Cantrell	Pervis Rodgers

Subscribed and sworn to before me this 27 day of November 1906

My Com Exp   J McDermott
July 25-1907   Notary Public.

Applications for Enrollment of Creek Newborn
Act of 1905 Volume XI

Copy

BIRTH AFFIDAVIT.
DEPARTMENT OF THE INTERIOR.
COMMISSION TO THE FIVE CIVILIZED TRIBES.

IN RE APPLICATION FOR ENROLLMENT, as a citizen of the Creek Nation, of Isreal Thompson, born on the 8 day of April, 1903

Name of Father: George Thompson   a citizen of the   Creek   Nation.
Tokpofka
Name of Mother: Emma Canard   a citizen of the   Creek   Nation.
Tulsa Can

                Postoffice   Senora Ind Ter

AFFIDAVIT OF MOTHER.

UNITED STATES OF AMERICA, Indian Territory,
     Western   DISTRICT.

     I, Emma Canard, on oath state that I am over 20 years of age and a citizen by blood, of the Creek Nation; that I ~~am~~ was formerly the lawful wife of George Thompson, who is a citizen, by blood of the Creek Nation; that a male child was born to me on the 8th day of April, 1903, that said child has been named Isreal Thompson, and was living March 4, 1905.   her
                                       Emma x Canard
Witnesses To Mark: mark
    { DC Skaggs
      Alex Posey

     Subscribed and sworn to before me this 30 day of June, 1905.

                                 Drennan C Skaggs
                                    Notary Public.

AFFIDAVIT OF ATTENDING PHYSICIAN OR MID-WIFE.

UNITED STATES OF AMERICA, Indian Territory,
     Western   DISTRICT.

     I, Melinda Hope, a midwife, on oath state that I attended on Mrs. Emma Canard, formerly wife of George Thompson on the 8 day of April, 1903; that there was born to her on said date a male child; that said child was living March 4, 1905, and is said to have been named Isreal Thompson   her
                                     Melinda x Hope
                                         mark

Applications for Enrollment of Creek Newborn
Act of 1905 Volume XI

Witnesses To Mark:
{ DC Skaggs
  Alex Posey

Subscribed and sworn to before me 30" day of June, 1905.

Drennan C Skaggs
Notary Public.

BIRTH AFFIDAVIT.
DEPARTMENT OF THE INTERIOR.
COMMISSION TO THE FIVE CIVILIZED TRIBES.

IN RE APPLICATION FOR ENROLLMENT, as a citizen of the Creek Nation, of Isreal Thompson, born on the 8 day of April, 1903

Name of Father: George Thompson   a citizen of the   Creek   Nation.
Name of Mother: Chot key Kinha   a citizen of the   Creek   Nation.
C R #7726

Postoffice   *(blank)*

AFFIDAVIT OF MOTHER.

UNITED STATES OF AMERICA, Indian Territory,
     Western   DISTRICT.

    I, Chotkey Kinha, on oath state that I am over 20 years of age and a citizen by blood, of the Creek Nation; that I am not the lawful wife of George Thompson, who is a citizen, by blood of the Creek Nation; that a male child was born to me on the 8 day of April, 1903, that said child has been named Isreal Thompson, and was living March 4, 1905.

Emma Canard

Witnesses To Mark:
{

Subscribed and sworn to before me this 27 day of November, 1906.
My Commission
Expires July 25" 1907   J McDermott
                                   Notary Public.

Applications for Enrollment of Creek Newborn
Act of 1905   Volume XI

BIRTH AFFIDAVIT.
DEPARTMENT OF THE INTERIOR.
COMMISSION TO THE FIVE CIVILIZED TRIBES.

IN RE APPLICATION FOR ENROLLMENT, as a citizen of the Creek Nation, of Israel Thompson, born on the 8 day of April, 1903

Name of Father: George Thompson   a citizen of the   Creek   Nation.
Tokpofka Town
Name of Mother: Emma Canard   a citizen of the   Creek   Nation.
Tulsa Canadian Town
                      Postoffice   Senora Ind Ter

AFFIDAVIT OF MOTHER.

UNITED STATES OF AMERICA, Indian Territory,
    Western   DISTRICT.

I, Emma Canard, on oath state that I am over 20 years of age and a citizen by blood, of the Creek Nation; that I ~~am~~ was formerly the lawful wife of George Thompson, who is a citizen, by blood of the Creek Nation; that a male child was born to me on the 8th day of April, 1903, that said child has been named Israel Thompson, and was living March 4, 1905.
                                 her
                         Emma x Canard
Witnesses To Mark: mark
  { DC Skaggs
    Alex Posey

Subscribed and sworn to before me this 30 day of June, 1905.

                            Drennan C Skaggs
                            Notary Public.

AFFIDAVIT OF ATTENDING PHYSICIAN OR MID-WIFE.

UNITED STATES OF AMERICA, Indian Territory,
    Western   DISTRICT.

I, Melinda Hope, a mid-wife, on oath state that I attended on Mrs. Emma Canard, former wife of George Thompson on the 8 day of April, 1903; that there was born to her on said date a male child; that said child was living March 4, 1905, and is said to have been named Israel Thompson   her
                        Melinda x Hope
                           mark

Applications for Enrollment of Creek Newborn
Act of 1905   Volume XI

Witnesses To Mark:
{ DC Skaggs
  Alex Posey

Subscribed and sworn to before me 30 day of June, 1905.

Drennan C Skaggs
Notary Public.

BIRTH AFFIDAVIT.
DEPARTMENT OF THE INTERIOR.
COMMISSION TO THE FIVE CIVILIZED TRIBES.

IN RE APPLICATION FOR ENROLLMENT, as a citizen of the Creek Nation, of Isrel Thompson , born on the 8th day of April , 1903

Name of Father: George Thompson   a citizen of the   Creek   Nation.
Name of Mother: Emma Thompson   a citizen of the   Creek   Nation.

Postoffice   Senora I.T.

AFFIDAVIT OF MOTHER.

UNITED STATES OF AMERICA, Indian Territory,
Western   DISTRICT.

I, Em ma Thompson , on oath state that I am Twenty years of age and a citizen by Blood , of the Creek Nation; that I am the lawful wife of George Thompson , who is a citizen, by Blood of the Creek Nation; that a Male child was born to me on the 8th day of April , 1903 , that said child has been named Isrel Thompson , and was living March 4, 1905.

Emma Thompson

Witnesses To Mark:
{

Subscribed and sworn to before me this 29th day of April , 1905.

MY COMMISSION EXPIRES JULY 13th, 1908   J.W. Fowler
Notary Public.

Applications for Enrollment of Creek Newborn
Act of 1905 Volume XI

AFFIDAVIT OF ATTENDING PHYSICIAN OR MID-WIFE.

UNITED STATES OF AMERICA, Indian Territory,
Western   DISTRICT.

I, Melinda Hope , a Mid-wife , on oath state that I attended on Mrs. Emma Thompson , wife of George Thompson on the 8th day of April , 1903 ; that there was born to her on said date a Male child; that said child was living March 4, 1905, and is said to have been named Isrel Thompson

                                           Her
                                  Melinda x Hope
                                      mark

Witnesses To Mark:
  Willie Hope
  John S Breshears

Subscribed and sworn to before me this 29th day of April , 1905.

MY COMMISSION EXPIRES JULY 13th, 1908   J.W. Fowler
                                                            Notary Public.

(The above Birth Affidavit given again.)

DEPARTMENT OF THE INTERIOR,
COMMISSIONER TO THE FIVE CIVILIZED TRIBES.
NEAR SENORA, I.T. APRIL 21, 1905.

In the matter of the application for the enrollment of certain new born children of "Snake" parents:

Asaf Jones, being duly sworn, testified as follows, through Alex Posey, Offician[sic] Interpreter: Also by Maria Kelley, and Sam Kelley.

Statement by Asaf Jones: George Thompson of Tookpafka Town and Emma Canard, of Tulwarthlocco, have a child named Isreal Thompson, the child is about three years old, the child is living. Senora is the post office address. Also Dick Marshall of Kialigee Town and Liza Marshall of Arbeka North Fork have a child a girl named Emma about three years old, living, post office, Senora.

Applications for Enrollment of Creek Newborn
Act of 1905   Volume XI

Muskogee, Indian Territory, May 2, 1905.

Mrs. Emma Thompson,
    Care George Thompson,
        Senora, Indian Territory.

Dear Madam:

The Commission is in receipt of an affidavit executed by you relative to the birth of your minor child, Isrel Thompson. It is stated in said affidavit that you and your husband, George Thompson, are citizens by blood of the Creek Nation.

Without further information, the Commission is unable to identify either of you on the approved roll as citizens by blood of said Nation. You are therefore requested to inform the Commission as to the roll numbers of yourself and your husband as the same appears on your deeds or allotment certificates.

                Respectfully,
                              Chairman.

NC 919

                Muskogee, Indian Territory, October 20, 1905.

Emma Canard,
    Senora, Indian Territory.

Dear Madam:

In the matter of the application for the enrollment of your minor child, Isrel or Israel Thompson, born April 8, 1903, this office is unable to identify you on its approved roll of citizens by blood of the Creek Nation; you are requested to state the different names under which you have been known, the name of your parents, the Creek Indian town to which you belong and the numbers which appear on your deeds and allotment certificates.

You are also requested to advise this office as to the correct spelling of the name of your said child, whether Isrel or Israel Thompson.

                Respectfully,
                              Commissioner.

Applications for Enrollment of Creek Newborn
Act of 1905   Volume XI

N C 919

JWH

Muskogee, Indian Territory, March 1, 1907.

Chotkey Kinha,
% George Thompson,
Senora, Indian Territory.

Dear Madam :--

You are hereby advised that on February 15, 1907, the Secretary of the Interior approved the enrollment of your minor child, Isreal Thompson, as a citizen by blood of the Creek Nation, and that the name of said child appears upon the roll of New Born citizens by blood of the Creek Nation, enrolled under the Act of Congress approved March 3, 1905, as number 1177.

This child is now entitled to allotment and application therefor should be made without delay at the Creek Land Office, Muskogee, Indian Territory.

Respectfully,
Commissioner.

NC 920.

Muskogee, Indian Territory, October 20, 1905.

Leoner Bruner,
Care Henry Bruner,
Edna, Indian Territory.

Dear Madam:

In the matter of the application for the enrollment of your minor children, Bettie Bruner, born July 10, 1903, and Jessie and Bessie Bruner, both born January 15, 1905, as citizens by blood of the Creek Nation; you state in your affidavits on file in said case that you are a citizen by marriage of the Creek Nation. You are advised that there are no citizens by marriage of the Creek Nation and that this office is unable to identify you on the final roll of either the freedmen or citizens by blood of the Creek Nation.

You are requested to advise this office whether you are not in fact a non-citizen of the Creek Nation. In the event that you are a non citizen, it will be necessary for you to

Applications for Enrollment of Creek Newborn
Act of 1905   Volume XI

furnish this office with either the original or a certified copy of your marriage license as proof of your marriage to Henry Bruner.

If you are a citizen of the Creek Nation, you are requested to state whether your name appear on the freedman or Indian roll, and if on either of said rolls, you will state under what name you are enrolled, the Creek Indian town to which you belong and the numbers which appear on your deeds and allotment certificate.

Respectfully,
Commissioner.

(The letter below typed as given.)

NC-920   (Copy)

Edna, I. T. Oct. 28th, 1905.

Commissioner.

Dear Sir

in regards to your letter of the 20th saying you wants to know wheather I am a citizen or a Non citizen I am a Non citizen. And was marred to Henry Bruner at Chandler I here inclose our morrage Citificate and you can send it back to me

Yours
(signed)   Mrs. L. A. Bruner.

NC-920

Muskogee, Indian Territory, November 3, 1905.

Mrs. L. A. Bruner,
    Care of Henry Bruner,
        Edna, Indian Territory.

Dear Madam:

In accordance with your request of October 28, 1905, there is herewith enclosed your certificate of marriage, a copy of which has been made and filed with the record in the matter of the application for the enrollment of your minor children, Bettie, Jessie and Bessie Bruner, as citizens by blood of the Creek Nation/

Respectfully,
Commissioner.

JYM-3-7

Applications for Enrollment of Creek Newborn
Act of 1905 Volume XI

NC-920

CERTIFICATE OF MARRIAGE.

I hereby certify that on the 14TH DAY OF April, A D. 1902, at Chandler, in the County of Lincoln, in the Territory of Oklahoma, according to law and authority

I DULY JOINED IN MARRIAGE

Mr. Henry Bruner of Beggs, Ind. Ter. and Miss Lena Slayden of Beggs Ind. Ter. in the presence of W. H. Smith of Chandler, Oklahoma and F. J. Lynch of Elba Oklahoma.

Given under my hand This 14th day of April, A.D. 1902.

(signed)   S. A. CORDELL

Official Title Probate Judge.

(SEAL)

INDIAN TERRITORY, Western District.   :   I, J. Y. Miller, a stenographer to the Commissioner to the Five Civilized Tribes, do hereby certify that the above and foregoing is a true and complete copy of its original.

JY Miller

Sworn to and subscribed before me
this the 4rd[sic] of November
1905.

Edw C Griesel
Notary Public.

BIRTH AFFIDAVIT.

DEPARTMENT OF THE INTERIOR.
COMMISSION TO THE FIVE CIVILIZED TRIBES.

IN RE APPLICATION FOR ENROLLMENT, as a citizen of the Creek Nation, of Bessie Bruner, born on the 15th day of Jan , 1905

Name of Father: Henry Bruner   a citizen of the   Creek   Nation.
Name of Mother: Leaner Bruner   a citizen of the   Creek   Nation.

Postoffice   Edna Ind Ter

317

Applications for Enrollment of Creek Newborn
Act of 1905   Volume XI

NB That Jessie and Bessie are twins

AFFIDAVIT OF MOTHER.

UNITED STATES OF AMERICA, Indian Territory, }
Western   DISTRICT.

I, Leaner Bruner , on oath state that I am 19 years of age and a citizen by marriage , of the Creek Nation; that I am the lawful wife of Henry Bruner , who is a citizen, by blood of the Creek Nation; that a female child was born to me on 15th day of Jan , 1905 , that said child has been named Bessie Bruner , and was living March 4, 1905.

Leaner Bruner

Witnesses To Mark:
{

Subscribed and sworn to before me this 4th day of April , 1905.

Richard J Hill
Notary Public.

My Commission expires March 25th 1909

AFFIDAVIT OF ATTENDING PHYSICIAN OR MID-WIFE.

UNITED STATES OF AMERICA, Indian Territory, }
Western   DISTRICT.

I, Minnie Saxton , a Mid wife , on oath state that I attended on Mrs. Leaner Bruner , wife of Henry Bruner on the 15th day of Jan. , 1905 ; that there was born to her on said date a female child; that said child was living March 4, 1905, and is said to have been named Bessie Bruner

Minnie Saxton

Witnesses To Mark:
{

Subscribed and sworn to before me this 11th day of April , 1905.

Richard J Hill
Notary Public.

My Commission expires March 25th 1909

Applications for Enrollment of Creek Newborn
Act of 1905 Volume XI

BIRTH AFFIDAVIT.
DEPARTMENT OF THE INTERIOR.
COMMISSION TO THE FIVE CIVILIZED TRIBES.

IN RE APPLICATION FOR ENROLLMENT, as a citizen of the Creek Nation, of Bettie Bruner, born on the 10th day of July, 1903

Name of Father: Henry Bruner   a citizen of the   Creek   Nation.
Name of Mother: Leaner Bruner   a citizen of the   Creek   Nation.

Postoffice   Edna Ind Ter

AFFIDAVIT OF MOTHER.

UNITED STATES OF AMERICA, Indian Territory,
Western   DISTRICT.

I, Leaner Bruner, on oath state that I am 19 years of age and a citizen by marriage, of the Creek Nation; that I am the lawful wife of Henry Bruner, who is a citizen, by blood of the Creek Nation; that a female child was born to me on the 10th day of July, 1903, that said child has been named Bettie Bruner, and was living March 4, 1905.

                         Leaner Bruner
Witnesses To Mark:

Subscribed and sworn to before me this 4th day of April, 1905.

                         Richard J Hill
                         Notary Public.
My Commission expires March 25th 1909

AFFIDAVIT OF ATTENDING PHYSICIAN OR MID-WIFE.

UNITED STATES OF AMERICA, Indian Territory,
Western   DISTRICT.

I, Harriet Bruner, a Mid wife, on oath state that I attended on Mrs. Leaner Bruner, wife of Henry Bruner on the 10th day of July, 1903 ; that there was born to her on said date a female child; that said child was living March 4, 1905, and is said to have been named Bettie Bruner
                                               her
                                           Harriet x Bruner
Witnesses To Mark: mark
   R.R. Bruner
   Jamie Bruner

Applications for Enrollment of Creek Newborn
Act of 1905   Volume XI

Subscribed and sworn to before me this *(blank)* day of *(blank)* , 190.....

                                    Richard J Hill
                                    Notary Public.
My Commission expires March 25th 1909

BIRTH AFFIDAVIT.

DEPARTMENT OF THE INTERIOR.
COMMISSION TO THE FIVE CIVILIZED TRIBES.

IN RE APPLICATION FOR ENROLLMENT, as a citizen of the Creek Nation, of Jessie Bruner, born on the 15th day of Jan , 1905

Name of Father: Henry Bruner	a citizen of the Creek	Nation.
Name of Mother: Leaner Bruner	a citizen of the Creek	Nation.

                    Postoffice   Edna Ind Ter

NB That Jessie and Bessie are twins

AFFIDAVIT OF MOTHER.

UNITED STATES OF AMERICA, Indian Territory,
    Western   **DISTRICT.**

    I, Leaner Bruner , on oath state that I am 19 years of age and a citizen by marriage , of the Creek Nation; that I am the lawful wife of Henry Bruner , who is a citizen, by blood of the Creek Nation; that a male child was born to me on 15th day of Jan , 1905 , that said child has been named Jessie Bruner , and was living March 4, 1905.

                                    Leaner Bruner

Witnesses To Mark:
{

    Subscribed and sworn to before me this 4th day of April , 1905.

                                  Richard J Hill
                                  Notary Public.
My Commission expires March 25th 1909

Applications for Enrollment of Creek Newborn
Act of 1905 Volume XI

AFFIDAVIT OF ATTENDING PHYSICIAN OR MID-WIFE.

UNITED STATES OF AMERICA, Indian Territory, }
 Western DISTRICT.

I, Minnie Saxton , a Mid wife , on oath state that I attended on Mrs. Leaner Bruner , wife of Henry Bruner on the 15th day of Jan. , 1905 ; that there was born to her on said date a female child; that said child was living March 4, 1905, and is said to have been named Jessie Bruner

Minnie Saxton

Witnesses To Mark:
{

Subscribed and sworn to before me this 11th day of April , 1905.

Richard J Hill
Notary Public.

My Commission expires March 25th 1909

NC 921

DEPARTMENT OF THE INTERIOR,
COMMISSIONER TO THE FIVE CIVILIZED TRIBES.
Paden, Indian Territory, October 10, 1906.

In the matter of the application for the enrollment of Sallo and Ella Coker as citizens by blood of the Creek Nation.

SAM DAVIS, being duly sworn, testified as follows:

BY COMMISSIONER:

Q What is your name? A Sam Davis.
Q What is your age? A About 36.
Q What is your postoffice address? A Paden, I.T.
Q Are you a Creek citizen? A Yes sir.
Q Do you know Charley Coker? A I do.
Q Do you know his wife Hettie Coker? A I do.
Q Do you know what her maiden name is? A Hettie Lena. I have her deeds here.

The witness presents allotment deeds issued to Hettie Lena Creek Roll No. 4834.

Applications for Enrollment of Creek Newborn
Act of 1905   Volume XI

---oooOOOooo---

I, Jesse McDermott, on oath state that the above and foregoing is a full and true transcript of my notes as taken in said cause on said date.

Jesse McDermott

Subscribed and sworn to before me this 10th day of December, 1906.

Alex Posey
Notary Public.

AFFIDAVIT OF DISINTERESTED WITNESS.

UNITED STATES OF AMERICA,
Western DISTRICT,   SS
INDIAN TERRITORY.

We, the undersigned, on oath state that we are personally acquainted with Hettie Coker nee Lena   wife of   Charley Coker   ; that there was born to her a   female child on or about the   28 day of   February   1902 ; that the said child has been named Sallo Coker   and was living March 4, 1905.

We further state that we have no interest in this case.

Witnesses: J McDermott	Sam Davis
	her
	Jinnie x Davis
Sam Davis	mark

Subscribed and sworn to before me this 10 day of October 1906.
My Commission
Expires July 25" 1907   J McDermott
Notary Public.

BIRTH AFFIDAVIT.

DEPARTMENT OF THE INTERIOR.
COMMISSION TO THE FIVE CIVILIZED TRIBES.

IN RE APPLICATION FOR ENROLLMENT, as a citizen of the Creek Nation, of Sallo Coker, born on the about 28   day of Feb , 1902

Name of Father: Charley Coker   a citizen of the   Creek   Nation.
Name of Mother: Hetty   "   a citizen of the   "   Nation.

Applications for Enrollment of Creek Newborn
Act of 1905 Volume XI

Postoffice   Paden

AFFIDAVIT OF ~~MOTHER~~.
father

UNITED STATES OF AMERICA, Indian Territory, ⎫
Western   DISTRICT.   ⎭

I, Charley Coker , on oath state that I am 43 years of age and a citizen by blood , of the Creek Nation; that I am the lawful ~~wife~~ husband of Hetty Coker , who is a citizen, by blood of the Creek Nation; that a girl child was born to me on about 28" day of February , 1902 , that said child has been named Sallo Coker , and was living March 4, 1905.

                                              his
Witnesses To Mark: Charley x Coker
⎰ HG Hains   mark
⎱ Alex Posey

Subscribed and sworn to before me this 1st day of May, 1905.

                                  Henry G. Hains
                                  Notary Public.

BIRTH AFFIDAVIT.
DEPARTMENT OF THE INTERIOR.
COMMISSION TO THE FIVE CIVILIZED TRIBES.

IN RE APPLICATION FOR ENROLLMENT, as a citizen of the Creek Nation, of Sallo Coker, born on the 28 day of Feb, 1902

Name of Father: Charley Coker   a citizen of the   Creek   Nation.
Name of Mother: Hetty   "   a citizen of the   "   Nation.

Postoffice   Paden

AFFIDAVIT OF MOTHER.

UNITED STATES OF AMERICA, Indian Territory, ⎫
Western   DISTRICT.   ⎭

I, Hetty Coker , on oath state that I am dont[sic] know years of age and a citizen by blood , of the Creek Nation; that I am the lawful wife of Charley Coker , who is a citizen, by blood of the Creek Nation; that a girl child was born to me on

Applications for Enrollment of Creek Newborn
Act of 1905 Volume XI

28 day of Feb , 1902 , that said child has been named Sallo Coker , and was living March 4, 1905.

Witnesses To Mark:
{ HG Hains
{ Alex Posey

                     her
            Hetty x Coker
                  mark

Subscribed and sworn to before me this 1 day of May , 1905.

                          Henry G Hains
                          Notary Public.

BIRTH AFFIDAVIT.

DEPARTMENT OF THE INTERIOR.
COMMISSION TO THE FIVE CIVILIZED TRIBES.

IN RE APPLICATION FOR ENROLLMENT, as a citizen of the Creek Nation, of Ella Coker, born on the 9 day of Dec , 1903

Name of Father: Charley Coker   a citizen of the   Creek   Nation.
Name of Mother: Hetty   "   a citizen of the   "   Nation.

                  Postoffice   Paden

AFFIDAVIT OF MOTHER.

UNITED STATES OF AMERICA, Indian Territory, }
     Western   DISTRICT. }

I, Charley Coker , on oath state that I am 43 years of age and a citizen by blood, of the Creek Nation; that I am the lawful ~~wife~~ husband of Hetty Coker , who is a citizen, by blood of the Creek Nation; that a girl child was born to me on about 9 day of Dec , 1903 , that said child has been named Ella Coker , and was living March 4, 1905.

                            his
                    Charley x Coker

Witnesses To Mark: mark
{ H.G. Hains
{ Alex Posey

Subscribed and sworn to before me this 1" day of May , 1905.

                          Henry G. Hains
                          Notary Public.

Applications for Enrollment of Creek Newborn
Act of 1905 Volume XI

BIRTH AFFIDAVIT.
DEPARTMENT OF THE INTERIOR.
COMMISSION TO THE FIVE CIVILIZED TRIBES.

IN RE APPLICATION FOR ENROLLMENT, as a citizen of the Creek Nation, of Ella Coker, born on the 9" day of Dec, 1903

Name of Father: Charley Coker   a citizen of the   Creek   Nation.
Name of Mother: Hetty   "   a citizen of the   "   Nation.

Postoffice   Paden

AFFIDAVIT OF MOTHER.

UNITED STATES OF AMERICA, Indian Territory,
Western   DISTRICT.

     I, Hetty Coker , on oath state that I am ------ years of age and a citizen by blood , of the Creek Nation; that I am the lawful wife of Charley Coker , who is a citizen, by blood of the Creek Nation; that a female child was born to me on 9" day of Dec , 1903 , that said child has been named Ella Coker , and was living March 4, 1905.

                                         her
Witnesses To Mark: Hetty x Coker
 { HG Hains   mark
   Alex Posey

     Subscribed and sworn to before me this 1 day of May , 1905.

                                 Henry G Hains
                                 Notary Public.

N.C. 921
                     Muskogee, Indian Territory, October 20, 1905.

Hetty Coker,
     Care Charley Coker,
         Paden, Indian Territory.

Dear Madam:

     In the matter of the application for the enrollment of your minor children, Sallie Coker, born February 28, 1902, and Ella Coker, born December 9, 1903, this office is unable to identify you on its final roll of citizens by blood of the Creek Nation; you are

Applications for Enrollment of Creek Newborn
Act of 1905   Volume XI

requested to state your maiden name, the names of your parents, the Creek Indian town to which you belong and the numbers which appear on your deeds and allotment certificate.

This office desires affidavit of the midwife or physician in attendance at the birth of said children and a blank for that purpose is enclosed herewith.

In the event that there was no physician or midwife in attendance when said children were born, it will be necessary for you to furnish this office with the affidavits of two disinterested witnesses relative to her birth. Said affidavits must set forth the names of said children, the date of their birth, the names of their parents and whether or not they were living on March 4, 1905.

                        Respectfully,
                                        Commissioner.
AG-5

                                                                JWH
N C 921
                        Muskogee, Indian Territory, March 1, 1907.

Hetty Coker,
    % Charley Coker,
        Paden, Indian Territory.

Dear Madam :--

You are hereby advised that on February 15, 1907, the Secretary of the Interior approved the enrollment of your minor children, Sallo and Ella Coker, as citizens by blood of the Creek Nation, enrolled under the Act of Congress approved March 3, 1905, as numbers 1178 and 1179, respectively.

These children are now entitled to allotment and application therefor should be made without delay at the Creek Land Office, Muskogee, Indian Territory.

                        Respectfully,
                                        Commissioner.

(Affidavit of Disinterested Witnesses given again.)

Index

ABRAMS
  Chas 202
ACKER
  Jessie 222
ADAIR
  J E 218
ADAMS
  Annie 12,13
  Bettie 181,182,183,184
  J F 218
  Lewis 12,13
  Mahaley 183
  Martha 11
  Mary 184
  T J 184
ADKINS
  Hattie 92,229
ALEXANDER
  Artie 286
  Arty 285
  Miley 285,286,287
  Nancy 285
ALLEN
  Geo W 65
  R C 83,92,228
ANDERSON
  J C 160
ARNOLD
  C O 189,190
ARPOIKA
  George 229,230,231,232,233, 234,235
  Sissia 233
  Sissie 230,231,232,234
  William 229,230,231,232,233, 234,235,236
ASBERY
  Josie 42
ASBURY
  Jesse 37
  Josephine 36,37,38,41,43,44
  Josie 35,37
  Lucy 143
  Mary 37
  Mose 143
  Moses 131,134
  Sallie 131

ATKINS
  Hattie 92
ATKINSON
  J C 280,281
BALL
  E J 202
BARBER
  Alice 74
  Alice A 79
  Cora 78,79,80,81
  E L 277,279
  John Thomas 78,79,80,81,82
  John W 76,78,79,80,81,82
  Lula F 73,75
BARKER
  N N 69,283,284
BARNETT
  Daniel 269,270
  Linda 269,270
  Pompey 293
  Samara 269,270
BARNHILL
  Fred E 45
BARTON
  B 5,75,76,80,81,123,125,157, 158,159
BASTABLE
  John 304
BAYNE
  R A 76
BEALL
  Wm O 52
BEAR
  Katie 234
BEAVER
  Harry 128,129,130,131,132
  Louisa 128,129,130,131,132
  Wilson 128,129,130,131,132
BEAVERS
  Bert J 6,229
BEAVERT
  Bert J 84
BEIDLEMAN
  Geo C 238,241
  George C 164,238,239,240,241
BEIDLEMAN & WINSTON 242

327

BENSON
  James 268
  Jim 258
  Kokey 259
  Mary 258
  Matilda 258,259
  William 32
BERRYHILL
  Aleck 26,27
  Alice 156,157,158,161,162
  Annie 26,27
  Arah Ann 96
  Archid 161
  Archie 158,160,161,162,163
  Arie 161
  Charlie S 188,189
  Clemantine 95,96
  Columbus 188,189,190
  Earl 122,123
  Emma 188,189,190
  Emma C 189,190
  Flora Edna 102,103,104
  G W 161
  George Franklin 95,96
  Jeanetta 18
  Joseph F 161
  Katie 26,27
  Leola May 18
  Lizzie B 104,105
  Lum 156,157,160,161,162,163
  May Bell 102
  May Belle 104,105
  Mrs A A 189,190
  Mrs Theodoria 104
  Mrs Theooria 105
  Nellie 102,103,104,105
  Nevada 161
  Pleasant 18,168
  Rilla 122,123,124,125,127
  Sam Bob 95,96
  Theo 126
  Theodore 122,123,124,125,127
  Thomas J 102,103
  Thos J 103,104,105
  Ves 124,125,127,128
  William 156,157,158,160,161,
    162,163

BIGPOND
  Rachel 203
BIRD
  Kizzie 165,166,167,168
  Mose 166,167
  Moses 165,167,168
  Sallie 165,167,168
  Sally 166
BIXBY
  Mr 122
  Tams 15,34,51,56,67,71,72,75,81,
    82,89,90,95,99,110,142,147,160,165,
    171,184,185,193,197,200,210,211,217,
    235,243,245,265,290,302
BLAKEMORE
  E P 273,274
BOON
  Ikey 10,11,12,13
  Isaac 10,11,12
  Martha 10,11,12,13
  Peter 10,11,12,13
BOONE
  Belle 115,116
  Imy R 115,116,117
  Ladossa Fredor 115,116
  Ladossa Fredre 116,117
  Mrs Imy R 116,117
BOSEN
  George 35,38,42,43,62
  Pearlie 35,36,37,38,42,43,44
BOSTON
  Ella 87,88,89,91
  Josephine 91
  Josephine (Posey) 89
BOWIE
  Minnie 147
BOWLEGS
  Caesar 250,251
BOWMAN
  J W 232,233
  Mary 207,209,215
BOZARTH
  Mark L 39,40
BOZEN
  George 41
  Pearlie 36,39,40,41
BRESHEARS

Index

John S 313
BRIDGES
  Bettie 54,55
  Patty 53
  Patty Bruner 56
  W E 55
  Wade 54,55
BROWN
  Jimsey 302,303
  Jimsy 303,304
  Lula 302,303,304
  Rosanna 302,303,304
  Susan 125
BRUNER
  Archie 297,300,301
  Arlinger 56
  Bessie 315,316,317,318
  Bettie 315,316,319
  Betty 297
  Daniel 297
  Harriet 319
  Henry ..315,316,317,318,319,320,321
  Hettie 248,250
  Jamie 319
  Jessie 315,316,318,320,321
  John 297,298,299,300,301
  Joseph 22
  L Beatrice 5
  Lady Beatrice 6
  Leaner 317,318,319,320,321
  Leoner 315
  Lucinda 2,3,4
  Magully 56
  Minnie 297,298,299,300
  Mrs L A 316
  Pamela 298
  Panela 297
  Patty 56
  Pemala 299,300,301
  Permela 297,298
  R R 319
  Richard 5,6
  Sarah 5,6
BUCK
  John 298
  Rosa 298
BUGESS
  Fannie 47
  Roman 47
  William 47
BURGESS
  Annie 107,108,109,110,115
  Bird 107,108,110,111,112,114
  Birdie 107
  Daniel 107,113,114
  Fannie 46,48,50,52
  Fanny 48,49,50,51,52
  James 107,108,109,110,111,112, 113,114,115
  Jim 47
  Roman 46,48,49,50,51,52
  Romn 47
  Susan 108
  Susanna 107,108,109,110,111,112, 113,114,115
  William 46,48,49,50,51,52
BURK
  Mahala 275
BURRUS
  Rhoda 152
BUSEY
  J T 168
CAMPBELL
  Henry 65
CANARD
  Annie 262,265
  Cilla 132,133,134,135
  Emma 306,308,309,310,311, 313,314
  Geo 264
  James 132,133,134,135
  Melissa 236
  Nellie 132,133,134,135
CANNARD 237
  James 236
  Malissa 240
  Martin 236,239,240,243
  Melissa 239
  Mellissa 243
  Minah 239,240,243
  Mineh 239
  Pitchee 236
CANTRELL

Index

Jim 308
CAP AH NEY 296
CA-PAH-NAY 295
CA-PAH-NEY 293
CARTER
   Anna 44,45
   Joe 44,45
   Mrs Joe 45
   William Thomas 44,45
CHAMBERLAIN
   Dewey 72
   John C 72
   Ruby 72
   Susie 70,71,72
CHAMBLEN
   Dewey 69,70,71,72
   Jno C 69,70
   John 71,72
   John C 68,69,70,71
   Rubey 72
   Ruby 68,69,70,71
   Sarah 69,169,256
   Susie 68,69,70,71
CHECOTAH
   Millie 185
CHECOTE
   Hettie 171
   Samuel 171
   Samuel J 169
CHENAH 29
CHENAULT
   M L 30
CHINAH 29
CHISSOE
   Sadie 6
CHITWOOD
   B B 168
CHRISTIAN
   B W 131
   N D 65
CLARK
   M G 120
CLARKE
   M G 121
CLAYTON
   Bud 136
   Charlie 136,137,138,139,140,141

Della 136,137,138
Della Jacobs 139,140,141
Ernest 137,139,140
Mrs 137
William McKinley 136,140,141
CLEMENT
   ? C 64
   Bettie 63,65,66
CLEMENTS
   Elizabeth 59
COKER
   Charley 321,322,323,324,325,326
   Ell 325
   Ella 321,324,325,326
   Hettie 321,322
   Hetty 322,323,324,325,326
   Sallie 325
   Sallo 321,322,323,324,326
COLBERT
   Louvina 270
COMBS
   Eli 96,97
COON
   Elmer 16
CORDELL
   John 251
   S A 317
COSAR
   Galvos 22,23
   Jennie 22,23
   Tom 22,23
COTT
   Wm 273
   Wm, MD 273
CRABTREE
   George 24,25
   Hattie 24,25
   Rebecca 25,26
CRANE
   C O 234
CRAWFORD
   J W 218
CROSSLAND
   Gracie 16
DANIEL
   Enah 226

Joseph 290
Mary 284,285
Miley 287,290
Robert 284,285,286,287,290
Unah 226,284,285,286,287,290
Unah, Jr 285,286
DANSBY
Lucinda 14,15,16
Vicey 14,15
Vicy 14,15,16
Walter 14,15,16
DAUSBY
Lucinda 15,17
Vicey 17
Walter 15,17
DAVIS
Alex 142,143,144,145,146
B F 246
Clarance B 274,275,278,279
Clarence B 274
Harvie 275
Harvie L 274,275,276,277
Hattie Johnson 82,83,84
Jinnie 322
Kizzie 82,83,84
Lewis 274,275,278
Lewis H 276,277,278,279
Lucy 142,143,144,145,146
Mary 145,146
Nellie 135
Nicey 142,143,144,145
Sam 275,321,322
Sisamma 277
Susanna 274,276,278,279
DAY
John N 68,69
DAYLEY
E B 7
J N 8
James 8
Mary A 8
Mary M 8
DEARSAW
Maggie 169
DEERE
Hattie Adkins 228
Sofarche 231

DERISAW
Hattie 171
DICKERSON
O K 286
DODSON
J S 127
J W 126
DOUGLAS
Duard C 86,87
Harry 86,87
Louie Mikey 86
Louis Mikey 87
DOYLE
Beulah 147,148,149,150,151,153,154
John 150
John N 147,149,151,152,153,
154,155,156
Limrod L 149
Nimrod L 147,150
Nimrod P 154,155
Rhoda 147,148,150,151,153,154
Timrod L 149
DRESBACK
N C 189,190
Nellie 270
Ralph 189,190,270
DYER
Eliza 221,222,223,224,225
Emmett 218,221,222,223,224
Fred S 219,221,222,223,224,225
Leotta 224,225

EGAN
John F 136
EMARTHLA
Leechie 305
Sam 305
ESKRIDGE
C C 31,32,33,86,87

FAR LO CON WE-NEY 294
FAR-CO-CON-WE-NA 295
FAR-LO-CAN-WE-NAY 293
FAR-LO-CON-WE-NAY 293
FIELDS
Annie 306
FIXICO

Locher..................................... 29
FLYNN
   T W 232,233,234
FORD
   Anna 125
FOSTER
   E A 152
   Edward 32
FOWLER
   C L 175,176
   E A 175,176
   J W 48,98,175,176,312,313
FREEMAN
   Chas R 218
FRY
   D W 218
FUSCINDA 29
FUSWA
   Kizzie 166
   Mose 166,167
   Sally 166

GARRIGUES
   Anna 46,119,174,237,259,275
GIBSON
   Hattie 169
   Hettie 168,169,170,171,172,173
   Joseph 168,169,170,171,172,173
   Martha 168,169,172,173
   Mattie 171,172
   Mottie 169,170
GIERKES
   Wm F A 12,13
GILLIS
   Lizzie 70
GIPSON
   Hettie 170
GLENN
   Elma 4,5
   Ida Estella 4,5
   R J 4,5
GOAT
   Alfred F 251
GOODWIN
   F M 255
GRAHAM
   M F 47

GRANT
   W H 280
GRAY
   Fannie 185,187,188
   Millie 185,186,187,188
   Siah 191
   Susie 185,186
   Willie 185,186,187,188
GRAYSON
   Buck 19,20,21
   George 182,183
   Joe 134,144
   Judie 25
   Lillie 20,21
   Mary 37
   Memene 21
   Menaney 20,21
   Menene 19,20
   Ollie 19,20
   Sarah 181,182,183,184
GREENWOOD
   C H 232,233
GREGORY
   Noah 293
GRIESEL
   E C .. 19,44,136,137,138,139,261,293
   Edw C 19,20,21,23,24,29,60,64,73,
      74,77,78,79,100,106,111,123,124,125,
      137,139,140,141,150,157,203,214,
      237,261,293,295,296,303,317

HAILSTONE
   Eliza 293
HAINS
   G H 231
   H G 9,44,229,286,287,323,324,325
   Henry 62
   Henry G .. 43,44,276,278,307,323,325
   Martha 259
HALEY
   Chas 68,69
   George Elmer 99,100,101,102
   Lena 99,100,101,102
   W D 101,102
   William D 100,101
   William David 99
HALLEYAMSON 129

Index

HAMILTON
  J O 304
HAMPTON
  C E 83
HANNAN
  Benjamin F 231
HANNBERG
  Dr J J 7
  J J 7
  Mamie 7
HARDRIDGE
  E E 130
HARJO
  Chissie 250,251
  Chofolup 29
  Hillis 305
  Maggie 168
  Mary 305
  Slow 306
HARRIS
  E B 96,97
HARRISON
  R P 76
  Robert P 77
HARRY
  Della 137
  Mollie 137
HAYNES
  Martha 260,261,264,267
  Sam 25,26
  Stella 167
HENRY
  Allen 54,55
  George W 58,59
  T A 55
HENSLEY
  E T 45
HEREFORD
  J O 137
  Mrs J O 136
HICKS
  Bunny 306
  Henry 306
  Joseph 306
  Kogee 306
  Louisa 306
HILL

Richard J 318,319,320,321
HODGE
  Johnson 215
  Maggie G 210
  Margaret 215
  Mary 204,206,207,209
HOFFMAN
  Ella 91
  Ella B 87,88,89,90
  Ella Boston 89,90
  Julius M 87,89
  Leola 87,88,89,90,91
HOGAN
  Belle 115
HOLDER
  W W 294
HOLLEYMAN
  Lula 209
  Lula Laura 213,215
  Lulu Laura 214,216,217
  Maggie 203,204,205,210,211
  Maggie G 204,205,206,207,208,
  209,210,211,212,213,214,215,216,217
  Marcella 205,206,208,209,210,
  211,212,213
  Marcellus 203,204,205,207,209,
  210,211,212,213
  T E 203,204,205,206,207,208,
  209,210,211,212,213,214,215,216,217
HOPE
  Henry 119,122,307,308
  Melinda 307,309,311,313
  Mind 175,176
  Mollie 119
  Willie 175,176,313
HOWELLS
  B P 7,8
HUCKABY
  Elcy 191,192,194,195,196
  Elsie 193,196
  Ora 193,195,196,197
  Ora May 191,194
  R W 191,192,193,194,195,196
  Randolph 191,192,193
HUCKAR
  Elsie 197
HULLQUIST

333

Index

C C 118
HUSTON
   J M 75
   James Madison 73,74
   Jesse May 73,74
   Lula F 73,74,75
   Thomas Addison.......................... 75
   Thomas Adison....................... 75,76
HUTTON
   Tooka................................. 24,25,26

ISAAC
   Louis... 270
ISPOKOGEE
   Belcher 1,3
   Jennie.. 1,3
   Sam.. 1,3,4

JACKSON
   W M.. 45
JACOBS
   Mollie 137
JANWAY
   Preston..................... 198,281,282
JENKINS
   Thos A 88
JOHNSON
   Alex 155
   Amandy 226,227
   Daniel 284
   Emma 58,63,64,65,66,67
   Enah... 226
   Fred... 119
   Isaac.. 83
   Jennie...............57,58,59,60,61,63,64,
   65,66,67,68
   Jinnie 67
   Joseph 289,292
   Kizzie 226,227
   Martin 57,59,60,61,62,66
   Miley Alexander........... 287,288,289,
   291,292
   Millie 292
   Mr... 156
   P 161
   Rev P 76,77
   Robert........284,286,287,288,291,292

Sandy..........57,58,59,60,61,62,63,64,
65,66,67,68
   Unah...226,286,287,288,289,291,292
   Unah Daniel 284,285
   Wicey 119,122
   Wiley..................................... 226,227
JOHNSTON
   Alex...................................... 154,155
JONES
   Asaf................................305,306,313
   S M.. 297,298
   A W... 152
JONSON
   P 160

KA PER NA 296
KANARD
   Cilla... 134
   Fannie 46,52
   Geo 260,261
   James 133,134,168
   Melissa 241
   Mellie 133
   Mineh 241
   Nellie 134
   Wash... 46
KANNARD
   Malissa 243
   Martin.....................237,238,241,242
   Melissa 237,238,242
   Mimah 237
   Minah 237,238,241,242
KA-PER-NA 295
KEATON
   Harwood......................102,288,289
KEIFER
   Clarance Ebert............................ 106
   Martha Lee 105,106
   Smith 106
KELLEY
   Maria 305,313
   Sam................................305,306,313
KENNEDY
   J A 31,33
   J A, MD..................................... 31,33
KEYS
   James 217,218,219,220,221

Index

Martha 218,219,220,221
Sam R 217,219,220,221
Samuel R 218,219,220,223
KIEFER
   Clarance Ebert 105
   Smith 105
KING
   Luila 306
   Mully 306
   Peter 306
   Sallie 306
KINHA
   Chot key 310
   Chotkey 307,310,315
KINNARD
   Melissa 238
KIRKPATRICK
   J ? 70
KIZZEE
   Harriet 26
KNIGHT
   C 277
   David 230,232,235
KRINKS
   Killie 294
   Lusanna 294

LAND
   Salina 57,61
LAWRENCE
   Eliza 150
LEE
   David A 100,101
LENA
   Hettie 321,322
LEWIS
   Albert 306
   Annie 306
   L L 58,59
   Sahala 306
LIKOWSKI
   Frank 97,98
   Matilda Agatha 97,98,99
   Senora 97,98
LINDESY
   Addie 254,255
   Hetty 254

LINDSAY
   Addie 246,247,250
   Hettie 246,247,250
   Walter 246,247,250
LINDSEY
   Addie 244,245,248,249,251,252,
   253,254
   Addoe 246
   Hattie 248,249
   Hettie .. 244,245,246,248,250,252,253
   Noah 252
   Walter 244,245,248,249,252
   Willie 252
LINSLEY
   Addie 246
   Walter 246
LIVINGSTON
   A H 218
LNCH
   Robert E 68
LOGAN
   F M 18
   S J 191
LONGFELLOW
   J M 234
LOVETT
   Annie 228,229
   Kizzie 228
LUMPKIN
   R W 92,118
LYNCH
   Elcy 195
   F J 317
   Robert E 59,66,70

MCADOO
   W C 168,286
MCDERMOTT
   J 2,3,30,35,39,46,58,103,104,
   105,111,119,152,159,174,182,244,259,
   261,263,275,308,310,322
   Jesse 21,23,28,46,60,74,78,79,104,
   105,107,111,119,202,258,263,295,296,
   302,307,308,322
MCINTOSH
   Jackson 118
   L G 24,25,26

Roley 198
T F 218,220
Thomas 198
Wm I 218
MCLAIN
Edward 16,17
MCNAC
Philip 119
Phillip 120,121
Tullie 119,120,121
Wicey 119,121
Wicy 120
MCNACK
Tullie 122
Wicey 122
MCQUEEN
W E 260,261,264
MARKS
Mattie 248,249,253
MARS
F L 61,67,68
G L 63
J J 67
J L 161
James J 3,4,161
P L 53,56,57
MARS AND MARS 67
MARSEY
Louisa 129
MARSHALL
Dick 306,313
Emma 306,313
Liza 306,313
Lizie 164
Lucy 164,165
Philip 238
Phillip 164,238
MARTINDALE
J A 7
W A 7
MASHBURN
Rebecca L 204,206
MATELOKA 229
MEEKS
Becky 280
William 280
MERITT

E B 255
MERRICK
Edward 226,230
Lona 8,94,229,230,231
MEYERS
J S 251,252
MICO
Henry 286
MIKEY
Enos Vay 199
Enos Vey 199,200,201
Josiah 199,200,201
Lizzie 199,200,201
Lizzy 199
Silwar 87
MILLER
Bluford 299,300
Effa 255,256
Effie 27,257,258
J Y 17,28,38,77,108,148,150,152,
159,303,317
John T 218,219
Martha 218,219,220
Sarah 255,256,257,258
Seborn 255,256,257,258
MILLS
B H 106
MINGO
Irene 91,92,94
Joseph 91,92,93,94
Robert 94
Robert J 91,92,93
MITCHELL
Hannah 304
Levi 230,233,235
MITCHENER
Dr W C 150
W C 151
MOORE
E H 256,299,300,301
MOORE & NOBLE 300
MORGAN
Barclay 36
Mr W B 39
W B 40
William B 41,42
MORON

336

Wm P 167
MORRISON
   Eliza 197,198
   Mary 197,198
   Watie 197,198
MORROW
   J B 117,217,218,219,220,221,
   222,223,224,225
MORTON
   Joseph C 175,176,177,178
   Joseph J 180
   Perry K 204,206
   T W 41
   Walter W 144
   Wm P 144
MOSELEY
   T P 210
MURPHY
   Mary 106
MUSKA 229
MYERS
   J B 215
   James B 179

NEKEEYAH
   David 271
   Davis 271,272
   Heness 271,272
   Mullie 271,272
NEWMAN
   Wm C 286,288
NOBLE
   E T 171
NOBLES
   Joe 149
   Mr 150
NOSEY 29

ODOM
   G W 218
OSBORNE
   J H 120

PAINE
   C W 277,279
PANTHER
   J F 298

PARKER
   Hon Gabe E 155
   Mr 155
PARRISH
   Zera E 17,94,137,139,148,283,293
   Zera Ellen 100
PARSINDER 29
PATTON
   D H 117
   F P 117
   Jennie 117
PAYNE
   C W 275
PEACOCK
   J L 77
PEMBERTON
   John 120
PETERS
   Isom 167
PETERSON
   Carr 297,299
   Cleo 298
PETTIGREW
   Annie 137
PHILLIPS
   Charles L 40
   Chas L 40,41
   J W 126,127
   John H 30,32
   Joseph W 126
PHILLIPS AND BOZARTH 39,40
PITMAN
   Ed 280,282
   Edward 280,281,282
   Moses 280,281,282
   Rose 282
   Susie 280,281,282
PLUMSTEAD
   Dr 138
   Dr M E 138
POSEY
   Albert W 7,8,9,10
   Alex .. 27,29,43,107,108,109,112,113,
   114,131,132,135,166,167,178,179,181,
   183,186,187,188,215,216,227,236,
   244,248,257,262,272,305,306,308,309,
   310,311,312,313,322,323,324,325

Carrie	228
Eloise	228
Frank	228
Mary A	7,9
Nina E	7,9
Ninna	9

POSTOAK
Eli	53,54,55,56
Lincoln	53,54,55,56
Maria	54,55

POTTER
R T	102

PRENCE
Nellie	279

QUINNER
Lena	236

RANDALL
Elie	47
Ulcey	111
Ulcy	108,112,114

REED
Mary	84

RICE
Benjamin F, Jr	70

RICHARD
Lizzie	199,201
Lizzy	199

RILEY
Louisa	306

RODGERS
Pervis	308

ROPER
J A	273

ROTHERY
John H	8

ROWELL
J R	127

RUBLE
G W	85

RUSSELL
R H	218
W H	210

SAPULPA
W A	22

SARTY
Hattie	82,84
Susan	6

SAXTON
Minnie	318

SCOTT
Emma	150
Kizzie	120,226
Luffus	306
Lumber	306
Mulley	188,227
Nicey	132,284
Polly	306
S W	231
Sanford	84
Turner	306

SECHALAGEE | 259

SELF
Alice	160,161
Maggie	125,157

SERANTON
Edith	88

SETTLE
Dr J A	117
J A	117

SEVERE
Lena	99

SEVIER
Amanda	174,175,177,178,180,181
Lena	101,102,173,174,176,177, 178,179,180
Lewis	174,175,176,177,179,180
Louis	178,181
Lucy	174
Solomon	178
Tom	173,174,175,179,180
Willie	178,179

SHELBY
David	1,19,21,23,60,74,78,79, 202,295,296

SHEPHERD
Annie	283,284
George	283,284
Sammie	283,284

SHERWOOD
L E	207,209,210

SIMMER

Lena 229,236
SIMPSON
　Ross M 85,86
SIMS
　E W 201
SKAGGS
　D C 27,30,35,43,58,109,112,113,
　　114,132,135,166,167,182,183,186,187,
　　188,227,244,248,257,262,272,286,
　　287,309,310,311,312
　Drennan C 18,19,27,42,43,49,109,
　　112,113,114,116,132,134,135,136,145,
　　146,151,152,166,167,170,183,186,
　　187,188,192,195,196,198,205,208,227,
　　248,249,258,262,263,272,307,309,
　　310,311,312
SLAYDEN
　Lena 317
SMITH
　D M 47
　Fred H 39,40,191,194
　M J 83
　W H 317
　Walter 16
SNAKEYA
　David 271,273
　Heness 271,273
　Molleanna 271,273
SNOW
　Ada 293,294,295,296
　Capohney 294
SPOKOGEE
　Belcher 2
　Jennie 2
　Sam 2
STANDWAITIE
　Toochee 22
STANFORD
　(Illegible) 289,290
STEEN
　Samantha 101,102
STEPHENS
　Jack W 241
STIDHAM
　Adline 25,26
STILLWELL
　H M 96,97

STINHA
　Chotkey 308
SUNDAY
　Bessie 259,261,262,265
　Matilda 259,261,265
　Tilda 262
　Willie 259,261,262,265
SUTTON
　Ray E 117
SWAFFORD
　J H 268,308
SZXTON
　Minnie 321
TAGGART
　T J 294
TAYLOR
　Arcichky 305
　David 305
　Leechie 305
　Lucile 117,118
　M D 5,75,158
　M D, MD 5,76,80,123,158
　Roley 305
　Rosa 118
　Rose 117,118
　Sallie 305
　William 117,118
THOMPSON
　Amanda 174,176,178,181
　Cassie D 95
　Em ma 312
　Emma 308,312,313,314
　Frank F 95
　George 306,307,308,309,310,311,
　　312,313,314,315
　Hagar 306
　Israel 311,314
　Isreal ... 306,307,308,309,310,313,315
　Isrel 312,313,314
　Josephine 38,41,42,43,44
　March 173
　Nancy 178
　Newman 307
　Soto 174
　Sotto 178
THOMSON

Isreal 308	Lonie 29
THORNBURGH	Malissa 29
Wright 288,289,290	Parcinder 29
TIGER	Parsender 33,34
John 202,203	Parsinda 28
Millie 202,203	Parsinder 30,31,32,33,34
Noty 273	Parsindie 31
Susannah 202,203	Robert 28,29,30,31,32,33,34
TOBLER	WILCAT
Pleasant 184	Matilda 268
Pleses 184	Mattie 268
TURK	WILDCAT
Peggie 198	Bessie 258,259,260,263,264,266,
TURNER	267,269
Bettie 277	Eliza 293
TURNHAM	Ka-ko-con-ney 295
Curley 85	Matilda 260,264,266,267,268
Joe 85	Sandy 259
Sillie May 85	Willie 259,260,263,264,269
	WILEY
UPTON	Melissa 186
Dan 264,265	Mellissa 186
	WILLHITE
VANN	Susan 98
Alice 140	WILLIAMS
VAUGHAN	Charley 202
J R 304	Eli 237,238
VAUGHN	WILLMOTT
C A 65	Jno W 249,250
	John W 249,250,251
WASHINGTON	WILSON
Maggie 284	Rilla 127
Wm 11	WINSTON
WATSON	J H 164,238,239,240
Fannie 46	James A 159
Fanny 48	Jas A 159,160
Mahala 275	John H 241
WEATHERLY	WOOD
Cora 76	W E 238
WEEKS	Wilford E 45
John M 57,62,65,125,126	WOODWARD
WESLEY 259	Amanda 118
Matilda 258,263,269	WRIGHT
WEST	C G 95
Elsie 28,29,30,31,32,33,34	Chester G 95
Feney 29	
J B 225	

www.ingramcontent.com/pod-product-compliance
Lightning Source LLC
Chambersburg PA
CBHW020243030426
42336CB00010B/590